MAPS

FOR HISTORIANS

MAPS
FOR HISTORIANS

Paul Hindle

Phillimore

First published 1998
Reprinted 2002 and 2006

Published by
PHILLIMORE & CO. LTD
Shopwyke Manor Barn, Chichester, West Sussex, England
www.phillimore.co.uk

ISBN 0-85033-934-0
ISBN 13 978-0-85033-934-5

Printed and bound in Great Britain by
CPI BATH

CONTENTS

ACKNOWLEDGEMENTS

Inevitably, in writing a book covering so many types of maps, I hope that, in trying to say the basics about each type of map, I have not over-simplified matters too much. If this book says nothing else, it must be that anyone using old maps must read the detailed references for each map type; this text can only be an introduction.

Particular assistance was received from Paul Laxton with the early large-scale county maps, and from Richard Oliver who read and gave very detailed comments on the Ordnance Survey chapter. I am also grateful to John Chapman, Brian Harley, Paul Harvey, Ralph Hyde, Gwyn Rowley and Rex Russell for their help.

For permission to reproduce maps I am grateful first to Harry Margary, who has allowed me to reproduce maps from his reprints, and second to the record offices, libraries and other individuals who are credited below.

Permission to reproduce maps was given by:

Harry Margary: Figures 2.9, 2.11, 2.12, 4.9, 5.12, 6.1; Paul Laxton: Figure 2.12; Tony Phillips: Figure 2.9; Rex C. Russell: Figures 3.13, 3.14, 3.17; Cumbria Record Office: Figures 3.11, 3.12, 5.7; Dyfed Record Office: Figures 4.4, 4.8; Essex Record Office: Figures 3.3, 3.4, 4.2; Kent Record Office: Figures 3.6, 3.7, 3.9; Lancashire Record Office: Figures 3.5 (DDX 10/3B) and 5.8 (DDCa 21/27), published with the permission of the County Archivist in whom copyright is reserved on behalf of the depositor; 5.9 (PDC 15), 5.14 (PDR 201), 5-15 (PDR 131), 5.16 (PDR 451); Nottinghamshire Record Office: Figures 3.1, 3.2 (by permission of Lord Savile and the Principal Archivist of the Nottinghamshire Archives Office); Warwick County Record Office: Figure 4.24; British Library: Figure 6.4; Brunel University Library: Figure 5.18; Guildhall Library, City of London: Figure 4.16; Rochdale Libraries: Figures 3.15, 3.16 (Local Studies Collection).

The geography departments at Manchester and Salford Universities have allowed me to use their map collections. Salford's Cartographer, Gustav Dobrzynski, drew the special maps, while the University Library obtained numerous articles for me—some of them in extremely obscure journals.

But, at the end of the day, only the author can take the blame for any errors of fact, omission or emphasis which may have crept in; these are his responsibility alone.

INTRODUCTION

'Maps are a dangerous type of evidence—they sap a man's critical faculties.'

'The historian wants written statements.'

Opinions such as these are extreme versions of a view commonly taken by historians—namely that old maps are not to be taken as 'good evidence'. Many historians would regard the mention of a water mill in a will or a topography as sound evidence for its existence, but they would probably not even contemplate looking for that same mill on a contemporary map. Historians who do consult maps often treat them only as illustrative matter and not as evidence. The various histories of Britain's railways are a case in point, rarely using contemporary maps as evidence of the different routes proposed and built, or of the disruption caused by them, especially within towns. On the other hand, some historians, particularly landscape historians and historical geographers, do use maps both as evidence and illustration.

At the very least, maps should be viewed as a particular type of historical evidence, no better nor worse intrinsically than the written word or any other source. Since it generally takes much longer (and costs more) to survey and draw, or often engrave, a map, one might expect the average map to be at least as good, or even a better source of evidence than the average written or printed document.

Both maps and documents can lie or mislead if what they have to say, and the way in which they say it, are not fully understood. To many people maps are written in a foreign language, but by learning a little of their grammar and vocabulary they can soon become intelligible. The fundamental aim of this book is to catalogue the great variety of old maps, and to show how they can be an indispensable and fascinating source of information for the historian, and for the student of local history and historical geography in particular.

There are, of course, many difficulties inherent in using old maps as evidence, especially if one is not familiar with their conventions and inaccuracies. All maps were made for a specific purpose and one has to be careful when using them for different ends.

A map is often a record of one person's perception, and is thus of unique value.

Context

Old maps have traditionally been studied in two ways. First, they may be studied as productions in their own right, as part of the history of cartography which concerns itself with the methods, techniques and skills of map-making especially with engraving and printing— but also encompasses other topics, from the paper and ink used, to looking at maps as works of art, and of course, as collectable items. The second approach is historical cartography—looking at the content of old maps—which is the main concern of this book. There is, however, a third area worthy of investigation, namely the *context* in which the maps were made. This has received relatively little attention, apart from in biographies of mapmakers, but it seems essential to study any map not just as a piece of historical geography or as an example of printing methods, but also as a product of the society and times in which it was produced. For our purposes, it is convenient in this respect to look at two people in particular: the map-*buyer* and the map-*maker*.

The 'demand' side of the equation of the map-making business has often been ignored. It is vital, though, to know why maps were made, and for whom. Some were no doubt bought as decorative items, and others for academic study, but most were surveyed, drawn and purchased for practical purposes. Most specialised maps, such as estate plans or road maps, have an obvious purpose, but more general maps such as those of a county or a town might have had a varied selection of buyers.

We must now consider the map-makers, and the conditions under which they worked. In fact, most were not 'map-makers' in the full sense of the term, rarely using original surveys, preferring instead to reprint their own and other publishers' maps. Emanuel Bowen, for example, was described as an 'engraver, printseller and publisher'. Such people were in the map business for profit, not for any academic geographical reasons. Nevertheless, many of them died in penury; Moses Pitt, for example, completed only four volumes of his projected 12-volume *English Atlas*, and was imprisoned in the Fleet for debt in 1689-91. Bowen, one of the most prolific map publishers of the following century, died poor and blind in 1767, despite having co-produced (with Thomas Kitchin) one of the most notable atlases of his day.

In the mid-18th century the principal map publishers in terms of output included Bowen, Kitchen, Sayer and the Bowles family, followed in the early years of the 19th century by Faden, Cary and Arrowsmith. We must also remember those who were real map-*makers* in the sense that they went out and produced or commissioned new and accurate surveys. The main result of their activities in England was the production of one-inch county maps, particularly in the 1760s and 1770s. The names which stand out here include those of Thomas Jefferys (also a prolific publisher) who mapped eight counties, and John Rocque who surveyed four.

These innovative cartographers must be distinguished from their more conservative brethren, who made their money solely in the engraving and publishing business. Some biographical details about map-makers are therefore needed in order to try to assess their general attitude. Had they been trained as practical surveyors, or, at the other extreme, were they simply carrying on the inherited family business? We need to know something of the people behind the maps, for they were ordinary mortals with their own perceptions and misconceptions of the world around them.

The English map trade was firmly centred on London; indeed many of the practitioners never seem to have strayed far from the capital, preferring instead to re-issue other publishers' maps (there being no effective copyright laws), usually without seeking to check, correct or improve them. Profit was often more important than accuracy. If this brief survey of some of the difficulties of looking at early maps has seemed critical of some aspects of the map trade, this is simply by way of warning researchers to be wary.

Maps must be considered from a number of viewpoints. It is not enough to look at what maps *show*, or to consider various aspects of map production. We also need to know the nature of the demand for maps, what they were required to show, and how the map-makers responded to this challenge. Only by putting the study of the content and cartography of early maps into a more general *context* can we begin to understand and interpret the maps themselves.

Survival

The survival rate of a map depends on many factors: how long ago it was made, how many copies were made in the first place, its purpose and where it has been kept since then. Thus the single copies of manuscript maps are less likely to survive than multiple printed copies of town plans or Ordnance Survey maps; cycling maps were used until they fell apart, whilst enclosure maps have been kept safe in official hands. It is particularly annoying to find a map referred to when it has not survived. Maps are more difficult to store than books; they don't fit neatly on shelves, and this is yet another reason why many maps have a low survival rate. Those of a size capable of being bound into atlases will thus survive better than large sheet maps.

Accuracy

There are two kinds of accuracy in a map. The first is planimetric or *geodetic accuracy*, that is, simply getting everything in the right place; towns, roads or fields are first correctly located with reference to each other, and then later with reference to latitude and longitude. There are a number of studies of this type of accuracy in early maps, the more statistical of which fall within the field termed 'historical cartometry'. These are generally of little importance to the local historian, who is much more interested in the *topographic accuracy* of an old map, the detail of settlement, industry, roads, fields and so on which it shows. It is important to know which maps are accurate in showing particular features and which are not; for example, the fields so often shown on late 18th-century county maps are nearly always grossly generalised, whereas estate plans from two centuries earlier will usually show accurate field boundaries, simply because they were drawn for that purpose, at a scale large enough to allow each field to be shown.

Generalisation

Maps usually have to generalise reality, simply because of the constraints of scale. A cartographer would have emphasised or exaggerated certain features, usually depending on who the map was intended for. From my window the main landscape feature is an electricity sub-station and 20 pylons, but the Ordnance map of the same area gives most prominence to roads and houses. Similarly, most old estate plans will depict the land of one landowner, ignoring land belonging to others. Estate plans usually ignore relief whereas a true 'Ordnance' map exaggerates features such as roads, woods, rivers and slopes, which would be of interest to an army commander. Road maps are another obvious example, where the road is shown far wider than its real width. Other features might have had to be displaced as a result, or simplified in some way. The ultimate form of generalisation is the *omission* of a particular feature. If a map does not show, say, a particular mill, it is not safe to say that the mill did not exist at the date of survey. The cartographer may have ignored or missed it, especially if mills were not central to his purpose in making the map. Maps do not show every detail of the landscape, and one should beware of trying to extract information from a map which it does not contain. Absence of evidence is not evidence of absence.

Finding maps

There are numerous repositories of maps, varying from national collections such as those at the Public Record Office, the Map Library of the British Library, and the National Library of Wales in Aberystwyth, through local record offices and local history libraries to a diverse group of other likely or unlikely locations. This last group includes some university libraries or departments of geography, private libraries or family records, or the records of solicitors, churches, insurance companies and the House of Lords Library—to name but a few. Wallis (1994) and Chibnall (1995) are useful starting points, listing the main holdings of map collections throughout the country.

Many libraries, however, present difficulties simply because of the way in which they catalogue maps. For a start, manuscript and printed maps are often kept separately, in some cases in entirely different departments, requiring separate searches to be made. This practice may have relevance to books, but it is hardly an important distinction with maps. A map is a map, and whether it is printed or in manuscript form is not usually important. Situations can arise where the few printed estate plans are kept (and indexed) separately from manuscript estate plans, or the manuscript Board of Health plans of c.1850 are kept apart from those similar plans which were printed. Most parish plans remained in manuscript, but some richer parishes had them printed; should the two types be kept separate? The simple answer is that all maps in a library should be listed in one index, even if they are stored separately.

Many libraries seem totally unsure of how to catalogue their maps. Some have no index at all and the majority have no separate and complete map index, listing maps only in their main catalogue—perhaps under the cartographer's name, or by map type, or by place. The root problem here is that librarians in the past have often felt little sympathy with maps, which fit neither the shelves nor the indexing systems designed for books. In some cases, maps lie in dusty corners, ignored, forgotten and uncatalogued.

I would therefore enter a plea for the clear cataloguing of maps, in a complete and separate index, in which both printed and manuscript maps should be included. Maps should be catalogued in three ways:
1. By place or area covered, whether parish, township or county.
2. By type (e.g. estate plans, enclosure maps, tithe maps, parish plans; railway maps, deposited plans)
3. By map-maker (both surveyor and publisher).

Within each section the maps should be in chronological order. This requires only three cards or entries for most maps. Ordnance Survey maps should be listed separately, under scale, then series or edition, then sheet number, and finally by date.

There are certain problems, with record offices in particular, which are connected with the reorganisation of the counties in 1974. Some counties were split up, others amalgamated, and each new county seems to have pursued a different policy since then. Cumbria, for example, took over Cumberland and Westmorland (which had record offices at Carlisle and Kendal, both still open); it also took over Furness and Cartmel from Lancashire, and it has now established record offices at Barrow-in-Furness and Whitehaven. The bulk of the records for Furness are still in the Lancashire Record Office at Preston, which also has the basic records for some areas now in Greater Manchester, Merseyside and Cheshire. The net result is that here, as in many other areas, a search may have to be made in more than one record office or local history collection for a particular map. The older the map, the more likely it is to have travelled from the area to which it relates.

Layout of the book

The content of chapters may at times appear arbitrary, simply because there is so much overlap between different types of maps. Chapter One is a brief survey of pre-Elizabethan maps; Chapter Two deals with county maps from the 16th to 19th centuries; Chapter Three mostly concerns manuscript maps of rural areas, whilst Chapter Four deals mainly with printed maps of urban areas. Chapter Five deals with specialised transport maps, and Chapter Six ends the story by looking at Ordnance Survey maps. The links between these main groups of maps are numerous: for example, roads and railways are depicted on almost all types of maps; tithe maps can include urban areas; some urban land ownership maps are much the same as rural estate plans, and eventually many types of maps were replaced by the products of the Ordnance Survey.

Within each chapter there are separate sections, each dealing with a particular type of map. Each section explains what maps of that type were drawn, and what areas were covered, what they show of the contemporary landscape—their content, amount of detail, accuracy, and the uses to which they can be put, and where the maps can now be found.

Coverage

The area covered is England and Wales, as the histories of Scottish and Irish cartography are different enough to have given them their own literature. The time period charted extends to about 1940. In terms of scale, the maps under consideration are local rather than national, though some of the latter kind are included for earlier periods, or when they show some local detail. Generally, the book deals with scales of 1 inch to the mile or greater. There is a technical distinction to be made here between 'maps' and 'plans': the latter are of larger scale, usually without any deliberate distortion of features such as roads or buildings. The Ordnance Survey now produces 'maps' at scales of up to 1:10,000 (about 6 inches to the mile); they become 'plans' from 1:2500, or about 25 inches to the mile. This distinction in terminology is not adhered to strictly in this book. A list of the main scales used, with their precise representative fractions and common names, is given in the Appendix.

References

Throughout, references are given to aid further, more detailed, reading and research; they are in the format (Bloggs, 1983) and are listed alphabetically in the Bibliography, thus avoiding the repetition which would otherwise have occurred. Reference to a particular page, where necessary is shown as (Bloggs, 1983, p.9). The Bibliography is not, of course, comprehensive but the references given will lead the reader to the original articles, which in turn will supply more detailed references.

It is always worth checking the recent publications of any local journal, whether historical, geographical, antiquarian or of a more general nature; items of great local significance are often reported in such journals, and they take time to reach the notice of anyone writing outside that local area.

Finally, a word about the maps reproduced in this book. It is often difficult to do full justice to those which are large or heavily coloured, while on others the ink has faded and the paper has become discoloured or torn. There is only one way to appreciate old maps, and that is to see and use the originals wherever possible. Original scale has not been maintained in the reproductions here, usually to #enable a larger area to be shown.

Note. A number of works not referred to elsewhere should be mentioned here; they are: Aston and Rowley, 1974; Barber & Board, 1993; Barker & Kain, 1991; Booth, 1977, 1979; Foot, 1994; Foster, 1989; Harley, 1968, 1988, 1989; Harvey, 1980; Hindle, 1985; Hoskins, 1967, 1972; Hunt and Smith, 1985; Koeman, 1968; Lambert, 1956; Lynam, 1953; Riden, 1983, 1987; Skelton, 1952; Smith, D., 1982, 1988; Stephens, 1977, 1981; Taylor, 1974; Tooley, 1979; and Warren, 1965.

1.1 *Map of Britain by Matthew Paris, c.1250. Virtually the only feature of interest to local historians is the central line of towns (from Newcastle to Dover) clearly representing a route.*

Chapter One

EARLY MAPS OF BRITAIN

THE EARLIEST MAPS of Britain were probably drawn by Ptolemy in Alexandria in about A.D. 150 (Crone, 1961, pp.21-2). None of his maps has survived, but he took the wise precaution of preserving their detail in the form of co-ordinates. Ptolemy's maps were reconstructed during the Middle Ages, and widely disseminated following the advent of printing. Numerous versions were printed from the 1470s onwards, even though better maps were by then available for many parts of the world, including Britain. Ptolemy's map of Britain is a valuable record of these islands in the years around A.D.100, showing rivers, tribal areas, towns and forts, but anyone wanting contemporary detail is probably better served by the Roman historians of the period, or by the lists of places given in later Roman documents such as the Antonine Itinerary or the *Notitia Digitatum*, the former being a list of the main post roads and the latter a book about administration.

What has been described as the earliest English school of cartography is represented by the maps of Matthew Paris, a monk working at St Albans in the middle of the 13th century (British Museum, 1928; Crone, 1961, pp.14-15). Four very similar maps of Britain survive, all drawn around the route from Dover to Durham, Newcastle or Berwick (Fig. 1.1). This route clearly forms the 'backbone' of each map, and other details are fitted in around it. The maps contain 252 geographical names, including 166 place names, and there is some attempt to denote the status of places by the use of different pictorial symbols. The maps are the first in northern Europe to have north at the top,

probably because of the dimensions of the page. One map has an interesting legend stating that 'if the size of the page had permitted, the island would have been shown larger than it is'—a sentence which should always be borne in mind when looking at any early map!

Despite certain inaccuracies, Matthew Paris had a general idea of the shape of Britain (though Scotland is shown as an island), and these maps provide one source of evidence for the study of medieval roads (Hindle, 1982). The same cannot, however, be said for a more diagrammatic map which Paris drew in his commonplace book, purporting to show the four great highways—Icknield Way, Foss Way, Ermine Street and Watling Street (Crone, 1961). This map contains half a dozen fundamental errors, including the intersection of all four roads at Dunstable.

The most important medieval map of Britain is the anonymous map named after the antiquarian Richard Gough who first noted its existence (Parsons, 1958; Hindle, 1980). It is usually dated *c*.1360, but it is likely that it was originally compiled in about 1280, the extant copy being a later revision. It is an outstanding map because of its overall depiction of the shape of the island. Although the promontories of Aberdeen and Caithness are missing, as is Cardigan Bay, it shows over six hundred settlements, and may 'justly boast itself the first among us wherein the roads and distances are laid down'. (Gough, 1780.)

On purely cartographic grounds it is evident that the roads and the topography have been drawn in relation to each other; the roads are no longer the salient feature, as was the case with the earlier maps of Matthew Paris in which all other features were subservient to the Newcastle to Dover route. Here, the delineation of the country is at its best where there is a bracing network of roads, and at its worst in Wales, Scotland and the south west of England where there are few or no roads shown. The sources of the map must have included written itineraries such as were used by travelling justices, carriers and traders, though Lynam (1944) believes that there must have been some sort of general survey of the country. Detail of East Anglia is shown in Fig. 1.2.

In terms of its overall depiction of Britain, it is arguably the best map made before the time of Saxton (1579), and its inclusion of road distances was not repeated until Thomas Jenner's map of England in 1671. Even the earliest road-book (giving distances in tabular form) was not published until 1570. Parsons comments:

It is possible that the Gough map represents a type, of which several copies were in circulation and that they were kept at London and other centres with local details added. This would account for the local roads in Lincolnshire and south-east Yorkshire. The map most probably owes its accuracy in overall proportion to a careful study of road distances … It is legitimate to suppose that it was an official compilation for carriers and other servants of the Crown who must have frequented the fourteenth-century highways. (Parsons, 1958, p.15.)

Perhaps the greatest compliment paid to the compiler of the map was that his distances

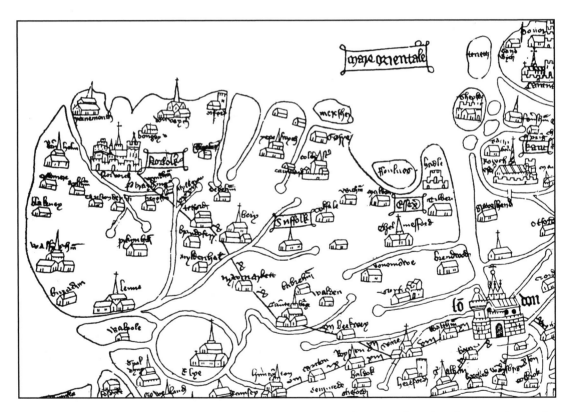

1.2 *Section of the 'Gough Map' (1280-1360). The map shows a large number of settlements, depicted pictorially, and a number of roads—the principal route in this extract is from Norwich to London.*

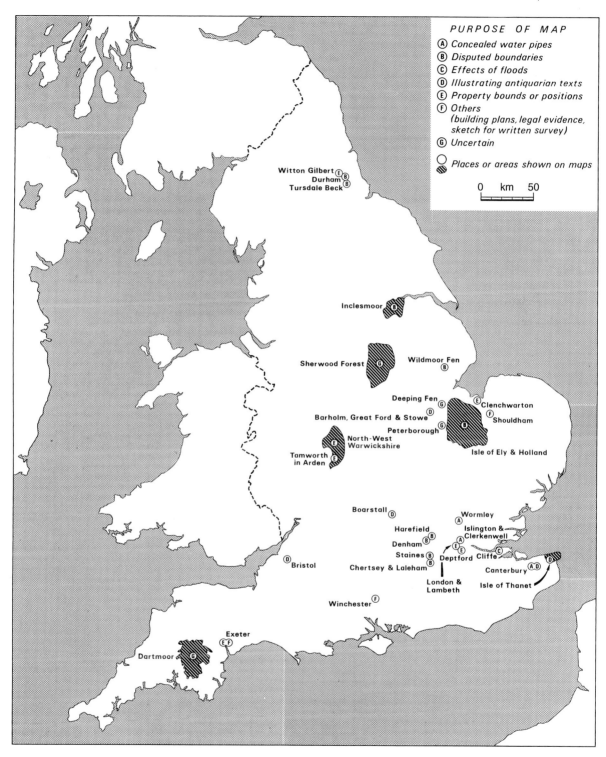

1.3 *Location and purpose of local maps and plans of England before 1500 (after Skelton and Harvey, 1986).*

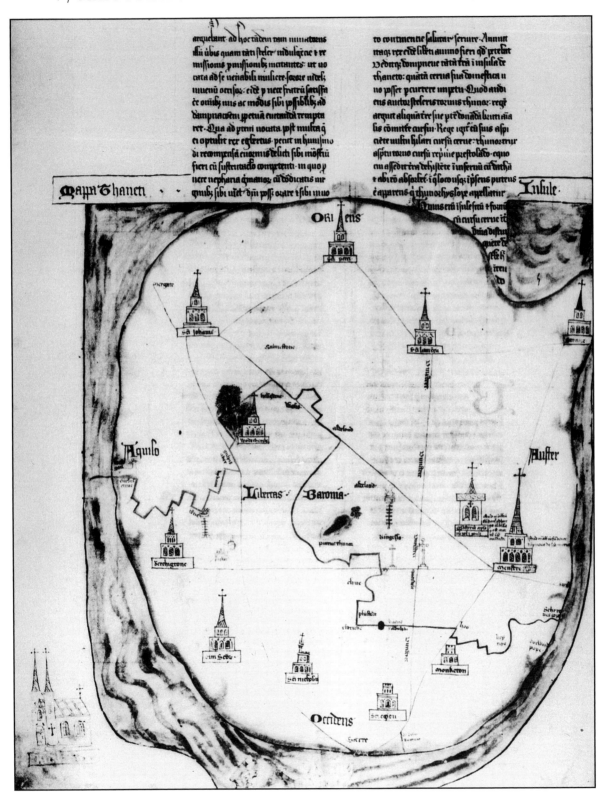

◄ **1.4** *Isle of Thanet, c.1400. East is at the top;
the original scale is roughly 2 inches to the mile.
Probably drawn by Thomas of Elmham to
illustrate a local legend.*

appear as computed mileages in Ogilby's
Britannia (1675), over 300 years later.

The great reputation which the Gough map
deservedly holds for its delineation of roads
cannot, however, be extended to its depiction
of settlements; the symbols themselves which
at first sight appear to be conventional signs,
falling into four fairly clear groups (single
houses, multiple houses, town walls, castles),
in fact give little indication of the importance
of a particular place. Moreover, the choice of
which settlements are shown appears to be
somewhat arbitrary, bearing little relationship
to either borough status or taxable value
(Hindle, 1980).

After the Gough map there is a period of
some 200 years from which there is little in
the cartographic record; in particular, the
national maps show little local detail, and are
often copied one from another (Crone, 1961).
However, surviving local maps and plans for
the period before 1500 have been gathered
together in a single, impressive volume by Paul
Harvey (Skelton and Harvey, 1986). Fig. 1.3
shows the areas covered by the 30 maps which
are reproduced. They are a diverse and scattered collection: seven show areas close to the
Wash, and a further seven are in or near London; at least nine different purposes for them
have been identified. Harvey notes that all
these maps have one thing in common, namely
their simple practicality. They each have a
single purpose and although each may be

accurate for its own purpose, it is usually
impossible to use it as evidence for anything
else. For example, the maps of buried water
pipes may be indispensable for locating the
pipes, but they cannot be used to locate any
other features. Fig. 1.4 depicts the Isle of
Thanet, showing a dozen churches pictorially,
and their linking roads (in red on the original).
The thicker line (in green) is an ecclesiastical
boundary called *cursus cerve*.

All the maps have a strong pictorial element, many using a combination of the plan
and bird's eye view, making them more like
diagrams than true maps. Harvey notes the
'maplessness' of medieval times and says that
this was due not to the low survival rate of
medieval plans but to the fact that map-making
was simply not done. 'Surveys' were commonly
carried out in medieval times, and measurements were taken, but the end result was a
written survey, not a plan or map. The index of
maps and plans in the Public Record Office lists
only four maps dating from before 1500, but 35
for the next 50 years. It is evident, for reasons
that are not entirely clear, that a revolution
occurred in surveying and mapmaking in the
first half of the 16th century. By Elizabethan
times, maps were commonly used by government officials and by the legal profession, and
the trade of the map-maker had been created.
The middle of the 16th century thus marks the
true beginning of English cartography (Harvey,
1993). Onto this Elizabethan stage stepped
Christopher Saxton to initiate the long history
of the English county map. Saxton later became
an estate surveyor, and the next two chapters
begin with his county and estate maps
respectively.

Chapter Two

COUNTY MAPS

Saxton and the early county maps

The flowering of English cartography in the middle of the 16th century saw its greatest achievement in the first complete set of county maps, surveyed by Christopher Saxton (Tyacke and Huddy, 1980). Little is known of Saxton's early life, nor of how he came to be England's first great map-maker. He certainly worked for John Rudd who had been preparing a map of England and Wales, and by the mid-1570s was working for Thomas Seckford, who in turn was employed by William Cecil, Lord Burghley. It is clear that Saxton's surveys had government backing, for Saxton was being rewarded by the Queen from 1574 onwards. The government must have felt the need for accurate and detailed surveys of the country, for all manner of administrative reasons, whether related to taxation or to defence, and the technology to survey the maps was newly available (Ravenhill, 1985, 1992). However, Saxton's were not the first regional maps of England and Wales; a map of 'debatable land' in Liddesdale, in the Scottish Borders, survives, drawn by Bullock in 1552, and the 'Burghley-Saxton' atlas includes maps of Durham, Northamptonshire and the area between Hull and Scarborough, all drawn in about 1570 (Tyacke and Huddy, pp.27-9).

Saxton produced his 34 county maps in an incredibly short period of time; the first was engraved in 1574 and the series was complete within five years; in 1576 alone no less than eight maps, covering 15 counties, were published. The dates of survey and publication are given in Evans and Lawrence (1979, pp.15-19). Saxton's maps vary in scale from 1½ miles to the inch (Monmouth) to almost 5 miles to the

inch (Kent, Lancashire, Lincoln and Northumberland), the scale of each map clearly depending on the size and shape of each county. Yorkshire had to be split across two plates, but nine of the maps show more than one county.

In order to understand what Saxton's maps show it is helpful to speculate on the means by which he actually conducted his survey. He was probably able to use some maps now lost to us, as well as written sources, but it is certain that direct observation in the field was the new and special element of his work. It seems that he used to ascend to some high position, such as a church tower, castle, or, more rarely, a hill, with locals who knew the country. He would then take bearings on surrounding towns, villages, hills and other components of the landscape, and the locals would tell him their names, giving him an idea how far away they were; all this information would be sketched, and Saxton would amalgamate his drawings and measurements later. There was clearly no attempt at the precise kind of triangulation undertaken by surveyors two centuries later, though Saxton may have used the rudimentary technique described by the Belgian cartographer Frisius in 1533.

Looking at a Saxton county map, two features immediately stand out: the hills and the settlements (Fig. 2.1). The relief is shown in crude perspective so these 'sugar-loaf' hills give a general impression of the topography, though only a few hills are actually named. The villages and towns are shown by a set of symbols. These appear to have been used rather randomly; they are often based on a minute drawing of a church with a tower, containing a circle and a dot, but

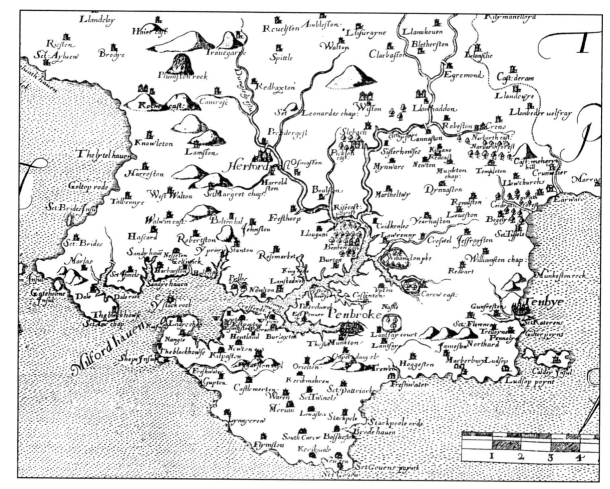

2.1 *Saxton: Pembrokeshire, 1578. Notice the relatively crude engraving, and the total absence of roads.*

the larger scale maps have a greater range of symbols. There is no key to these, and their different sizes do not give any accurate reflection of the size or status of a place. In fact, the size of the lettering is a better guide. The maps do, however, give a clear depiction of the coastline and of rivers and lakes, some bridges are shown, as are parks (surrounded by a pale), trees, and, on five maps only, the hundreds of the county. But the greatest omission is of roads, which reduces the usefulness of the maps considerably; this is all the more surprising as Saxton in his travels must have been in a uniquely fortunate position to be able to survey and then depict the main routes.

The maps also contain a title and scale bar, a local crest or two, and the names of adjacent counties. It should be noted that they were printed in black only; any colouring was added by hand later. No one could claim that Saxton's maps are jewels of the cartographer's art, yet the detail which he provides for England and Wales as a whole was not to be surpassed for over 200 years. Indeed, his original copper plates were sold or passed on. They were probably last used in 1770, having been variously altered in the meantime by, for example, William Webb, in 1645, Philip Lea, in *c*.1690, George Willdey, in *c*.1730, and Thomas Jefferys, in *c*.1750 (Tyacke and Huddy, pp.37-9). Saxton was not the only cartographer producing county maps in the 16th century, although he was certainly the only one who completed the mapping of the whole of England and Wales.

John Norden was perhaps the most important of the later Elizabethan cartographers (Kitchen, 1997). He wanted to produce a set of county descriptions which would be entitled *Speculum Britanniae*, containing new maps, and a text with much archaeological and historic detail. Of this series only Middlesex and Hertfordshire were published in his lifetime,

but Cornwall was printed in 1728 and has been reprinted (Norden, 1966a). During the 1590s Norden produced manuscript maps of several counties in southern England, but due to shortages of money only five were printed in his lifetime (Middlesex, Hertfordshire, Surrey, Sussex and Hampshire). The other surveys, of Kent, Northamptonshire, Essex, Cornwall, the Isle of Wight, Guernsey and Jersey remained in manuscript. Norden may well also have surveyed Norfolk, Suffolk, and Warwickshire, but these maps have either been lost or have

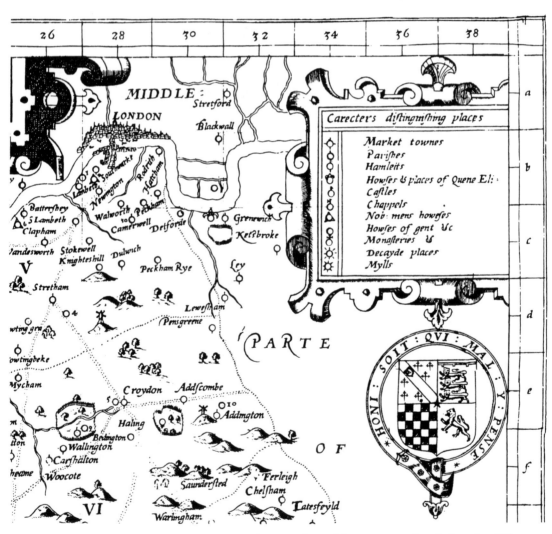

2.2 *Norden: Surrey, 1594. Norden's maps show roads, and have conventional signs for different places.*

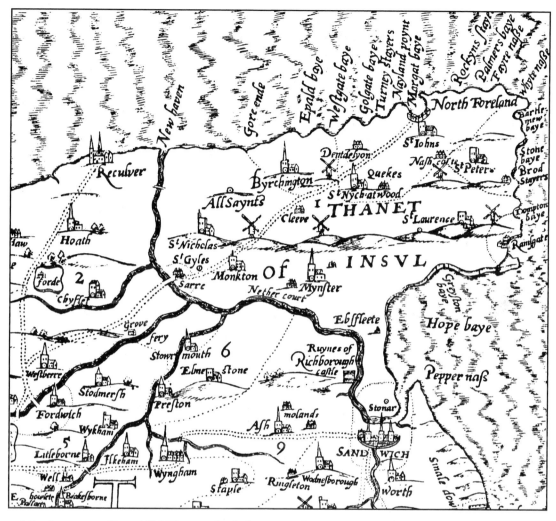

2.3 *Symonson: Kent, 1596. The standard of cartography is improving, but there is still little detail—no more in fact than in the map drawn two hundred years earlier (Fig. 1.4).*

survived only in doubtful versions copied by other hands (Skelton 1952, p.53; Tooley, 1970, p.66).

Norden's maps contain several improvements compared to those of Saxton. First, most show roads and hundred boundaries; second, they have a gazetteer with a referencing system in the margins; third, they have distance tables; and fourth, they use conventional signs, with a key, for the first time on a British map (Fig. 2.2). Norden's improvements were such that his maps were preferred to those of Saxton where they were available. Sadly, however,

Norden received little encouragement, and remained poor throughout his life.

Other original maps of this period include 12 by William Smith, drawn in *c.*1602-3. Two are probably based on original work (Lancashire and Cheshire), eight are based on Saxton (Essex, Warwickshire, Leicestershire, Suffolk, Norfolk, Northamptonshire, Worcester and Staffordshire) and two on Norden (Surrey and Hertfordshire). He probably obtained his additional information from local correspondents. Philip Symonson produced a map of Kent in 1596, which has been reprinted by the Ordnance

2.4 *Speed: Isle of Man, 1605. Based on a survey by Thomas Durham in 1595. Note the strange distortion of the surrounding coastlines.*

2.5 *Morden: Lancashire, 1695. One of the Saxton/Speed maps, updated to include roads and sandbanks.* ➤

Survey. It is the best county map of its time, showing roads and using symbols to distinguish churches with spires from those with towers (Fig. 2.3).

Saxton's and Norden's maps were extensively copied by later cartographers, a few of whom added or corrected details, but most of whom simply redesigned the maps (often making errors) without setting foot outside their workshops (Skelton, 1970). Among the earliest copies are those in Camden's *Britannia* of 1607, which credits 41 maps to Saxton and six to Norden; nine maps have no cartographer's name. The most famous copies, however, are those issued by John Speed after 1610 (Nicolson & Hawkyard, 1988). He was quite open about his sources, admitting, 'I have put my sickle into other mens corne'. In fact Speed borrowed freely from Saxton, Norden, Smith, Symonson and others, but his maps are more decorative, have some extra places named,

mostly show the hundreds, and above all have plans of one or two towns on each sheet (see Chapter 4). Speed attempted to revise his information about some counties, but only by obtaining notes from local antiquaries; he did, however, print maps of the Isles of Man and Wight for the first time, although these were based on earlier surveys (Fig. 2.4).

The place names on these early county maps have been much studied—often to see which were omitted or included. The precise spelling of the place names can give clear clues to the process of copying. For example, if we take the places named in West Derby hundred (Lancashire) on the maps of Saxton (1577), Smith (1603) and Speed (1610) the 'odd one out' in the spelling is nearly always Smith. In fact, of the 102 places named by both Saxton and Speed only 19 have different spellings, nine of which differ only by one letter (usually a terminal 'e'). Moreover, Speed has added four

places not recorded by Saxton. Smith gives 37 spellings which appear in neither Saxton nor Speed, many of which are distinctly different. Thus from this evidence alone it is reasonable to infer that Speed copied Saxton, adding a few places, whilst Smith's map was more original.

Speed's maps were themselves copied until about 1770; for example, the Dutch firm of Blaeu produced particularly artistic versions of Speed's work in 1645. Perhaps the greatest single improvement to these county maps, however, was the addition of roads, using the information in Ogilby's road book (*Britannia*) of 1675. Philip Lea added roads to his version of Saxton's atlas (1689-93), as did Morden to his versions of Speed's maps produced for another edition of Camden's *Britannia* in 1695 (Morden, 1695) (Fig. 2.5). Morden had set about his task with the high aim of producing 'new' maps, but in fact his are composite documents incorporating the county maps of Norden, Smith and Speed; such later surveys as were available; Ogilby's roads; and, in the case of coastal counties, some detail from coasting charts, such as those made by Collins. Morden

says that his maps had been sent to 'knowing gentlemen' in each county for comment. One result of this was that the roads do not generally agree with those in Ogilby's *Britannia*.

The 17th century was clearly the age of the map *publisher* as opposed to the map surveyor; there was no copyright law, and it seems that each and every publisher copied every other publisher's maps without permission, hindrance or even acknowledgement—and only very rarely with any revision.

Perhaps the most sobering fact about all these early county maps is their sheer profusion; writing over 80 years ago, Fordham (1914) was able to note 43 different maps of Hertfordshire between Saxton and the next original large scale survey (1766). He also noted 106 reprints of those maps; many were small copies deriving ultimately from Saxton and Norden (Fig. 2.6), although Seller's map of 1676 was a rare attempt at a fresh survey. It was not until the 1720s that a new, larger map of the county appeared. Much the same is true for every other county, although Hertfordshire was better served than most.

2.6 *Speed: Hertfordshire, 1627. One of the many reduced sized derivative county maps; this is an early example from Speed's Pocket Atlas.*

Bibliographies of County Maps

Bedford: Tooley, 1978; Chambers, 1983
Berkshire: Tooley, 1979; Burden, 1988
Brecon: Lewis, 1972
Buckingham: Wyatt, 1978; Tooley, 1981
Cambridge: Tooley, 1981
Cardigan: Lewis, 1955
Cheshire: Tooley, 1981
Cornwall: Tooley, 1982
Cumberland: Tooley, 1982; Higham, 1997
Derbyshire: Handford, 1971; Tooley, 1984
Devon: Tooley, 1985; Batten & Bennett, 1996
Dorset: Tooley, 1985
Durham: Tooley, 1986
Essex: Emmison, 1955; Tooley, 1986
Gloucester: Tooley, 1987
Hampshire: Rodger, 1989
Hereford: Rodger, 1990
Hertford: Hodson, 1974; Rodger, 1992
Isle of Man: Cubbon, 1967; Coakley (forthcoming)
Isle of Wight: Rodger, 1995
Kent: Bergess, 1992
Lancashire: Whitaker, 1938; Bagley & Hodgkiss, 1985

Leicester: Baum, 1972
Lincoln: Carroll, 1996
London, Hyde, 1975; Howgego, 1978
Merioneth: Lewis, 1949
Monmouth: Michael, 1985
Montgomery: Jones, 1987
Norfolk: Chubb & Stephen, 1928; Frostick (forthcoming)
Northants: Whitaker, 1948
Northumberland: Whitaker, 1949
Nottingham: Wadsworth, 1930
Oxford: Leighfield (forthcoming)
Radnor: Lewis, 1977
Rutland: Goldmark & Traylen, 1985
Shropshire: Cowling, 1959
Somerset: Needell, 1995
Stafford: King, 1988
Surrey: Sharp, 1929
Sussex: Kingsley, 1982
Warwick: Harvey & Thorpe, 1959
Westmorland: Curwen, 1918
Wiltshire: Chubb, 1912
Yorkshire: Whitaker, 1933; Raistrick, 1969

Note: most of these bibliographies refer only to printed maps. Limited lists exist for most other counties; see Armitage (1990/95)

A useful bibliography is given by Tooley (1970, pp.72-4); however, it is vital to check for up to date literature on each county (see list above). Studies such as that by Chambers (1983) on Bedfordshire continue the tradition of carto-bibliography begun by Fordham, Harrison, Whitaker and Chubb in the early years of this century, while more general descriptions such as that of Lancashire by Bagley and Hodgkiss (1985) are of great use and interest, even if they do not contain a complete list of all county maps. Certain non-county areas may also have been the subject of such a list (for example the Fens).

The basic starting-point for national bibliographies is the work of Chubb (1927), Skelton (1970), Rodger (1972) and Shirley (1980, 1988).

The cartographers themselves are detailed in Eden (1975-9), whilst a contribution on early 18th-century county atlases is to be found in Hodson (1984, 1989).

After the great cartographic steps forward taken in the Elizabethan period there was little further progress, other than the reprinting and plagiarism already noted, until towards the end of the 17th century. A few new county surveys were undertaken, however: for example, Plot's Oxfordshire (1677) and Staffordshire (1682); Ogilby's Essex (1678) and Middlesex (1677), shown in Fig. 2.7, and Seller's Hertfordshire (1676), Kent (1680) and Middlesex (1680). Seller also surveyed Surrey, Buckinghamshire, and Oxford, and both he and Ogilby had plans to produce new 'English Atlases' (Skelton, 1952,

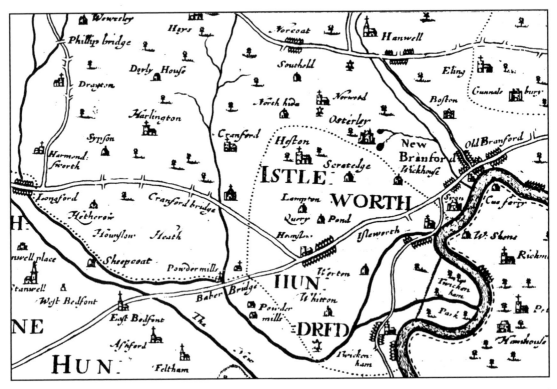

2.7 *Ogilby: Middlesex, 1677. Ogilby had undertaken a survey of all the main roads in England and Wales; this county map shows them clearly.*

pp.70-4; Harley, 1972, p.69). The method of survey of Warburton's Yorkshire (1720), one of the last of this generation of 'primitive' maps, is known in some detail (Crump, 1928).

During this period, county maps became increasingly embellished. The London map trade became well established, though sadly not on the basis of new survey work. A brief run through the leading map publishers might have included Overton, Lea, Bowles, Senex, Sayer, Moll, Bowen, and Kitchin, whose catalogues would include Saxton's maps alongside their 'newest surveys'. But as Richard Gough remarked at the end of the 18th century, 'as to the several sets of county maps professing to be drawn from the *latest* observations, they are almost invariably copies of those that preceded them'. He singled out Bowen and Kitchin for particular criticism in this regard.

Large scale county surveys

The 18th century saw a slow but steady trickle of newly surveyed county maps: 20 appeared between 1699 and 1761, but between 1765 and 1783 no less than 29 new county maps were produced. Thus, for the first time since Saxton's day, two hundred years before, there was now a virtually complete new survey of England. By 1800 only Cambridgeshire among English counties remained unsurveyed (although a survey had been started by Mason in the 1750s). In Wales the only unsurveyed counties in 1800 were Pembrokeshire, Cardigan, Carmarthen, Radnor and Brecon. Taken together, these new county maps are probably among the most important cartographic sources for the student of local history.

The reason for this great upsurge of carto-graphic activity is often attributed to the offer

Large scale county maps of England (1699-1839) (after Laxton, 1976)

County	Cartographer Date *Facsimile: [Publisher, Date; Author of commentary]* Maps in **bold** were awarded a prize by the Society of Arts
Bedford:	Gordon 1736; Jefferys 1765 *[?, c.1990]*; Greenwood 1826; Bryant 1826
Berkshire:	Rocque 1761 *[Margary, 1973; Laxton]*; Greenwood 1824
Buckingham:	Jefferys 1770; Bryant 1825
Cambridge:	Baker 1821
Cheshire:	Burdett 1777 *[Hist. Soc. Lancs. & Ches., 1974; Harley & Laxton]*; Greenwood 1819; Swire & Hutchings 1830; Bryant 1831
Cornwall:	Gascoyne 1699 *[Devon & Cornwall Rec. Soc., 1991; Ravenhill & Padel]*; Martyn 1748; Greenwood 1827
Cumberland:	Donald 1774; Greenwood 1823
Derby:	**Burdett 1767** *[Derbys. Arch. Soc., 1975; Fowkes, Harley & Harvey]*; Greenwood 1825; Sanderson 1836
Devon:	**Donn 1765** *[Devon & Cornwall Rec. Soc., 1965; Ravenhill]*; Greenwood 1827
Dorset:	Taylor 1765; Greenwood 1826; Outhett 1826
Durham:	Armstrong 1768; Greenwood 1820; Hobson 1839
Essex:	Warburton 1726; Chapman & André 1777 *[Essex R. O., 1950; Emmison]* *[Margary, 1972]*; Greenwood 1825
Gloucester:	Taylor 1777 *[Bristol & Gloucs. Arch. Soc., 1961]*; Greenwood 1824; Bryant 1824
Hampshire:	Taylor 1759; **Milne 1791**; Greenwood 1826 *[ALL: Margary, 1977; Laxton]*
Hereford:	Taylor 1754; Price 1817; Bryant 1835
Hertford:	Warburton 1725/49[2]; Andrews & Dury 1766[1]; Bryant 1822[2] *[ALL: Herts. Libraries, [1]1980, [2]1985; Hodson]*
Huntingdon:	Gordon 1731; Jefferys 1768; Ellis 1825; Greenwood 1831
Kent:	Andrews, Dury & Herbert 1769 *[Margary, 1969]*; Greenwood 1821
Lancashire:	**Yates 1786** *[Hist. Soc. Lancs. & Ches., 1968; Harley]* *[Richardson, 1982]*; Greenwood 1818; Hennett 1830
Leicester:	**Prior 1779** *[Leics. Libraries, 1984; Leics. Ind. Hist. Soc.]*; Greenwood 1826
Lincoln:	Armstrong 1779; Bryant 1828; Greenwood 1830
Middlesex:	Warburton 1725/49 *[G.L.C., 1967]*; Rocque 1754 *[Middx. Arch. Soc., 196?]*; Cary 1786; Greenwood 1819
Monmouth:	Snell 1785; Price 1823; Greenwood 1830

Norfolk:	Foster 1739; Donald & Milne 1797 [*Norfolk Rec. Soc., 1975; Barringer*] [*Lark's Press, 1989; Barringer*]; Bryant 1826
Northampton:	Jefferys 1779 [*Northants. Libraries, 1975; Hatley*]; Greenwood 1826; Bryant 1827 [*Northants. Libraries, 1988; Hatley*]
Northumberland:	**Armstrong 1769**; Fryer 1820; Greenwood 1828
Nottingham:	Chapman 1776; Greenwood 1826; Ellis 1827; Sanderson 1835
Oxford:	Overton 1715; Jefferys 1767; **Davis 1797** [*Riden, 1975*]; Bryant 1824
Rutland:	Armstrong 1780; Greenwood 1826
Shropshire:	Wood 1710; Rocque 1752; **Baugh 1808** [*Shrops. Arch. Soc., 1983; Trinder*]; Greenwood 1827
Somerset:	**Day & Masters 1782**; Greenwood 1822 [*BOTH: Som. Arch. Soc., 1981; Dunning & Harley*]
Stafford:	Yates 1775 [*Staffs. Rec. Soc./Margary, 1984; Phillips*]; Greenwood 1820; Phillips & Hutchings 1832
Suffolk:	Kirby 1736; **Hodskinson 1783** [*Suffolk Rec. Soc., 1972; Dymond*]; Greenwood 1825; Bryant 1826
Surrey:	Senex 1729; Rocque c.1768[3]; Lindley & Crosley 1792[3]; Greenwood 1823[3] [[3] *Margary, 1974; Ravenhill*]; Bryant 1823
Sussex:	Budgen 1724; Yeakell & Gardner 1783[4] (southern half only; completed by **Gream 1793**[4]); Greenwood 1825[4] [[4] *Margary, 1970; Skelton*]
Warwick:	Beighton c.1727; Yates 1793; Greenwood 1822
Westmorland:	Jefferys 1770; Greenwood 1824; Hodgson 1828
Wiltshire:	Andrews & Dury 1773 [*Wilts. Arch. & Nat. Hist. Soc., 1952; Crittall*]
Worcester:	Taylor 1772; Greenwood 1822
Yorkshire:	Jefferys 1771 [*Margary, 1973; Harley & Harvey*]; Greenwood 1817; Bryant 1829 (East Riding only)

Welsh county maps (in chronological order) (excluding Monmouth)

Denbigh/Flint:	William 1720
North Wales (Anglesey/Flint/Denbigh/Caernarvon/Merioneth/Montgomery):	
	Evans 1795
Glamorgan:	Yates 1799 [*S. Wales Rec. Soc., 1984; James & Walters*]
Cardigan:	**Singer 1803**
Brecon/Glamorgan/Radnor:	
	Greenwood 1828

A fuller list of large scale county maps with their various reprints and copies is given in Rodger (1972); but see also Tooley (1978-87), Rodger (1989-95) and Armitage (1990/95). For Wales see Walters (1968).

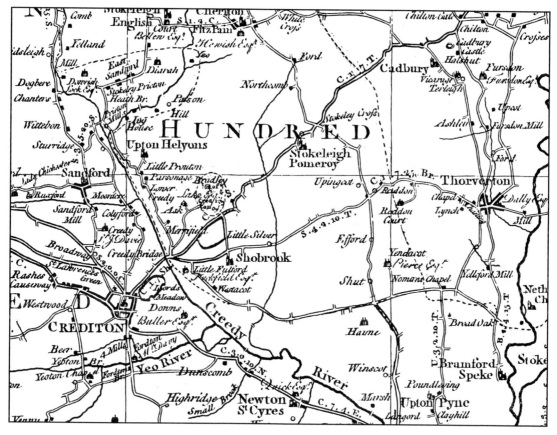

2.8 *Donn: Devon, 1765. Part of the first large scale county map to win a Society of Arts prize; note that minor roads are not shown.*

of a premium by the Society of Arts for new and accurate county surveys. However, as we shall see, local demand was just as important (if not more so) in encouraging cartographers.

The Society of Arts first offered its premium of £100 in 1759 and this continued intermittently until 1808 (Harley, 1963-4; 1965). The first prize in 1765 was won by Benjamin Donn for his map of Devon, shown in Fig. 2.8. In fact only three premiums were awarded in the first 20 years of the scheme, and only a further ten in the last 30 years; of the 48 maps published during the whole period, only 23 were even submitted for an award. The influence of the Society's premiums, however, was greater than these figures suggest, because they encouraged and speeded up the survey work which had

been going on sporadically for the previous 80 years.

Some cartographers, such as Thomas Jefferys (who had a hand in the mapping of eight counties in all, including Yorkshire), had their surveys turned down for reasons which were more bureaucratic than cartographic. Indeed the extra expense of having to commission his own surveys helped lead to Jefferys' bankruptcy in 1766. It is important to bear in mind that even if a cartographer received the full prize of £100 this would only pay for a small part of the total cost of a county survey: the cheapest recorded was Armstrong's Northumberland whose costs totalled £516, while Yeakell and Gardner estimated that a full survey of Sussex (at double the scale) would have cost £2,400.

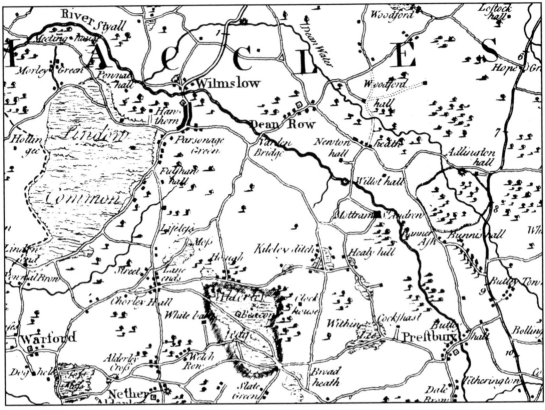

2.9 *Burdett: Cheshire, 1777. An accurate map, but lacking in detail.*

In total, over 50 years, the Society paid out only £460, eight prize-winners receiving gold or silver medals—or a silver palette instead. Most of the maps were in fact promoted and sponsored by local patrons and wealthy residents who often had their names and houses engraved on the maps.

Many cartographers were local to the areas they mapped. Of the first three recipients of awards, Donn was a teacher, Burdett an amateur surveyor (Fig. 2.9), and Armstrong an army lieutenant. It was not until 1783 that Hodskinson, a professional London map-maker, won a prize for his map of Suffolk. Perhaps the whole business of providing original maps was too expensive and risky for the London map trade to undertake. But, as a sad footnote, many of the plates produced by the local map-makers later fell into the hands of

London cartographers (particularly William Faden) who then made profits where they had failed to invest (see Fig. 2.10). Thus many of these county maps continued to be published, often with little or no revision, until well into the 19th century. They were also used as the basis for many smaller scale maps. This was exactly the same fate as that which had befallen Saxton's maps two centuries earlier.

The contribution of the Society of Arts was thus significant. It gave direct encouragement to a few cartographers, often amateurs, many of whom (such as Armstrong) continued to produce further maps, and it also encouraged the art of cartography in a more general way. More important was the fact that there was a demand within each county for new and accurate surveys. These were mainly produced on a subscription basis, with a couple of hundred

2.10 *Yates: Stafford-shire, 1775. Additions and changes made to the south-west sheet by William Faden for his 1799 edition (Phillips, 1984).*

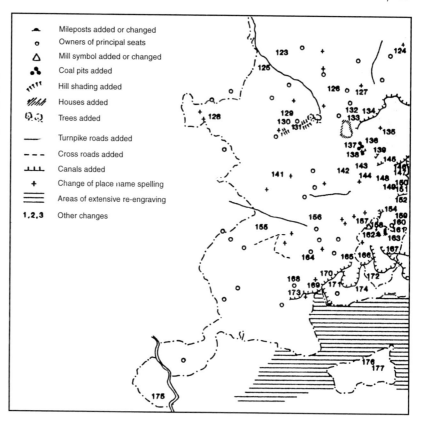

Key:
- ▲ Mileposts added or changed
- ○ Owners of principal seats
- △ Mill symbol added or changed
- ♣ Coal pits added
- ꙮ Hill shading added
- ﹍ Houses added
- ☍ Trees added
- —— Turnpike roads added
- - - - Cross roads added
- ⊥⊥⊥ Canals added
- + Change of place name spelling
- ═══ Areas of extensive re-engraving
- **1,2,3** Other changes

subscribers paying part of the cost in advance. This demand was the real *raison d'être* of the great period of English county maps.

The new county maps were based on accurate triangulation rather than the sketch/traverse method before; some maps even included the triangulation diagrams. Indeed, in 1759 the Society of Arts had stipulated: (a) a trigonometrical survey; (b) the accurate measurement of road distances; (c) correct latitude and longitude; (d) that a survey should be completed in one, or at the most, two years; and (e) perhaps most important, that a scale of one inch to one mile be used (some surveys were published at larger scales—often two miles to the inch). Finally, the Society aimed to check the accuracy of the maps submitted to it.

These maps often provide the first detailed cartographic source for many features of the rural landscape, showing land use, industrial sites, communications and towns. Most counties have a series of maps which, when followed by the productions of the Ordnance Survey, give a continuing record of changes in the landscape for over 200 years.

The first problem may be to establish the date of the map. The date of engraving and publication could have been long after the survey was begun; moreover, different parts of a county would have been surveyed at different dates. Day and Master's Somerset (1728) took seven years to survey, whilst Yates' Lancashire, published in 1786, had been surveyed in the early 1770s. Rocque's Berkshire was begun in 1752, and not completed until 1761. These are all relatively short periods of time, but they may help to explain omissions or inconsistencies.

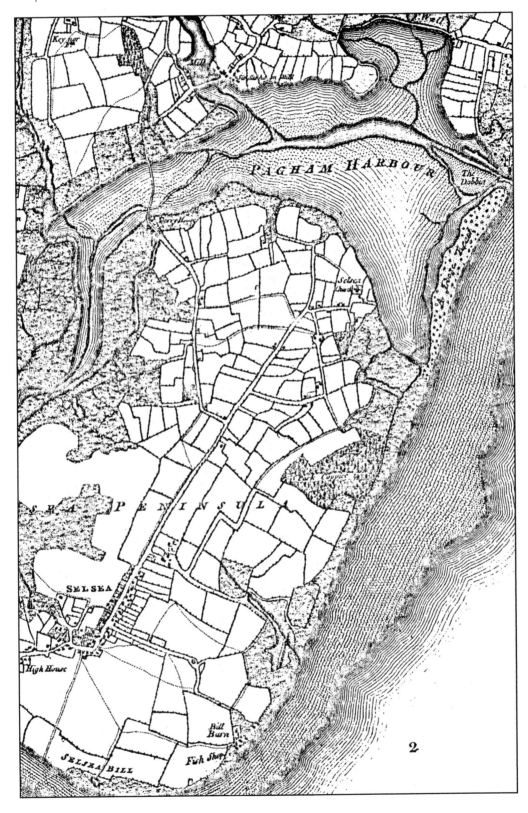

The surveyors of these maps were human, and individual, each with his own eye for the country around him; thus each would concentrate more on certain features than others. One might faithfully record every windmill and coal-mine, while the next might concentrate more on antiquarian features. Rocque, for example, had been a landscape architect, and thus he shows parks in great detail. Therefore, it is important to know a little about each surveyor in order to try to determine how he might have seen the landscape.

We like to assume that all these 18th-century surveys were original, but it is hard to envisage any surveyor ignoring the existence of any estate maps which would save him time and effort, especially if the surveyor himself was also in the business of making estate plans.

Some later editions of these maps were altered when they were re-issued by subsequent owners of the plates. For example, William Faden re-issued Yates' Staffordshire in 1799, almost a quarter of a century after its first appearance. He re-engraved one sheet extensively, and made numerous small changes to the rest. He incorporated some information from other surveys and added a plan of Lichfield. The changes included the addition of the seats of nobility and gentry, the correction of place name spellings and the marking of new turnpikes, canals and some industrial sites. The result was a clarification and improvement of the map—but not a full revision (Phillips, 1984, pp.xxiii-xxx) (see Fig. 2.10.). However, the scale of changes made here was unusually large: most reissues had far fewer alterations, and some had none at all. The facsimile of Taylor's Gloucestershire of 1777 (listed above) is in fact Faden's 'second edition' published in 1800. Donald's Cumberland (1774)

was reissued by Faden in 1802 (unchanged) and then corrected by Fryer in 1818. It was also published at ½-inch scale in 1783 (revised in 1810). The area around Keswick was issued as a single sheet environs map (clearly aimed at the early tourists) in 1789.

Local historians will be interested principally in the depiction of various topographical features and their accuracy and reliability. We must not expect the same standards as those set by modern O.S. maps, but we must try to assess how much topographical detail has been faithfully recorded. There seems to be an inverse relationship between geodetic accuracy and the amount of topographic detail; for example, the maps of Burdett, Prior, Armstrong and Donn are accurate but thin on detail (see Fig. 2.9.). On the other hand, Yeakell and Gardner's 2-inch survey of Sussex (1783) contains some very fine topographical detail (Fig. 2.11).

It is important to assess the accuracy of specific features on each map separately. In this respect, the depiction of field boundaries and land use has attracted most attention (Laxton, 1976, pp.44-7; Wallis, 1981, p.46). Perhaps the best way to put this topic into perspective is to look at the similar scale modern 1:50,000 map, which makes no attempt to show individual houses or field boundaries, and illustrates only a few types of land use—such as woodland, orchards and parks; no attempt is made to distinguish between different types of farming land. It is not until we look at the modern 1:25,000 map that field boundaries appear, and in fact, of all the early county maps, only Yeakell and Gardner's 2-inch map of Sussex (1783) claimed to show all the fields individually (Fig. 2.11).

Rocque's Berkshire (1761), also published at the 2-inch scale, appears at first glance to show individual fields and types of land use (Fig. 2.12), but on closer examination it is clear that the fields are drawn far too large, and we have to ask whether the land use depicted is

◄ **2.11** *Yeakell and Gardner: Sussex, 1783. This uncompleted map of Sussex shows much topographical detail—at a scale of 2 inches to the mile.*

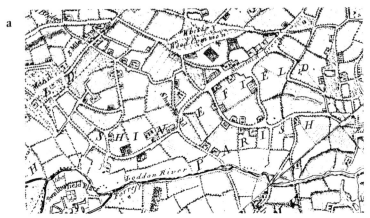

a

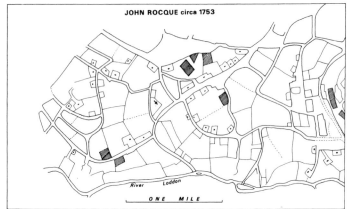

b

JOHN ROCQUE circa 1753

River Loddon

ONE MILE

◁ **2.12** *Rocque: Berkshire, 1761. (a) The area around Shinfield (surveyed c.1753) appears to give a detailed depiction of the fields, but a comparison of Rocque's field boundaries (b) with two later surveys (c, d) shows the extent of his generalisations. (Laxton, 1976)*

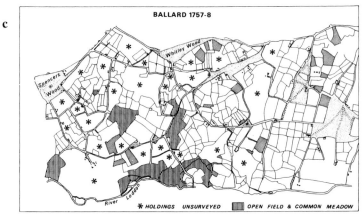

c

BALLARD 1757-8

Whitley Wood

Spencers Wood

River Loddon

* *HOLDINGS UNSURVEYED*   ▥ *OPEN FIELD & COMMON MEADOW*

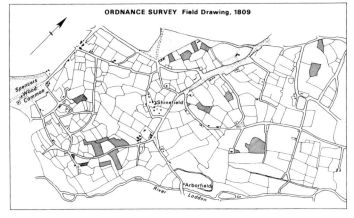

d

ORDNANCE SURVEY Field Drawing, 1809

Spencers Wood Common

Shinfield

Arborfield

River Loddon

2.13 *Donald: Cumberland, 1774. The turnpikes from White-haven, enacted in 1738, are shown, complete with distances and the location of toll bars. A number of patrons have their names engraved on the map.* ➤

pure invention or an attempt to 'generalise' what actually existed. Laxton (1976) has compared Rocque's map with more detailed estate plans, notably with those done by Josiah Ballard, who probably also surveyed Rocque's map. Ballard's estate plans are all dated after the equivalent parts of Rocque's map and it is likely that Ballard did his detailed plans after completing the county survey. Laxton concludes that, generally, the map is a reasonable record of major features such as woodland, roads, settlement, heaths and commons, and that the balance in the map between arable and grassland is probably realistic. The large open arable fields are depicted with some degree of accuracy, but, on the other hand, Rocque's field boundaries are pure fiction; he shows only 10-15 per cent of the actual number of fields. Even the Ordnance Survey Field Drawings of

1809 (also done at 2-inch scale) do not contain all the necessary detail, and we have to wait until the first 6-inch survey of 1872-7 for an accurate depiction of field boundaries. It is a great pity that no field drawings survive for these early county maps. On Yates' map of Staffordshire (1775) it is possible to distinguish moor, moss, heath, woodland, forest and parkland, although there is no attempt to show agricultural land use (Phillips, 1984, pp.xi-xv). Similar work would have to be done to determine the land use accuracy of any of the maps.

Some industrial sites are found on all these county maps—most commonly wind- or watermills, indicated either by name or by symbol (Smith, 1990). Jefferys' map of Yorkshire (1775) shows 736 watermills and 184 windmills, but we need to know whether this is anywhere near the real total, whether certain

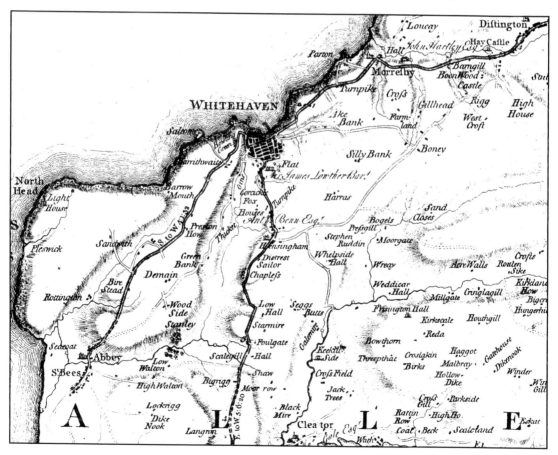

types of mill were more likely to be missed, whether mills which were not working are shown, whether the type of mill (if given) is correct, and so on. Jefferys used three surveyors for different parts of the county (Ainslie, Donald and Hodskinson), and it is extremely unlikely that they all surveyed to the same standards. Equally, it may be difficult to compare the detail on this map with that given by different cartographers for neighbouring counties. It is thus hard to use the map evidence without documentary or archaeological back-up; all three types of evidence need to be taken in conjunction with one another. Laxton indicates some ways through this difficult area (Laxton, 1976, pp.47-9).

Mills are the best depicted indication of industry—watermills because the rivers were nearly always accurately surveyed (partly due to a concern for possible navigation) and windmills because they were prominent features in the landscape. Other forms of industry are less well shown. Burdett's depiction of sites of the Cheshire salt industry in the 1770s bears little resemblance to reality; Yates' map of Lancashire is equally difficult to use for the study of coal-mining, and Yates' Staffordshire gives no indication of the Burslem pottery industry.

Communications are usually well depicted on these maps, for they show not only the main roads which had been shown on older county maps since the end of the 17th century, but also a range of lesser roads. By this time many of the main roads had been turnpiked, and these are usually shown distinctly, often by the use of thicker lines; milestones and toll-bars are also shown (Fig. 2.13). In the absence of detailed turnpike plans, these maps are often of great use in determining the routes taken by early turnpikes; the information given in the Turnpike Acts themselves is usually rather brief (Hindle, 1984, pp.138-41; 1993, pp.105-30).

These county maps were the first attempt to map local roads in any detail; they were certainly not all carefully traversed, and of course many are omitted, but nevertheless the road network depicted is usually very full. Fig. 2.14 shows the area around Wolverhampton on Yates' map of 1775, where the turnpikes and roads are depicted in some detail. The transport feature which stands out most clearly here though is the canal system, principally the Birmingham Canal (opened in 1772), looping its way past Tipton on its original route, since much altered. Yates also shows one canal further north-west in the county which was never built. It was quite common for county maps to show canal routes drawn from plans

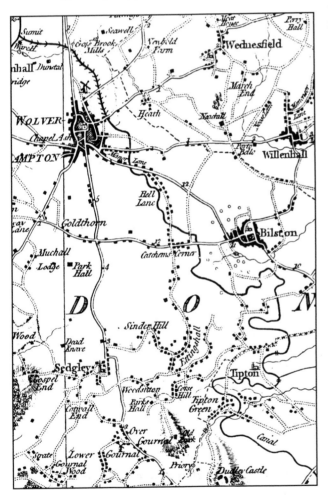

2.14 *Yates: Staffordshire, 1775. A remarkable number of roads appear, as well as the new canal, and various industrial sites.*

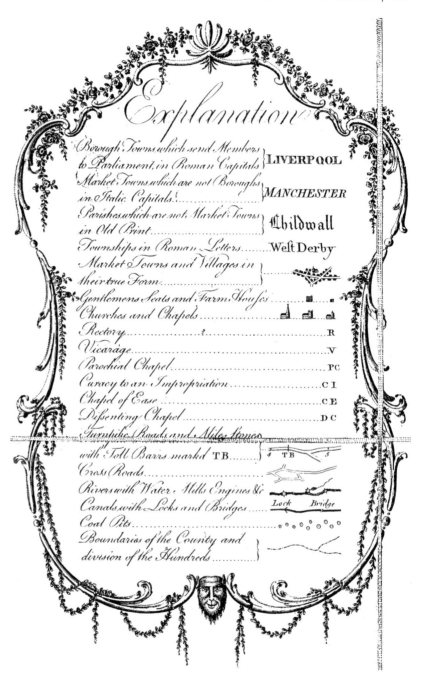

2.15 *Yates: Lancashire, 1786. A full and detailed key is given.*

issued by their promoters. Often such plans were changed, or never came to fruition at all.

Parish boundaries are shown on a handful of maps; for example, Martyn's Cornwall (1748); and Rocque's Middlesex (1754) and Berkshire (1761). It must have been difficult to get this information into map form, and it is hardly surprising that few cartographers attempted it.

Finally, settlements are shown, but again only in a generalised way. Individual country houses, and many farms, are usually clearly shown, though comparison with estate plans will show how much generalisation has occurred. As with modern maps at similar scales, villages and towns are shown in outline—an improvement on the symbols used by Saxton and his copiers. Many maps have the names of subscribers engraved on the map next to their residence; even in remote Cumberland, Donald engraved 96 names, though surprisingly none is in Carlisle (Fig. 2.13). Most of the maps have a key, with perhaps ten to twenty headings; the 'explanation' on Yates' map of Lancashire is one of the more extensive though it curiously fails to include windmills (Fig. 2.15).

The end of this story can be briefly told. A general re-survey was undertaken by Christopher Greenwood and his competitors in the 20-year period after the Napoleonic Wars, between 1817 and 1839. Indeed, a further 46 county maps were published in the 1820s alone. The demand for these maps was largely due to the great changes that had occurred in the landscape since the earlier surveys, most of which had been carried out in the previous century. New turnpikes and canals had been created, more land had been enclosed and the population had grown and spread along with increasing industrialisation.

2.16 *Greenwood: Worcestershire, 1822. The roads and canals leading south from Birmingham stand out on this map.*

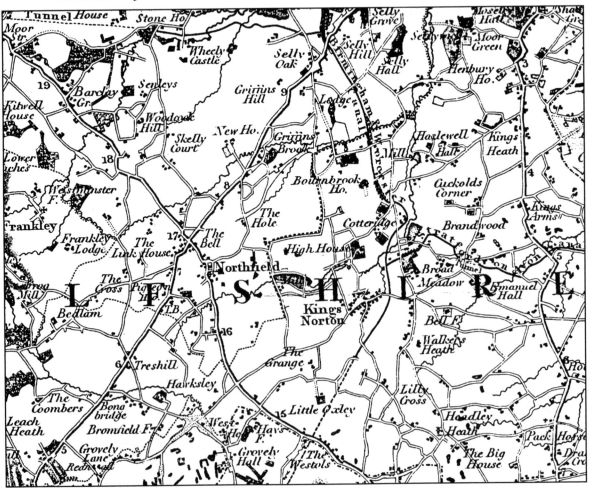

Christopher Greenwood began by publishing his map of his home county, Yorkshire, in 1817, and managed to complete a further 36 counties in the remarkably short space of 15 years, with the aim of producing a uniform atlas of England and Wales; only seven counties remained unsurveyed by him. His technique was to advertise not only for subscribers but also for existing local surveys in order to speed up publication; thus the quality of his maps was somewhat variable. In parts of southern England his maps appeared after those of the Ordnance Survey—but he does not seem to have copied from their maps. Greenwood was also able to use a variety of printed sources, from the census through to guide books and directories (Fig. 2.16).

Greenwood's main competitor was Andrew Bryant, who published maps of 13 counties mostly at the larger scale of 1½ inches to the mile (Fig. 2.17). The situation began to get faintly ludicrous, with surveys of Surrey, Gloucester, Suffolk and Northamptonshire appearing from both firms within a year of each other. At times they must have been following each other around—not to mention the Ordnance surveyors. The latter's maps effectively took away the market for the county map as

2.17 *Bryant: Buckinghamshire, 1824. A more spacious map, at a scale of 1½ inches to the mile, emphasising the main roads.*

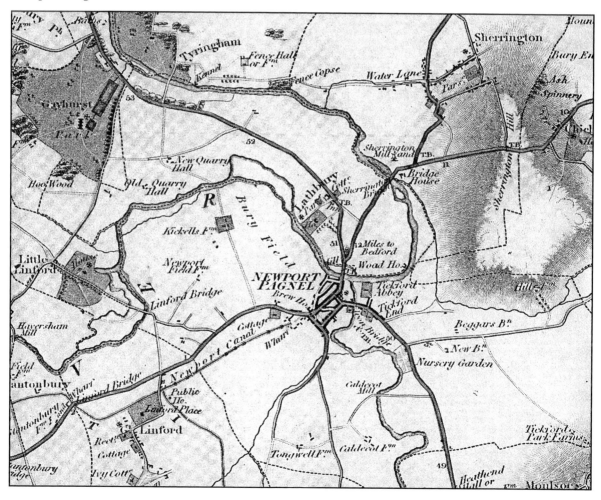

their surveyors worked their way northwards across the country (see Chapter Six). Neither Greenwood nor Bryant achieved their aim of completing a national survey, though Greenwood did issue an atlas of England in 1834, and by the mid-century the county surveyor had virtually disappeared. Yet the maps continued to be reproduced, often in smaller scale versions. The map publishers involved in this trade included Smith, Cary, Darton, Teesdale, Moule, Pigot, Walker and Fullerton, who did little other than add the new railways to their maps after 1830. A set of Moule's county maps from the 1830s has recently been reprinted (Moule, 1990). The sheer number of county maps is astonishing; the recent listing of Devon county maps up to 1836 gives a total of 117, not including reprints and later editions (Batten & Bennett, 1996); only two were based on original surveys. One famous oddity was Hobson's *Fox-Hunting Atlas* (1850), based on an earlier Walker atlas, which showed the location of each hunt. The many Victorian county maps simply used existing maps, and added railways, roads, curiosities, resorts, cycling routes, geological features and electoral districts (Smith, 1985).

Environs maps, covering county-sized areas around particular towns, were also produced. The first such map was probably that of Ogilby and Morgan, which was a ½-inch map, extending up to 20 miles around London. The demand for such maps grew, as the better-off began to live further away from the towns and as leisure became more important (especially in the late 19th and early 20th centuries, with improvements in transport). Environs maps were in the same cartographic style as the contemporaneous county maps; they covered a similar-sized area at similar scales, but had the great advantage of being able to ignore 'irrelevant' county boundaries, placing the town (wherein lay their market) at the centre of the map. They also ignored town and city boundaries, thus showing developing suburbs and neighbouring towns. Environs maps of the West Riding towns were quite common, illustrating neither the whole county nor the riding, but including many closely spaced though administratively separate areas; two early examples are a map of the area for 20 miles around Leeds, published in 1712 by Sutton Nicholls, and a '10 miles around Leeds' map produced by Thomas Wright in 1797. Environs maps were the forerunners of the Ordnance Survey plans in that they moved away from the use of the county as a cartographic unit.

Other types of environs maps were produced, including guides for travellers and visitors—and even cab-fare maps (Hyde, 1979; Smith, 1985). Although numerous and varied, these maps were in most cases based on existing plans, and thus give relatively little new information of interest to the local historian. The cycling map blossomed after the arrival of the touring bicycle and the pneumatic tyre in the mid-1880s; many of these maps were centred on London and other large towns. Some were old excursion maps with a new title. Hyde (1975, p.36) mentions 'Mogg's Twenty Four Miles Round London' which first appeared in 1805; by 1859 its title had the addition 'and Crystal Palace Excursion Map', and by 1881 the addition read 'and Bicycle Excursion Map'. The content of the map had meanwhile scarcely altered at all.

Note. Further references useful to the subject of this chapter are: Andrews and Dury, 1952; Bagley, 1971; Booth, 1979; Bowen and Kitchin, 1971; Chambers, 1964; Crosthwaite, 1968; Harvey, 1981; Hodson, 1984a; Lawrence, 1981; Lawrence and Hoyle, 1981; Norden, 1966; Raistrick, 1969; Ravenhill, 1972, 1983; Rawnsley, 1970; Symonson, 1918; Walters, 1970; Yates, 1968.

Chapter Three

ESTATE, ENCLOSURE AND TITHE MAPS

MOST OF THE MAPS discussed in this chapter are manuscript plans of rural areas. Urban estate plans—some of which were printed—are mentioned in both this chapter and the next. The three types of maps discussed here cover a span of over 300 years, encompassing most of the improvements which occurred in the production of manuscript maps. That they were hand-drawn by a host of different individuals raises particular problems in the use of estate, enclosure and tithe maps. The competence of the surveyor, and the techniques which he employed, must be assessed. Some of these maps are little more than sketches; others are fully triangulated, cadastral surveys showing the extent, value and ownership of land, for taxation purposes (Kain & Baigent, 1992). It is not safe to assume that accuracy improved with time; there are a few 16th-century estate plans which are more accurate than some of the tithe maps drawn almost three centuries later. Harley (1972, pp.36-9) suggests that in order to establish fully the accuracy of the maps available, recourse ought to be made to the professional papers of surveyors, or to their working drawings. Few such documents survive, however, and contemporary manuals may be the only guide to the general standards of surveying at a particular date.

It is, of course, possible to run some basic checks on the accuracy of these maps most simply by comparing them with the large scale surveyor's drawings for the Old Series One-Inch (usually at between 2 in. and 6 in. to the mile), with the first edition of the 6-in. or 25-in. Ordnance Survey plans, or with a modern plan. An estate plan can be compared with another drawn up at a different date, or with an enclosure or tithe map. Harley says that the internal content of all local manuscript maps should, as a matter of routine, be compared with other topographical sources. In fact, estate plans developed from *written* surveys, and in many cases both continued to be produced, one complementing the other. Equally, enclosure and tithe maps have their written 'awards', without which they should not be used. Thus these maps must be used alongside written sources.

Some parts of a map may be more accurate than others. For example, some of the poorer tithe maps incorporated pre-existing surveys and only used new survey work to update detail or to fill in gaps. It is a general rule that *all* maps show certain features more clearly than others, and will omit what is not required for their purpose. Thus any of the types of maps discussed in this chapter, all essentially depicting land areas and boundaries, may not give an accurate (or indeed *any*) depiction of such features as settlements, buildings, industrial sites, rights of way or relief. Land use is often shown on the maps in this chapter; a fuller treatment of land use mapping is given by Wallis (1981).

In purely cartographic terms there was often no standardisation of symbols on these maps and, in the absence of a key, it is unwise to assume, for example, that a road depicted by dashed lines was running across open country (i.e. without hedges or walls); different surveyors used different symbols for different features. Equally, with regard to terminology, one surveyor's 'rough pasture' may be another's 'common and waste'; 'pasture', 'grassland' and 'meadow' may or may not be the same thing.

Some areas, nonetheless, will possess a sequence of estate, enclosure and tithe maps which will present details of the changing landscape over a long period. If examples of two or three of these plans exist for the first half of the 19th century they can be amalgamated into composite plans, using the strengths of each to give a very full picture of the countryside at that date (see *Victoria County History* volumes for Oxfordshire and Wiltshire; volume 8 onwards in each case).

There are clearly difficulties involved in using manuscript plans. But if the problems of determining their accuracy can be overcome (and in most cases they can), then we have a group of maps which gives great insight into much of the landscape of Britain from the Elizabethan through to the Victorian age.

Estate maps

Estate surveys carried out before the mid-16th century were usually presented in written form, and any map would be used merely as an illustration. The transition from the almost picture-like maps of the late medieval period, which had little cartographic accuracy, to the detailed estate maps drawn at a consistent scale which were being produced by the end of the Elizabethan age has still to be studied in detail (Harvey, 1985). It is clear, nonetheless, that changes were brought about by two interrelated factors: first, by the increasing demand by landowners for estate surveys in map as well as in written form and, second, by the improvement in surveying techniques. The possibility of obtaining an accurate map no doubt helped to create this demand. Unlike the old rough sketches, the new, accurately scaled, maps showed the relative size of each field far more clearly than any written survey. The landowner could then envisage subdivisions or enclosures, boundary disputes could be more easily settled, and, if the worst came to the worst, the courts could see more clearly what was involved in legal battles over land. Nevertheless, it is difficult to understand how the 'maplessness' of the period before 1550 was overcome so rapidly; it requires a large mental jump to move from the 'bird's eye view', which is the perspective obtained from a hill or a tower, to the plan view, which was not actually *seen* by anyone until the invention of balloons and aeroplanes. Even today there are many people who find maps incomprehensible, finding it impossible to relate the landscape they can see to the map in their hand.

The rudiments of compass survey and basic triangulation had first appeared in book form in English in 1559, and various instruments such as the theodolite, circumferentor and plane-table had come into more general use by the end of the century (Richeson, 1966; Evans and Lawrence, 1979, pp.42-4). The improvement in survey techniques is evidenced by the increasing number of books published at this time on the practical aspects of surveying, such as Norden's *Surveyors Dialogue* of 1607.

England's rise as a maritime power required an increased competence in navigation, which meant accurate instruments and maps. Meanwhile, military surveyors had become involved in the laying out of defensive works, and in the geometry of gunnery. A number of military topographical maps survive from the end of the reign of Henry VIII, some made by masons who were extending their drawing abilities from buildings to larger areas (Tyacke and Huddy, 1980, pp.11-15). How much the military surveyors contributed to mapping in general is not as yet clearly understood.

Estate maps started to appear in the 1570s, but even at this time 'surveying' still usually meant measuring the land (i.e. the size of each field) rather than drawing up a plan. The best known of the early estate map-makers is probably Christopher Saxton, who, after completing his county maps, returned to Yorkshire in the mid-1580s to become a professional land surveyor. Twenty-five of his estate maps survive, and he also made written surveys (Evans and Lawrence, 1979, pp.74-121). The scale of his maps varies from 16 perches to the inch to half a mile to the inch, and he usually gives a scale of perches. The standard perch was 16½ feet, but others were in use locally, varying between 9 and 26 feet; Saxton never states which one he used. Assuming that he used the standard perch, his largest scale was thus 20 in. to the mile. North is always at the top of his maps; his hills are shown as 'sugarloaves' as on the county maps, and many features of the landscape are depicted by conventional signs—including trees, bridges, parks and windmills. Buildings are also depicted conventionally, but in perspective, while larger houses and churches are more elaborate (Figs. 3.1 and 3.2). Although early in date, Saxton's are typical of many estate maps: they show

what was required with a minimum amount of fuss or decoration, and no attempt is made to fill in any empty spaces. These are not decorative maps; they are functional, each designed for a specific purpose. Most of Saxton's plans are of estates, though a handful are of rivers demonstrating their importance for the provision of both power and drinking water, and as boundaries (the maps being all the more vital if the rivers changed their courses).

Saxton is known to have carried out two urban surveys, one of Manchester for John Dee (now lost) and one of Dewsbury, though this is really a map of the River Calder for a mile or so upstream from the town. Evidently Christopher Saxton of Dunningley had become the local estate surveyor for the area around the Aire and Calder valleys, although he also worked further afield. A full list of his known surveys (and their present whereabouts) is given

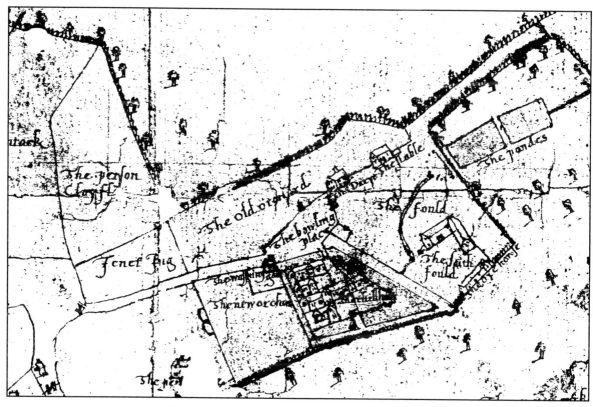

3.1 *Saxton: Thornhill Hall, 1602, showing the buildings and fields around the hall.*

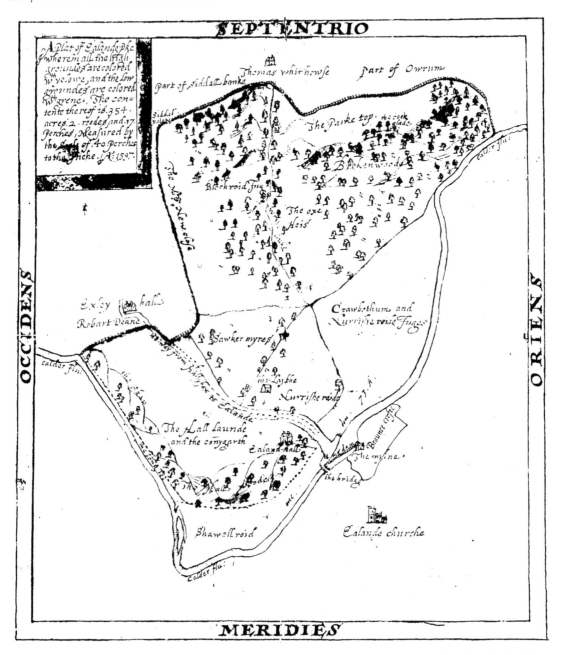

3.2 *Saxton: Elland Park, 1597. Saxton's 'sugar-loaf' hills depict relief, and other detail includes the river Calder, and 'the way from Hallyfax to Ealande'.*

by Evans and Lawrence (p.79). (It is interesting to note that, of the 25 maps known, seven are in the Public Record Office, six are in private hands, five are in Nottingham Record Office, while the remaining seven are scattered singly from North Yorkshire to Kent. In fact, 17 are no longer in the county to which they refer, making reference to them difficult. One can only hope that each county record office has tried to obtain a copy of all estate maps of their county which are held elsewhere, whether in public or private collections.)

Of course, Saxton was not the only estate surveyor at work at this time; his own son Robert followed in his footsteps, and other notable practitioners of his period included John Norden, Ralph Agas, John Walker (senior and junior), Thomas Langdon and William Senior. Norden clearly put into practice what he had preached in his *Surveyors Dialogue*; he surveyed manors in southern England and South Wales (especially in the Duchy of Cornwall, where he was the official surveyor) and also made maps of several of the King's forests. An

interesting example of his work is his survey of the Suffolk coastal area behind Orford Ness, carried out in 1600-1, which as well as being a survey of the countryside also gives a detailed picture of the coastline at that date (Norden, 1966; Kitchen, 1997).

Among the early surveyors, the two John Walkers stand out, having produced maps which were both accurate and artistic (Edwards and Newton, 1984). Over thirty of their maps have reached the Essex Record Office, dating from 1586 to 1615 (Figs. 3.3 and 3.4). Three more Elizabethan estate surveyors have been described in detail by Peter Eden (Tyacke, 1983,

3.3 *Walker: Moulsham, 1591. This estate map shows detail of the hamlet very clearly, as well as detail of the fields.*

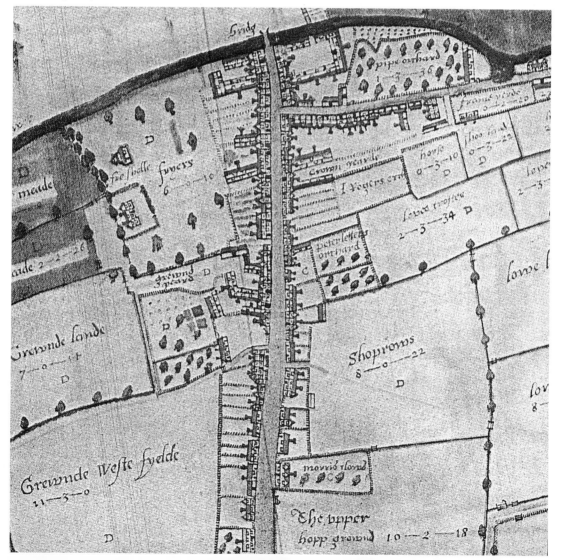

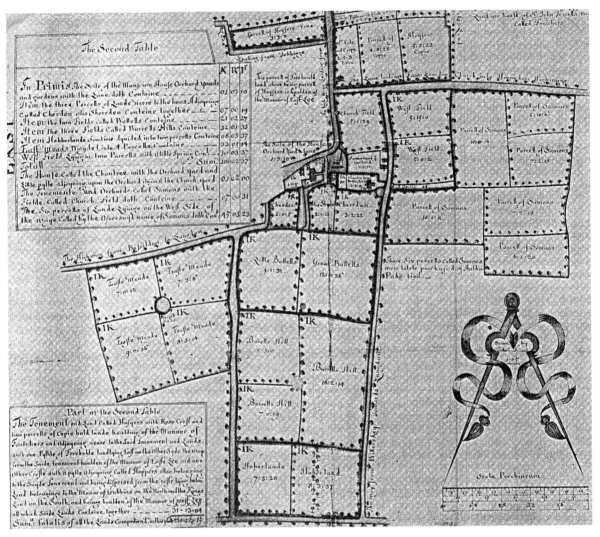

3.4 *Laindon, 1702. This map is probably a copy of a now lost map by John Walker, drawn in about 1600.*

pp.68-84), while a study of draft estate maps has helped to show how measurements in the field were translated into the finished map (Woolgar, 1985). The estate maps of Christ Church, Oxford, have recently been described by Fletcher (1995).

During the 18th century estate plans became generally better drawn, and the crude perspectives of buildings and hills were replaced by more accurate representations. Not only did these surveys develop a certain uniformity of style, but they also increased greatly in number. For example, in the list of private estate maps in Essex, the period up to 1700 covers some eight pages, while the following 150 years require 29 pages (Emmison, 1947). This period from 1700 to 1850 has been described by Harley as the 'golden age of the local land surveyor', with vast numbers of surveys, only brought to an end by the appearance of enclosure, tithe and Ordnance Survey large scale plans. Even after this, some estates added their own details to Ordnance maps. In terms of quality, both of the surveying and of the draughtsmanship, the surveys of the Goodwood estates carried out by Yeakell and Gardner in the 1780s are fine examples of the map-maker's art (Steer, 1962) as is their county map of southern Sussex (see Chapter Two).

Maps very similar to estate plans occur in the records of the various Courts of Sewers. The word 'sewer' referred to a small river which drained low-lying land into the sea, and from the early 15th century various Commissions of Sewers were set up to keep these drains clear, as well as to build or maintain sea-walls and occasionally even to improve river navigation (Willan, 1936, pp.16-23). From time to time the Commissioners would require a map to be drawn of the area or 'level' for which they were responsible. In the Essex collections, Courts of Sewers maps exist for the 18th and 19th centuries (Emmison, 1947). An example is the first map listed there, which covers East Ham, Barking, Dagenham and Hornchurch, showing owners, occupiers, sewers, green walls, ponds, troughs, a church, a house and a post-mill (1735-41). The last map in the collection was drawn up as recently as 1861-2. Figure 3.5 is a plan drawn in 1778 of land affected by the flooding of the River Alt on the west Lancashire coast. It shows the proposed improvements in drainage which were to be made.

The total number of surviving estate maps is probably close to 30,000, and consequently it is extremely difficult to generalise about them. Despite their fundamental similarity of purpose, they were drawn by a large number of individual surveyors, and thus vary greatly in terms of scale, size, extent, content, detail and ornament (Figs. 3.6 and 3.7). As a basic minimum, they usually show part or all of a

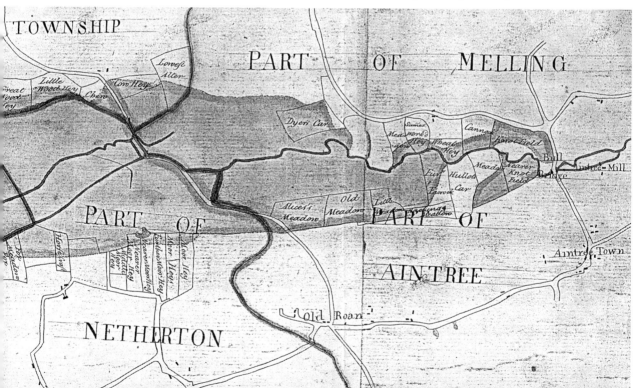

3.5 *Plan of the damaged lands adjoining the river Alt, with the intended cuts for draining the same, 1778. The land affected by flooding has been shaded.*

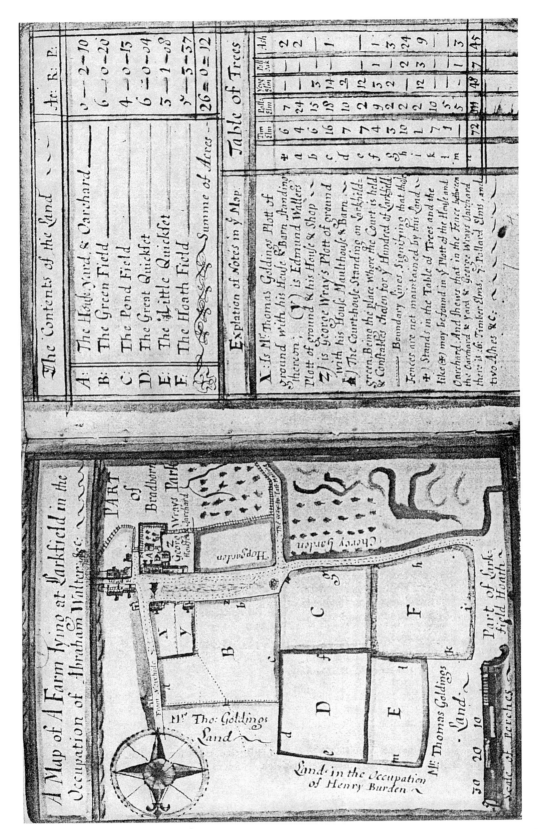

▲ **3.6** *Walter: Larkfield, East Malling, 1681. Abraham Walter's survey of his own farm, with an unusual 'Table of Trees'.*

3.7 *Watts: Thurnham Manor, 1709. John Watts of Boxley employs a reference grid on this Kent estate map.*

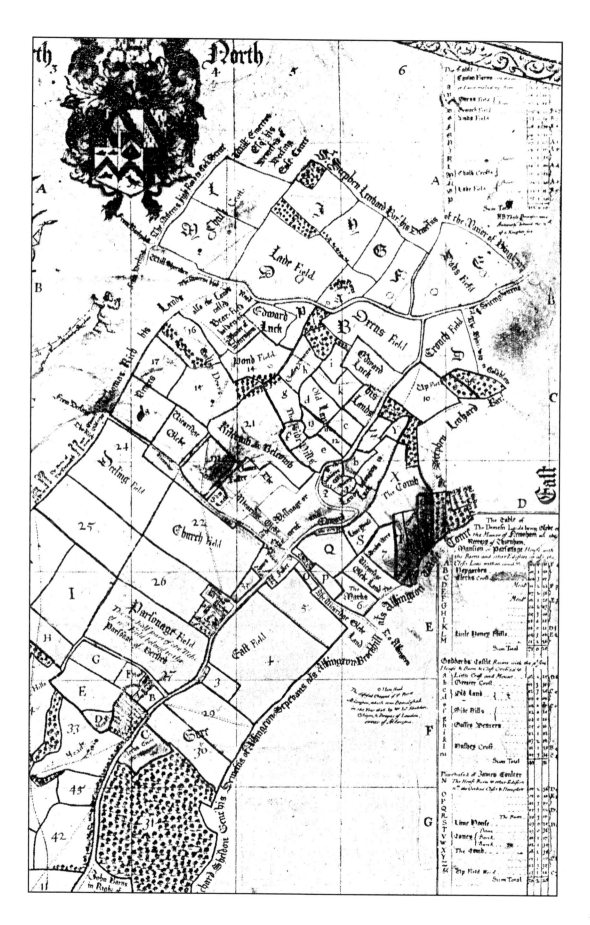

single landowner's holdings; some show only one farm, but about one in ten covers a whole parish or a larger estate extending over several parishes. Typically they show the individual fields, together with hedges, walls and access routes, and often give the acreage of each areal unit. If the fields were still sub-divided into strips, then each strip would be shown, usually with the name of the tenant or farmer.

Looking at an estate plan, one of the first tasks is to establish its scale; the modern equivalent is the O.S. 25-inch plan (1:2500), but it must be borne in mind that the 6-inch (1:10,000) and 50-inch (1:1250) scales mark the extreme limits used by estate surveyors. Clearly, a scale within this range allows comparatively small features such as streams or buildings to be shown with some accuracy, should that particular feature have been of importance to the landowner and therefore to the map-maker. In fact, because most estate surveys are concerned with land and in particular with the acreage of fields, rather than with settlement, the depiction of buildings may be unreliable. Nevertheless, where a village is shown, the detail may be sufficient to say a great deal about that settlement's size and shape, even if virtually every building is conventionally illustrated. The larger buildings, such as the church, manor house or school, may be shown in greater detail—either in perspective or in plan. Roads and tracks leading from one village to another or to the fields may be shown in some detail, giving valuable local information rarely recorded elsewhere. The village of Padbury (Buckinghamshire) is illustrated in an estate plan of 1591 which shows a radial network of seven lanes leading out of the village in a very irregular fashion, with numerous branches and cross routes (Hindle, 1982, pp.21, 45). Most of these routes end up in the fields, and only a few reach the parish boundary; 'Buckingham Waye', leading to the county town (only three miles away) is nothing more than a track as it leaves the parish (Fig. 3.8).

It is the fields which are usually best recorded and estate maps are sometimes accompanied by a written survey giving further detail about each plot of land. Precise details of cultivation or land use are not always given; colour is sometimes used, often to depict meadow or woodland. The estate map will usually give field names which can be of interest in themselves, and not only to the student of place names. For example, a 'town field' in the middle of the countryside may indicate some lost settlement, 'Coal Pit Field' an old industrial site, and 'Street Field' a lost road. Any publication of the English Place-Name Society will furnish examples, as will a dictionary of field names (Field, 1972). Some surveyors put in earthworks, and even, occasionally, the remains of lost villages. For example, a map of Heath (Shropshire) drawn in 1771 shows many remains of the medieval landscape—including 'Moat Meadow' (i.e. the deserted village site) and the medieval fishponds (Rowley, 1972, pp.113-15). Such detail is all the more important now that so many hedges have been grubbed up and so much ridge and furrow ploughed out in recent years, changing the rural landscape more dramatically than at any period since the open fields were enclosed several centuries ago.

Beyond the fields, areas of woodland and wasteland, streams, ponds, marsh, fen or moor may be shown (though often only the edge of such land is depicted). Parish boundaries are often shown, while special local features such as orchards and parks, or rural industrial sites such as iron works, mills and limekilns would not always be ignored.

J.B. Harley (1972, pp.27-8) notes the existence of estate plans of industrial areas, which have often been overlooked. These include both general estate plans showing much industrial detail, and maps drawn specifically of industrial areas. Common examples occur in areas where minerals were extracted at the surface (as lead was in Derbyshire, for example), or

3.8 *The estate map of Padbury, 1591, redrawn to show the open fields and the many roads and tracks within the parish.*

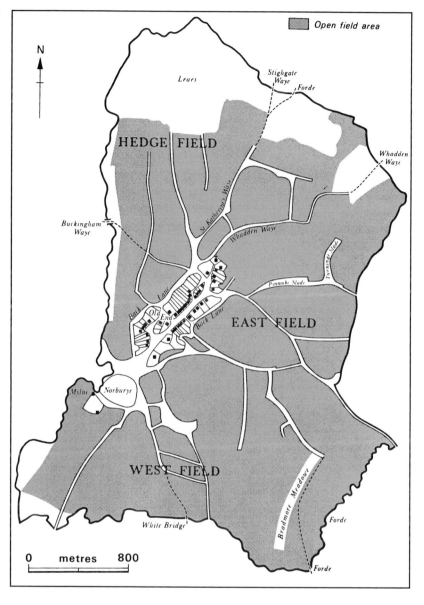

where minerals existed beneath the ground and the landowner wished to establish the extent of mineral rights (Fig. 3.9). A few estate plans were printed, either for wealthy landowners, or when multiple copies were needed, as for example when an estate was to be sold (Fig. 3.10).

In short, estate maps may show virtually any feature of the rural landscape which was of interest to the landowner or his surveyor.

Any single estate map will illustrate only a *partial* selection of the landscape's features, and the fact that a particular feature is *not* shown does not mean that it was not in existence when the survey was carried out. As always, maps can only be used as evidence when they *do* show the existence of a feature; the omission of a feature does not mean that it was not there.

It is not the purpose of this book to discuss the myriad uses to which estate plans have been

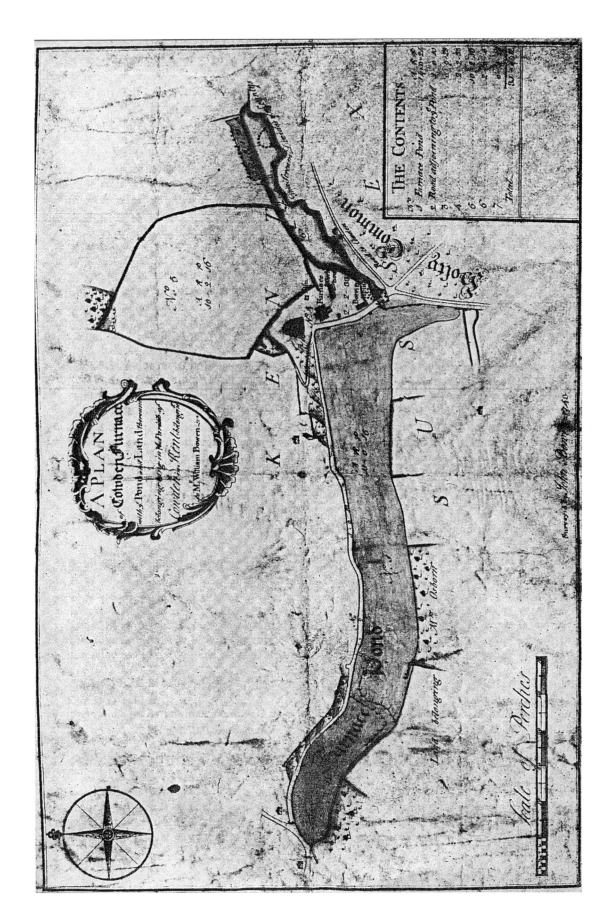

⊲ **3.9** *An estate plan of an industrial site—Cowden Furnace, on the Kent-Sussex border, drawn in 1743.*

⌃ **3.10** *A plan of the Middleton estates, south of Leeds, 1853. The land has been divided into lots for sale by auction.*

put, so a few examples will have to suffice. Maurice Beresford, in his *History on the Ground* (1984), subtitled 'Six Studies in Maps and Landscapes', discusses a plan of Salford (Bedfordshire) of 1596 which was altered in 1769 to show the enclosure of part of the open fields, while a map of Maids Moreton (Buckinghamshire) also of 1596 shows some fields already enclosed. A plan of the deserted village site at Whatborough (Leicestershire) of

1586 shows the place where the 'towne' once stood, as well as the line of a hedge thrown up in 1494 when part of Whatborough was transferred to the neighbouring village. Finally, two plans of Holdenby (Northamptonshire) of 1580 and 1587 show the changes wrought by the creation of a park.

At Cuxham, in Oxfordshire, Paul Harvey (1965) was able to effect a substantial reconstruction of medieval farming practices by combining an estate map of 1767, still showing the arable fields (not enclosed until 1846), with the written records going back to the 14th century which survive in Merton College, Oxford. Other books worth consulting include Hoskins (1955 and 1967), Baker and Harley (1973), Rogers and Rowley (1974), Beresford and St Joseph (1979), Cantor (1982) and Aston (1985). The books in the series *The Making of the English Landscape* frequently use early estate plans; Rowley's (1972) volume on Shropshire, for example, employs estate plans to illustrate the history of such diverse topics as forest, grazing rights, fields, settlements, enclosure, emparking, coal-mining, charcoal production and the early iron industry.

Emmison (1974) says that 'well-drawn, detailed and accurate estate maps are the greatest treasures for the local historian'. However, there are three basic problems to be overcome in the use of estate maps: first, plans may not have been drawn for the particular area or date in which the researcher is interested; second, they may not have survived (for these were nearly always done in manuscript, and thus usually only ever existed in single copies); third, the plans may be difficult to track down. Many estate plans are still in private hands, in estate offices, solicitors' offices, Oxford and Cambridge colleges and among the records of the landed gentry. The owners may not even know what maps they have, and sometimes, even if their maps have been catalogued, may not allow easy access to them. Fortunately, many estate maps have found their way into county collections, usually held in local record offices or local history libraries. A few counties have published estate map catalogues (e.g. Essex, by Emmison and Mason; Cambridge by Bendall; Glamorgan by Thomas; Sussex by Steer; and Buckingham by Elvey), but in most cases a full search has to be made through the general parish index and any other relevant lists. Maps may be hidden within entries listing written surveys of estates. Many counties do now have up to date indexes of their collections of estate maps, while others provide some information in the more general format of guides to the whole of each collection. Local plans also occur in national collections, and reference should be made to the various published indexes of manuscript holdings in the British Museum, the Public Record Office and the National Library of Wales (Davies, 1982). Maps for the Crown estates are held in the Public Record Office or by the Crown Estate Commissioners. A major difficulty with any printed list, however, is that it is always out of date.

A final problem, already demonstrated by the scattered locations of the Saxton estate maps, is that such maps do not always remain in the county to which they refer, and thus a full search would have to involve trips to repositories in (at least) adjacent counties to consult their indexes. Ideally, all map holdings should be available for consultation via computer links so that a searcher seated at a terminal in one library or record office could call up the holdings of every major repository in the country for his or her particular parish. Such a happy situation still seems remote.

Enclosure maps

The enclosure of individual fields has been a feature of the English landscape since medieval times. Even a village with open fields might have had some enclosures, perhaps to contain young animals but, as medieval populations grew, villagers were given permission to bring more land into cultivation ('assarting'), and waste land, usually unproductive woodland, moor or fen around the village, was enclosed. In the open fields themselves, some tenants might have arranged for their scattered holdings to be amalgamated into a single block, and, by this means too, enclosed fields were created. In some parts of the country, where open fields had never been common, an enclosed landscape was the norm. Thus by

Elizabethan times many areas were already largely enclosed.

At this time a second type of enclosure was occurring, namely the enclosing of part or all of their open fields by landlords wishing to pasture sheep, cattle or even deer instead of allowing the land to remain as arable; this sometimes aroused local or even national opposition. Such enclosures proceeded in a piecemeal fashion by local agreement or by the landowner imposing his will on his tenants. The net result was that, by the middle of the 18th century, large areas of England were already enclosed. Unfortunately very few documents or maps survive to tell the tale in any detail. Occasionally, however, an estate plan will show the landscape as it had appeared prior to enclosure, or detailing the changes which enclosure had wrought (Beresford, 1984).

From about 1760 onwards, a third type of enclosure became common: enclosure by Act of Parliament. This was usually of arable land, but, especially after 1795, of common or waste land too. The process became more standardised as time went on, with the passing of the General Enclosure Acts of 1801, 1836 and 1845; the normal procedure was that the local promoters of enclosure placed a bill before Parliament, which might or might not be opposed, and it would usually become an Enclosure Act. The Act allowed the promoters to nominate commissioners who re-allocated the land holdings of all the landowners into coherent units so that each landowner should have the same *value* of land (not acreage) as before, usually in the form of a single field; they also arranged for the whole area to be hedged or walled. One of the commissioners' first jobs was to appoint a surveyor, who began by drawing up a 'true and exact plan and admeasurement' of the lands as they were (i.e. a written survey *and* plan) upon which the new layout would be based. (Unfortunately, few of these plans of the old landscape survive, especially from before 1830.) When the legal claims and counter-claims had all been settled, the agreed changes were embodied in the 'Enclosure Award'—a large book, with the surveyor's new plan appended. For large enclosures many years sometimes separated the act and award—16 in the case of the 1803 Act for Inglewood Forest in Cumbria. The original award was then given to the incumbent of the parish (so that it would be kept in the parish chest and be available for local reference), while an enrolled copy was usually given to the county. These second copies are now often held in local record offices.

The 'awards' depict in great detail the new system of land ownership, indicating field boundaries and roads, often laid out afresh by the surveyor. In short, these 'enclosure awards' and maps give uniquely valuable information about large areas of the country, principally for the reign of George III (1760-1820) but in some cases for as early as 1720 or as late as 1900. Over 5,000 Acts covered almost seven million acres, of which about two-thirds was open field arable land and one-third common and waste land. Overall, 21 per cent of England was enclosed by Act of Parliament, but the percentage varied widely from place to place. The table overleaf shows those counties with a higher percentage of land enclosed.

The temporal pattern of parliamentary enclosure is even more complicated. In terms of open field arable land, over one-third of the area of both Leicester and Northampton was enclosed before 1793, while almost as much of Bedford, Cambridge and Huntingdon was enclosed in the war years of 1793-1815. Fifteen per cent of Cumberland was enclosed from common and waste land during those same war years (Turner, M., 1980, pp.186-9). Yet there was only a small amount of parliamentary enclosure in some counties, either because there was little existing open field agriculture or because the land had already been enclosed (either from open field or from waste) at an earlier date. Cheshire, Cornwall, Devon, Essex, Hereford, the Isle of Wight, Kent, Lancashire, Monmouth,

Counties with a higher percentage of enclosed land

	%		%		%
Oxford	54	Rutland	45	Wiltshire	29
Cambridge	53	Lincoln	39	Middlesex	28
Northants	53	Nottingham	36	Cumberland	28 *
Huntingdon	50	Buckingham	35	Gloucester	26
Bedford	49	Berkshire	34	Yorks West Riding	24 *
Leicester	47	Warwick	32	Derby	23
Yorks East Riding	45	Norfolk	31	Westmorland	21 *

*Only these three counties in this list had more common and waste than open field enclosure.   (Turner, 1980, pp.180-1)

Shropshire and Sussex each had less than ten per cent of their area enclosed by Act of Parliament. Thus the picture of the landscape given by the awards and maps is particularly incomplete for these counties. There is still a chance, however, that a particular parish being researched was one of the few to have an Enclosure Act: it is worth checking the records to find out.

A good deal has been written about the general aspects of enclosure. A short list would include Hoskins (1955), Russell (1974, 1977), Chapman (1987), Yelling (1977) and Turner, M. (1980, 1984); a full list of references up to 1970, including local studies, is in Brewer (1972). A good example of a local study is that by Harris (1961) of the East Riding between 1700 and 1850, while Tate's list of awards for Somerset (1948) has a useful introductory essay, and a list of maps.

Enclosure awards and their maps can be used in two main ways; the first is as a record of the planning of the new landscape by the surveyors. It is important to remember that enclosure maps are planning maps of what the surveyor intended should be created, and not maps of what existed. Comparison with later maps will tell how much of the surveyor's plans were implemented. The maps vary in the amount of topographical detail they give, so

they should be used in conjunction with the awards, which give more precise information about the routes and widths of new roads and watercourses and the re-allotment of land. Each plot is numbered, described and located, and details of ownership and acreage given; plot number, owner and size usually appear on the map. There were also certain special allotments, which included 'glebeland', 'commutation of tithes' (see next section), 'rights of warren' and land to be given to the parish for the provision of road stone (i.e. quarries). The maps may also show land which was already enclosed ('old enclosures'), roads which had been stopped up, occasionally the position of some buildings, and even rural industrial sites (Figs. 3.11 and 3.12).

The main feature of enclosed landscapes is their regularity; roads and field boundaries are straight and right-angled corners common. New roads are wide (usually 40, 50 or 60 feet [12, 15 or 18 metres]), often leading straight to the parish boundary. Because enclosure was carried out area by area at different dates, there is often a slight bend in the road as it crosses the parish boundary, indicating the work of two different surveyors at two different dates (Hindle, 1984, pp.164-72; 1993, pp.131-7).

The second use of enclosure awards and maps is to reconstruct the landscape *before* it

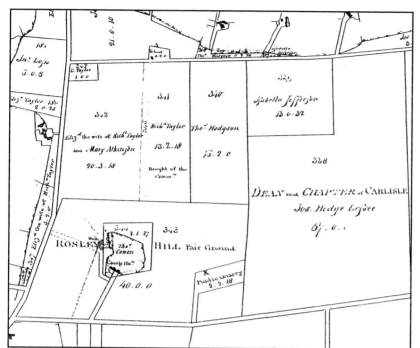

3.11 *Enclosure map of Rosley, Cumberland, 1822 shows the enclosure of the long established cattle fairground. Note the 'public quarry' which was needed to provide roadstone.*

3.12 *Enclosure map of Hutton End, part of the massive enclosure of Inglewood Forest, 1819. The planned straight roads within the area to be enclosed contrast with the existing roads at the edge.*

was enclosed; in many instances it had remained little changed since the Middle Ages. In a few cases this can be done by using the original map which the surveyor drew of the area to be enclosed. Unfortunately few of these maps survive. It is often possible, however, to reconstruct the former landscape by combining details of former holdings given in the award with the new holdings shown on the final map. A series of studies along these lines was carried out by Russell and Russell (1982, 1983, 1985) who looked in detail at landscape changes due to enclosure in many parts of northern Lincolnshire. In almost every case they were able to draw a map of the pre-enclosure landscape (Figs. 3.13 and 3.14), only being defeated in a few parishes by the wording of the award. In some parishes enclosure occurred so late in the 19th century that the Ordnance Survey surveyors were charting unenclosed landscapes.

Most county record offices have updated lists of the enclosure awards and maps in their keeping. On a national scale, finding out whether an enclosure map exists for an area,

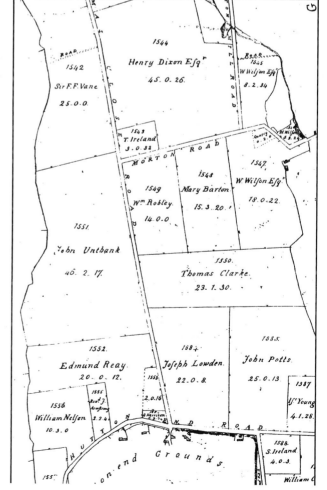

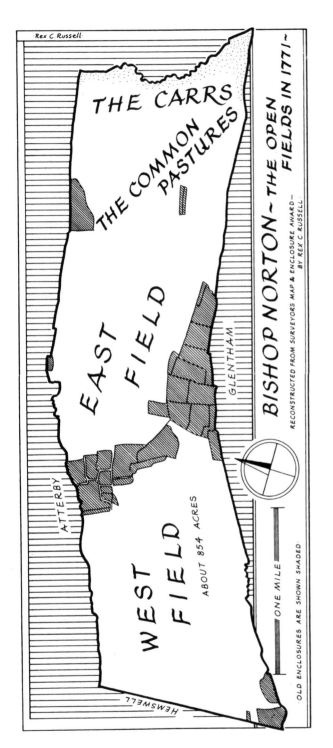

The following text appears within the left map:

- Rex C. Russell
- THE CARRS
- THE COMMON PASTURES
- EAST FIELD
- WEST FIELD
- GLENTHAM
- ATTERBY
- HEMSWELL
- ABOUT 854 ACRES
- BISHOP NORTON ~ THE OPEN FIELDS IN 1771 ~
- RECONSTRUCTED FROM SURVEYORS MAP & ENCLOSURE AWARD ~ BY REX C. RUSSELL
- ONE MILE
- OLD ENCLOSURES ARE SHOWN SHADED.

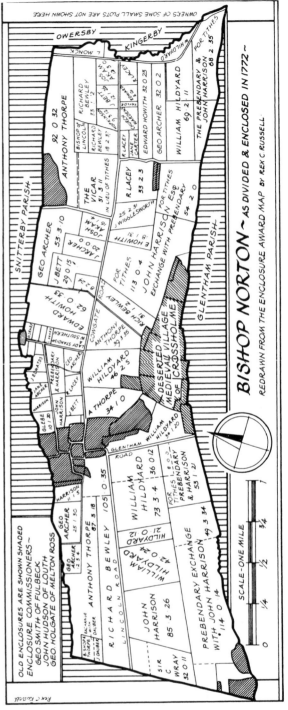

The following text appears within the right map:

- OWNERS OF SOME SMALL PLOTS ARE NOT SHOWN HERE
- OWERSBY
- KINGERBY
- L. MONCK
- ANTHONY THORPE 92 0 32
- BISHOP OF LINCOLN 33 · · 2
- RICHARD BEWLEY
- RICHARD BEWLEY 18 2 37
- EDWARD HOWITH 32 0 25
- GEO ARCHER 32 0 2
- WILLIAM HILDYARD 69 2 11
- THE PREBENDARY & FOR TITHES JOHN HARRISON 68 2 35
- SNITTERBY PARISH
- GEO ARCHER 53 3 10
- THE VICAR 51 3 11 IN LIEU OF TITHES
- J BETT 29 0 15
- J ARCHER 20 0 0
- JOSH ADAM
- R LACEY 33 2 3
- JANE CARTER
- R LACEY 25 2 3
- WIGGLESWORTH
- E HOWITH
- JOHN HARRISON FOR TITHES EXCHANGE WITH PREBENDARY 54 2 0
- FOR TITHES 113 0 4
- EDWARD HOWITH 62 0 33
- RICH BEWLEY
- COWGATE ROAD
- SOUTHERN
- LADY STANDISH
- GEO HARRISON
- JANE EDWARDS
- GLEBE
- JANE HARRISON
- PREBENDARY & HARRISON
- JOHN HARRISON
- R LACEY
- J BETT
- ANTHONY THORPE
- WILLIAM HILDYARD 46 2 5
- A THORPE 34 1 0
- DESERTED MEDIEVAL VILLAGE OF CROSSHOLME
- GLENTHAM PARISH
- GLENTHAM ROAD
- OLD ENCLOSURES ARE SHOWN SHADED
- ENCLOSURE COMMISSIONERS ~
- GEO SMITH OF FULBECK
- JOHN HUDSON OF LOUTH
- GEO HOLGATE OF MELTON ROSS
- GEO HARRISON 25 1 30
- GEO ARCHER 2 3 4
- ANTHONY THORPE 87 1 18
- RICHARD BEWLEY 105 0 35
- LINCOLN ROAD
- WILLIAM HILDYARD 73 3 4
- HILDYARD 21 0 12
- WILLIAM HILDYARD 36 0 12
- FOR TITHES PREBENDARY & HARRISON 53 1 2
- SIR C WRAY 52 0 11
- JOHN HARRISON 85 3 26
- PREBENDARY EXCHANGE WITH JOHN HARRISON 49 3 34 114 0 14
- BISHOP NORTON ~ AS DIVIDED & ENCLOSED IN 1772 ~
- REDRAWN FROM THE ENCLOSURE AWARD MAP BY REX C. RUSSELL
- SCALE-ONE MILE
- Rex C. Russell

▲ **3.13** *The enclosure of Bishop Norton, 1772. These redrawn maps show the parish before and after enclosure from details in the surveyor's map and the award. (R.C. Russell)*

3.14 *The enclosure of East Keal, 1774. For this parish there is an estate map by John Grundy in 1757 (left), plus the detail in the enclosure award and map by John Hudson (centre and right). (Redrawn by R.C. Russell)* ➤

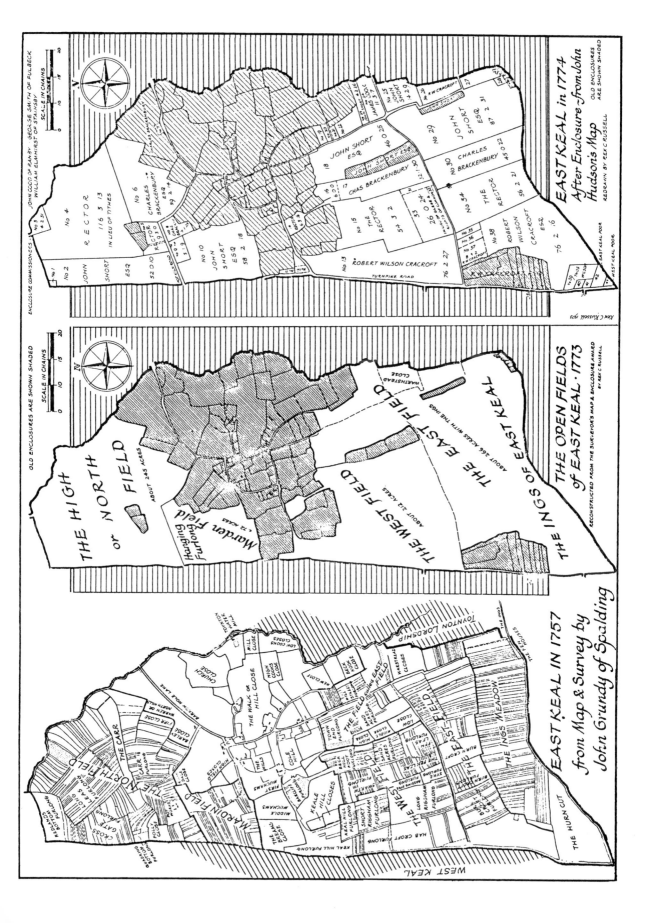

EAST KEAL in 1774
After Enclosure-from John
Hudson's Map

OLD ENCLOSURES
ARE SHOWN SHADED

REDRAWN BY REX C. RUSSELL

THE OPEN FIELDS
of EAST KEAL · 1773

RECONSTRUCTED FROM THE SURVEYOR'S MAP & ENCLOSURE AWARD
BY REX C. RUSSELL

OLD ENCLOSURES ARE SHOWN SHADED

EAST KEAL IN 1757
from Map & Survey by
John Grundy of Spalding

and where it can be consulted, has become very much easier in recent years, largely due to the work of W. E. Tate, whose English county listings, many of which had been published separately, were finally completed posthumously in 1978 (Tate and Turner). This *Domesday* has an introduction, largely concerned with the process of parliamentary enclosure (from the bill's passage through the Commons to the work of the commissioners) but its main bulk consists of a county by county list of the acts and awards, together with the acreages involved and the location of copies (usually the second, enrolled copy). For each county the acts are divided first into those containing some arable land, and those containing none, and second into those enclosures carried out by private act or under the 1836 and later acts. The presence of the plan with the award is indicated by an asterisk. Some counties, such as Cumberland, have a plan for virtually every award, while others have few.

In total, about 70 per cent of all enclosure maps have survived, though this proportion improves for later maps; of maps made before 1789 only 45 per cent survive, as opposed to 85 per cent of those made between 1790 and 1839. If a map is not housed with its award, then Tate and Turner sometimes note where the original or a copy can be consulted. A glance through the Oxfordshire pages, where the County Record Office lacks the maps for most awards before 1800, reveals maps in the hands of various solicitors, banks, libraries, parish councils and Oxford colleges. Tate and Turner also note where pre-enclosure maps are attached to the awards. There are probably some 4,500 places for which an enclosure map survives.

If no original enclosure map is known to have survived, then we must look for a draft version or a copy made at or near the time of enclosure, though such maps are few in number. As a last resort, a conjectural map can be drawn. A number of these have been made, in particular for Worcestershire, where there are a dozen such plans for enclosures before 1778, a period from which only a handful of original plans, copies or tracings survive. A final point to remember is that occasionally a pre-enclosure estate plan is included among the commissioners' papers, collected as part of their evidence about the original state of the parish.

In Wales enclosure was never as extensive as it was in most of England (Bower, 1914; Dodd, 1951; Thomas, 1963). Chapman (1992) details the 227 enclosures in Wales.

Tithe maps

By the early 19th century the payment to the Church by the lay population of one-tenth of all produce (whether crops, animals or industrial goods) had been an established practice for about a thousand years. But by then there was much wrong with the system, and much opposition to it. For example, some clergy held more than one living simultaneously, while other curates had to seek extra work in order to survive. Some livings brought in very little, and the ups and downs of agricultural production meant that the level of income was variable. Certain laymen also received tithes, often payments which had once been made to the long-since dissolved monasteries; indeed, by 1836 about a quarter of all tithes went into lay hands. Tithes seemed an increasingly irrelevant charge on village communities, especially as the growing urban and industrial sectors largely escaped them. Even some of the landed gentry were affected; if an enterprising landlord increased his agricultural production, the Church still took its percentage, despite having made no contribution to the capital expended. Clearly, a change was needed. Many enclosure awards had already commuted tithes, either into an allotment of land (clearly indicated on the enclosure maps) or, more rarely, into a fixed cash payment. Tithe owners usually obtained very generous terms; at Yarburgh (Lincolnshire) for example, the enclosures of

1807-13 gave the rector 216 acres in lieu of tithes out of a newly enclosed area of 940 acres—and this in a parish of only 1,330 acres (Russell and Russell, 1983). In this process each landowner lost about a seventh of his land, while the Church's estates increased by about 60 per cent (Kain and Prince, 1985, p.23).

In fact, out of a total of 4,166 enclosure acts, tithes had been commuted in 2,230 cases by 1835. We must bear in mind, however, that about one-third of the acts were concerned with common and wasteland, where commutation was rarer. A combination of high taxes, an economic slump and agrarian uprisings eventually caused Parliament to pass the Tithe Commutation Act in 1836. The whole process is described in great detail by Kain and Prince (1985), and the definitive description and analysis of the maps is given in Kain and Oliver (1995); much of what follows is based on their work. The Welsh tithe maps will be described by Davies (forthcoming). Shorter accounts can be found in Beech (1985) and Evans and Crosby (1997).

Under the new system, the country was divided into 14,829 tithe districts (usually townships in the north of England and parishes elsewhere); tithes were already extinct in 2,096 of these districts. Next, the total value of tithes paid over the previous seven years and the rent charges were calculated and checked. Once agreed, the rent charge was then apportioned amongst the land holders, depending on the acreage and quality of their land—the latter usually assessed by observing the state of cultivation of each field. In order to perform this complicated task accurately, detailed surveys were needed; each field had to be precisely measured and its state of cultivation recorded as 'arable', 'grass', 'meadow', 'pasture', 'common', 'wood', 'coppice', 'plantation', 'orchard', 'hop-ground' or 'market garden'.

The surveys were usually undertaken by local surveyors, who received detailed instruction and supervision. In overall charge of the survey was R.K. Dawson, who right from the start suggested that there should be a cadastral survey of the *whole* of England and Wales, at a scale of three chains to one inch (26.7 inches to the mile) which he said would only cost a fifth more than just surveying the titheable areas at that scale. Parliament did not accept this proposal, and, moreover, the original strict requirements for the maps were relaxed. Thus the maps made for the tithe commissioners were not standardised in either scale or detail, and were done over a much longer period than Dawson had originally envisaged. In the event, the maps were surveyed over 20 years. They fell into two distinct groups. The 'first-class' maps were produced in line with Dawson's original proposals; these were detailed and accurate enough to serve as legal evidence of boundaries and areas. Most, however, fell into the 'second-class' category. These were maps which failed the Commission's tests, or were not put forward by their surveyors to be tested at all. A common reason for this was that many tithe maps were copied from existing estate or parish maps, which were not on a large enough scale; the Commission required at least 4 chains to an inch (20 inches to the mile) for 'first-class' maps [1 chain = 22 yards]. Field boundaries and buildings shown on the map being copied would be brought up to date, previously unsurveyed areas completed, and then the map would be re-drawn to comply with the basic requirements of the Commissioners. Most of these 'second-class' maps were accurate enough for their immediate purpose. The main reason for opting for a 'second-class' map was cost; Dawson's general estimate was that a first-class survey would cost 9d. an acre but this was clearly too much for many parishes (despite the obvious advantages of having such a map), especially for those in the north which had large tracts of moorland, or in parishes where only part of the area still had tithes. In the event, only 1,458 maps out of 11,785 were rated as 'first-class'—just

12 per cent of the total. In parts of southern England the percentage was much higher (notably in Kent, which has virtually complete tithe map coverage).

The geographical coverage of the tithe maps varies; overall, about three-quarters of England and Wales was covered, but for some counties, where enclosure acts had already commuted the tithes, there are few tithe maps. Thus only about a quarter of Northamptonshire has tithe maps, the figure for Leicester is about 30 per cent, and it is between 35 and 40 per cent for Bedford, Huntingdon, Rutland and the East Riding. At the other extreme, Cheshire, Cornwall, Devon, Kent, Monmouth and Shropshire all have more than 89 per cent coverage. East Anglia and Wales were also well covered.

In general, enclosure and tithe maps tend to complement each other, but there are many exceptions to the 'parliamentary enclosure equals no tithe map' rule, most obviously when enclosure did not commute the tithes, or where there was less titheable land. Sussex has tithe maps for virtually every parish, but only the small remnants of tithe lands were surveyed. For a few areas two tithe maps of different dates exist, usually due either to substantial alterations in apportionment or to major changes such as the development of suburbs or railways.

Clearly, the most useful tithe maps are those at the larger scales—usually at 3 or 4 chains to the inch (i.e. 26.7 or 20 inches to the mile). Forty-six per cent of all tithe maps are at these scales. The peak period was 1839-41,

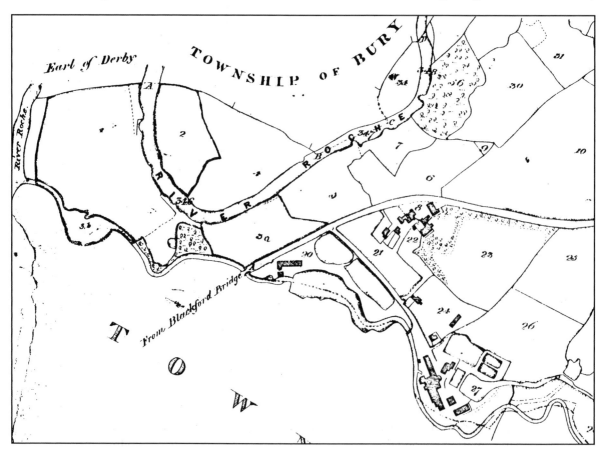

3.15 *Tithe map of Pilsworth, Lancashire, drawn by William Bell in 1838. A good example of artistic simplicity in these maps.*

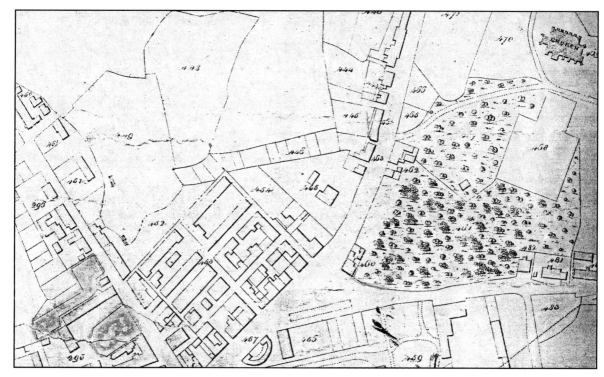

3.16 *Tithe map of Middleton, Lancashire, 1839, which includes a generalised depiction of the town and its parish church.*

when one-third of all tithe maps were produced. Such maps usually pre-date the Ordnance Survey 25-inch plans by many years (see Chapter Six) and provide for a great number of areas the first detailed cadastral surveys, delineating the rural landscape of the 1840s. In addition, many towns were surveyed and recorded, either on large scale plans inset into the maps or on completely separate maps.

There is no such thing as a 'typical' tithe map. The bottom line is that they show the boundaries of a tithe district and of tithe areas within it (Fig. 3.15). The usual convention was to show enclosed fields by a solid line, and boundaries of and within unenclosed fields by dotted or dashed lines. Each field was then numbered, for reference to the apportionment; sometimes the owner's name is inscribed on the map. Any information beyond this is a bonus. Many tithe maps show watercourses, woods, roads, paths and buildings; sometimes

different types of cultivation are indicated by the conventional signs proposed by Dawson or by a system of colouring. Settlements were sometimes drawn separately at a larger scale, in order to allow for extra detail, and large scales of 1 and 2 chains to the inch are not unknown (i.e. about 80 or 40 inches to the mile). Where settlement is shown on the ordinary plan, buildings may have been coloured (often red for houses and grey for others) and particular buildings, whether churches, inns, industrial works, or the more important houses, may be specifically named (Fig. 3.16). The use of colour in these maps seems to vary regionally.

One odd feature of tithe maps is the fact that first-class maps are often plain in appearance, indicating the importance of accuracy rather than decorativeness. When using a tithe map it is important to find out which class it belonged to: first-class maps are more accurate (indeed many were used to plot the course of

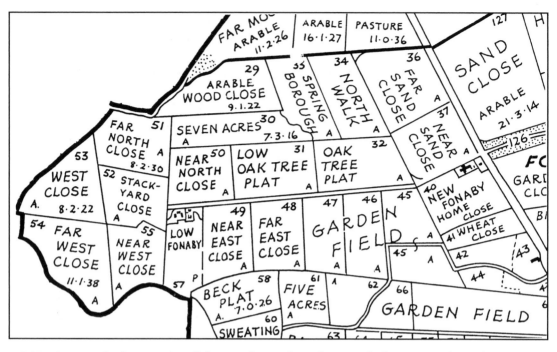

3.17 *Section of tithe map of Audleby, Hundon and Fonaby, Lincolnshire, 1841. This redrawn map shows field names, acreages and land use (A = arable, P = pasture). (R.C. Russell)*

the new railways) whereas second-class maps vary enormously in reliability. Work on second-class tithe maps in Devon has shown them to be much better than their 19th-century detractors claimed: linear measurements were found to average less than 3 per cent error, and areal measurements less than 4 per cent (Hooke and Perry, 1976). For the purpose of studying the 19th-century landscape they are quite accurate enough. Examples of both maps and awards can be seen in Kain and Prince (pp.89-102), Kain and Oliver (1995), and in West's *Village Records* (1997, pp.201-21).

In order to interpret a tithe map fully, the schedule of apportionment must also be consulted. These large sheets enumerate and name each tithe area (typically several hundred in each district, though sometimes several thousand in unenclosed areas) giving details of ownership, the state of cultivation (or the actual crop planted), the acreage and the amount of rent payable. Entries are arranged

in alphabetical order of owners' names. The tithe areas were usually fields, and so there is also a full list of field names. Other areas such as 'house and garden' are often briefly described (Fig. 3.17). Finally, there are the tithe files, which give more detailed information on farming (Kain, 1984, 1986; List and Index Society, 1986).

Overall, the tithe maps and awards are a mine of information:

They contain examples of every type of land holding, from scattered plots in the remaining open fields to the great estates of the landed proprietors. We can find from them how much titheable land belonged to estates of various kinds, how much land was owned by the universities, the Church and later by the railway companies. We can find out how much land remained unenclosed in 1840, where it was and who owned it. We can find out what land was farmed by owner-occupiers and what by tenants. The proportion of land under different cropping patterns is given and can be usefully compared with present land uses and related to the underlying geology or to the soil ...

(Morgan, 1979, pp.58-9)

By any standards, the tithe maps and awards are one of the most complete records ever made of agriculture in England and Wales. For detailed examples of the uses to which they can be put, the reader is once again referred to Kain and Prince, who look in turn at field systems, land use (including settlement), farming, farms, landowners and rural social structure.

A Parliamentary paper, *Return of all Tithes Commuted* (1887), provides a convenient list of all parishes for which records should exist. The tithe documents were prepared in triplicate, the original for central government records, a copy for the local diocese, and another copy for the tithe district. The three copies are not always identical in content. The originals are now in the Public Record Office at Kew, for which catalogues have been published (List and Index Society, 1971-2); photographic prints of the documents for particular areas can be obtained. For Wales, all the diocesan copies are in the National Library of Wales. The copies intended to be kept in the parish chest have often been damaged, over-used, misused or lost, but many of these, along with those from the diocesan archives, have now been transferred to local record offices or libraries. Most counties have hundreds of tithe maps, though they do not all have complete sets; they may have two copies for some parishes, and none for others. Kain and Prince give a list of the published guides and lists (pp.117-19), most of which are contained within more general guides. They also advise looking elsewhere for copies: in university, municipal or ecclesiastical archives, for example, or in local libraries. There is an *Index to the Tithe Survey*, which was a special printing by the Ordnance Survey of the first edition 1-inch maps on which the parish boundaries have been added.

Note. Further references useful to the subject of this chapter: Bagley, 1971; Baptist, 1967; Carpenter, 1967; Eden, 1983; Evans, 1968, 1978; Munby, 1969; Newton, 1969-70; Phillips, 1980, 1981; Ravenhill, 1973; Smith, B.S., 1967, 1967a; Thomas, 1966.

Chapter Four

TOWN PLANS

Speed and other early plans

As was the case with county maps and estate plans, town plans were a product of the arrival of the Elizabethan surveyors with their new skills. Political factors encouraged the making of county maps in the 1570s, and changes in the countryside had the same effect on the production of estate plans, which began to appear in volume towards the end of the century. The making of town plans was a slightly later activity marked in particular by the publication of the numerous town plans in Speed's set of county maps in 1612.

Continental cartographers had been publishing perspective or bird's eye views of towns since the middle of the 16th century.

(Technically speaking, a perspective view is one which might be obtained from some vantage point, such as a hill or a tower, whilst a bird's eye view looks down from a much higher angle of between 30° and 60°.) Braun and Hogenberg published five volumes of their *Civitates Orbis Terrarum* before 1600, and included plans of eight English towns—originally drawn by English surveyors such as William Smith (maker of several manuscript county maps). The towns were Bath, Bristol, Cambridge, Canterbury, Chester, London, Norwich and Oxford (Skelton, 1952a; Fordham, A., 1965). The sixth volume of *Civitates Orbis Terrarum*, published in 1617, was able to draw on Speed's plans. Meanwhile, John Norden had been surveying

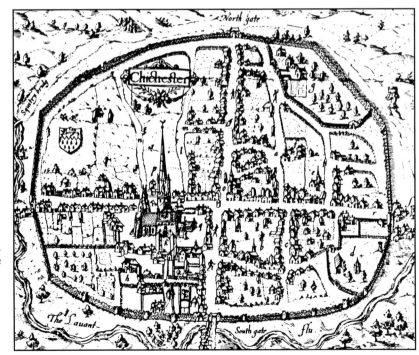

4.1 *Norden: Chichester, 1595. A small town plan inset on the county map of Sussex.*

towns for his county descriptions, suggesting that 'the most principall townes Cyties and castles within evrry Shire shoulde be breefly and expertly plotted out, in estate and forme as at this day they were'. He had already mapped Higham Ferrers and Peterborough in 1591 for his patron Lord Burghley, to try to convince him of this need (Beresford, 1984, pp.154-8). The Higham Ferrers plan is still a rather crude mixture of plan and perspective. Norden's plan of Chichester appears on his map of Sussex (Fig. 4.1), while London and Westminster appear on his map of Middlesex (1593); all three were to be used later by Speed. One of Norden's later estate maps (1607) includes a plan of Windsor.

There are only a few surviving town plans from the period before 1612; the earliest known is the manuscript sketch of Bristol done by Ricard in about 1479 (Skelton and Harvey, 1986). The first printed plan is William Cuningham's Norwich (1559), and the list also includes Lyne's Cambridge (1574), Hooker's Exeter (1587), Agas' Oxford (1578), Hamond's Cambridge (1592) and Patteson's Durham (Constable, 1932). All of these were printed, often on the continent, but we must not forget the equally early manuscript plans of towns which were drawn when a single landowner held a town; these might equally be classed as estate plans. Good examples are John Walker's 'trew platt of the Mannor and towne of Chellmisforde', drawn in 1591 (Fig. 4.2) and the estate plan of Sherborne in Dorset (Harvey, 1965a). Also in this category are plans of Bristol, Salisbury, Leicester, Canterbury, Norwich and London (Tooley, 1970, p.67). William Smith prepared, but never published, seven bird's eye views, adding Rochester to the list of towns surveyed. Only his plan of Bristol was original (Elliot, 1987).

These early plans often exaggerate certain features; thus Lyne's Cambridge overemphasises the colleges and churches whilst showing the suburbs at a smaller scale. Cuningham's

Norwich suffers from the same problem, giving an impression of a town filled with grand houses to the extent that 'one is left … to wonder where the poor lived' (J. Campbell in Lobel, 1975). There are other problems too: the amount of open space may have been reduced to make way for the enlarged depiction of buildings, and some cartographers were less accurate than others when it came to the depiction of buildings or the spelling of street names.

John Speed's *Theatre of the Empire of Great Britaine* was published in 1612, and has a comprehensive and standardised collection of town plans (Skelton, 1952a; Nicolson & Hawkyard, 1988). About 50 of the 70 town plans and views which he inserted into his new versions of Saxton's English and Welsh county maps were probably based on his own surveys. Thus the charge of plagiarism correctly levelled at the county maps themselves should not be extended to the town plans. They have a uniformity of style, are done in plan rather than bird's eye view, and most have a key to the more important buildings, churches and streets of a town. Speed suggests that the surveys which he undertook himself can be identified as those having a 'Scale of Pases' (he says that he took a pace to be five feet, i.e. *two* strides). In most cases there were no maps for Speed to copy, so he had to conduct his own surveys. The sources for Speed's town plans are listed in the following table:

A. *Town plans with a 'Scale of Pases' and thus assumed to be by Speed* (44):
Bangor, Beaumaris, Bedford, Brecon, Buckingham, Caernarfon, Canterbury, Cardiff, Cardigan, Carmarthen, Colchester, Denbigh, Derby, Dorchester, Ely, Flint, Harlech, Hereford, Hertford, Hull, Huntingdon, Ipswich, Lancaster, Lichfield, Lincoln, Monmouth, Montgomery, Newport, Nottingham, Oakham, Pembroke, Radnor, Reading, St Asaph, St Davids, Salisbury, Shrewsbury, Southampton, Stafford, Stamford, Warwick, Winchester, Worcester, York.

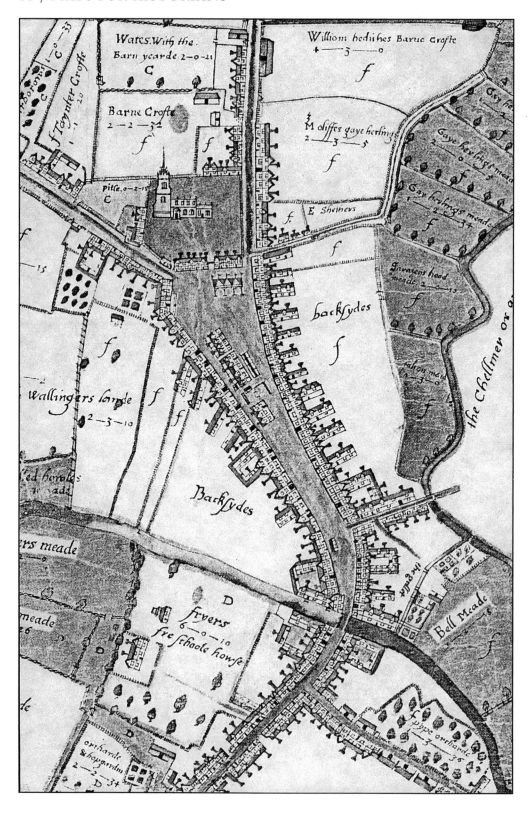

B. *Plans having a 'Scale of Pases' but possibly copied* (5):
Berwick (Cotton MSS), Chester (Smith), Newcastle (Mathew), Northampton (Norden), Peterborough (Norden).
C. *Plans with no 'Scale of Pases', origin unknown* (8)
Coventry, Gloucester, Kendal, Leicester, Llandaff, Richmond, Rochester, St Albans (Verulamium).
D. *Plans with no 'Scale of Pases'; probable origin indicated* (13):
Bath (Jones), Bristol (Smith), Cambridge (Hammond), Carlisle (Cotton MSS), Chichester (Norden), Durham (Patteson), Exeter (Hooker), Launceston (Norden), London (Norden), Norwich (Smith), Oxford (Agas), Westminster (Norden), Windsor (Hoefnagel).

Speed's maps are generally square, or slightly rectangular, usually measuring 6 in.

by between 5 in. and 8 in. Most have magnetic north at the top, along with a compass rose. The scale of the plans varies between 5 and 10 inches to the mile, and thus much detail had to be omitted. Where he copied from other plans, the generalisation and coarsening can often be seen—as in the case of Chichester, which Speed copied from Norden's county map (Fig. 4.1). For his own maps, it is hardly likely that he would have spent more than a few days in each town, and his technique probably involved little more than pacing the main streets and sketching in the principal buildings. It is highly unlikely that Speed used any more sophisticated techniques.

In attempting a plan view, however crude, Speed moved away from the perspective views which had been so popular at the end of the previous century. He did not renounce the old

4.2 *Walker: Chelmsford, 1591. The town is shown as part of an estate plan of the manor of Bishop's Hall.*

4.3 *Speed: Hereford, 1610. A typical Speed town plan showing street names, gates, bridges, walls and churches.*

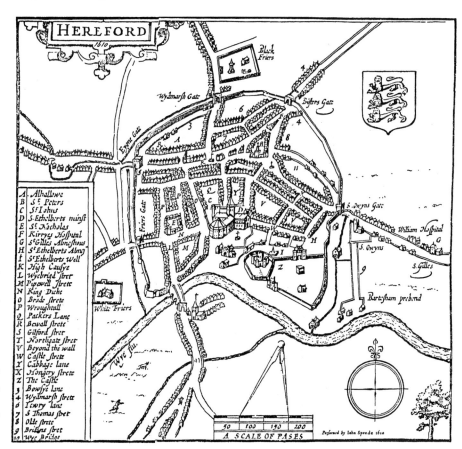

style entirely, however. Most features are still shown in perspective but they are positioned on a roughly measured plan (Fig. 4.3).

The cartographic accuracy of Speed's maps can be checked against a modern map, but this is not of great importance as Speed was clearly not attempting a precise survey. More important are the details which his maps show, not only of the main buildings, but also of other lesser features such as mills, market crosses, bridges, monastic precincts, gallows, limekilns and stocks. The little houses which line the streets are, however, conventionally drawn and do not represent the exact number of dwellings. It is always important to check whether

a plan was Speed's own, or whether it was copied from some earlier source whose reliability and accuracy might have been different.

On all the town plans, up to and including Speed's, Lobel (1968) notes two major problems: the exaggeration or reduction of certain features, and the variable accuracy of street, building and place names. However, she mentions four features for which Speed's maps provide valuable evidence: the street plan, the siting of town walls and gates, the siting of churches and buildings later demolished and the extent of suburban development at this date. Speed's map of Hereford, for example (Fig. 4.3), gives us unique information about

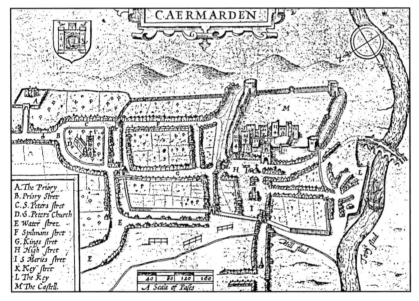

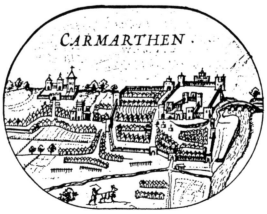

4.4 *Speed: Carmarthen. The rectangular version is more detailed, but the oval version (originally much smaller than the first) is different in several respects, notably in its depiction of the Priory (top left).*

the castle and its surroundings, about the siting of two churches demolished after the Civil War and about the extent of the suburbs in *c*.1610. Equally, Speed's map of Gloucester depicts the town walls as they were before the 17th-century alterations and shows the appearance of two churches and the existence of a bridge over the Severn. For Carmarthen there are two versions of the map, with some differences between them (Fig. 4.4).

Speed's idea of adding town plans to county maps established a fashion which was to continue for many years. Indeed, his original plans continued to be reproduced, unrevised, by some map publishers, for over 150 years. Speed's use of a measured plan as a base was important, and later surveyors could no longer get away with sketched surveys.

Urban plans of a very different sort, and at a much larger scale, were also being drawn at this time. For example, several plans showing individual blocks of property in London, drawn by Ralph Treswell in *c*.1612, have survived (Schofield, 1983). Although most of these plans depict only a few houses, some allow the reconstruction of the layout of larger areas (especially useful if the area was destroyed by the Great Fire in 1666); they can also give valuable information on room size and use and other minute details. Many such maps are in fact urban estate plans.

A full history of town plans has yet to be written. In order to illustrate the changes which occurred, and the various types of maps which were drawn, it will be useful to look briefly at the various maps which were made of London because it has a far greater number of plans than anywhere else and has been the subject of much detailed study (Glanville, 1972; Hyde, 1975; Howgego, 1978). Because London's maps have received so much attention no examples of general plans are included; it would in any case be almost impossible to pick out only three or four from the many produced. London is in fact untypical in having so many maps; never-

theless, the following section will provide a broad cartographic history, to which the maps of other towns can be related.

Maps of London

The first maps of London were essentially bird's eye views, though many were drawn to a reasonably consistent horizontal scale. The earliest surviving map is part of a large scale plan, perhaps drawn by Wyngaerde in the 1550s, of which only two plates survive. This was copied in a map once attributed to Ralph Agas which can be dated from internal evidence to the 1560s (Elliot, 1987). Next come Hogenberg's plan of 1572, a French woodcut of 1575 and Norden's plan of 1593—subsequently used by Speed in 1612. All these plans are at quite small scales (3½ to 6½ inches to the mile). In all, Howgego lists 15 maps dating from before the fire of 1666 and a further 45 between then and 1700—depicting at first the ravages of fire, and then the rebuilt city. Plans were drawn up for the rebuilding of the city by Wren, Evelyn, Hooke and Knight, though none was ever carried out.

The first large scale plan made after the fire was published by John Leake in 1667. It is described by Lobel (1968) as 'a most authoritative map, and the first scientific survey of the centre of the city'. If nothing else, the fire certainly encouraged the map trade! John Ogilby lost his shop in the fire, together with '£3,000 of stock', but the City appointed Ogilby and William Morgan to draw maps to help with the replanning of London and to settle disputes. Their map of the city (53 in. to the mile) appeared in 1676, the year of Ogilby's death; Morgan's own, reduced, map (17½ in. to the mile) was published in 1681-2. This last map was the only one to cover the whole built-up area until Rocque's map of 1746. All these plans and many others of London have been reprinted by H. Margary (see Bibliography). Some of these early maps were of enormous size: the twenty sheets of Ogilby and Morgan, for example, measure 60 in. × 97 in. overall.

Ogilby and Morgan also published the first 'environs' map of the area around London in 1683, including roads—a rare detail at this date. The map covers the area between Waltham Abbey, Gravesend, Sevenoaks and Colnbrook, at a scale of ½ inch to the mile (one sheet; 12 in. × 15 in.) and is effectively a 'county' map.

Hollar's map of 1685 (9½ in. to the mile) is interesting in many ways. Its title terms it, 'A New Mapp ... Being a ready guide for all Strangers to find any place therein. Drawne by W. Holler, the like never done before ...' The last point was certainly true; Hollar had died in 1677! Howgego adds that 'the draughtsman, whoever he was, attempted to disarm criticism ... with a rather sad-faced female figure brandishing a pair of dividers in her left hand, while holding in her right hand a scroll with the legend: *The Scale's but small, Expect not truth in all*.' (Howgego, 1978, p.15.) The immediate lesson is clear!

Evidently the London map trade was by now well established. Hollar's map invited buyers to the Rose and Crowne in Budge Row, 'Where you may have all sorts of Mapps'. Maps were already being copied from one another, and such phrases as 'A New Map' often meant very little. In fact, after Morgan's plan (1682) no new survey of London was made until Rocque's map of 1746. Instead, there were only new editions of old maps, with plates passing from father to son and from one firm to another. Notable map publishers included Stent, Overton, Sayer, Morden, Lea, Bowles, Seller, Bowen, Kitchin, and Jefferys—many of whom we have already mentioned in connection with the production of county maps. Partly as a result of unacknowledged plagiarism, Parliament passed an Act in 1734 granting a 14-year copyright period, imposing draconian penalties on anyone infringing the act. One result was that the original plates changed hands more frequently, and the names on the maps were

changed legally; this however did little to improve the content of the maps themselves.

The arrival of John Rocque from France in the 1730s was to bring about great improvements in cartography. He began work as a surveyor, and in 1737 started work on his new survey of London, which took him over nine years to complete. It was eventually finished in 1746, at a scale of 26 in. to the mile. The whole map is covered by a numbered grid, and an index of streets (and other features) was issued with it (Davies, 1987). Reduced versions were made by Rocque in 1749 (6 in.) and 1755 (13 in.) and new editions of the original appeared in 1749, 1761, 1770 and 1775 (this last one by Jefferys). Rocque also published an 'environs' map in 1746 (52 in.) but the most extensive of these was by John Andrews in 1774-7, extending as far as Bedford, Margate, the Isle of Wight and Newbury, at just less than 1 in. to the mile (20 sheets), drawing on the fruits of the county surveyors.

John Cary was one of the few English publishers at this time who took any care to keep his maps up to date. Starting his business in 1783, he published his 'New and Accurate Plan' of London at 6½-inch scale in 1787; it went through at least 20 editions before 1825.

During the 18th century a series of ward maps was produced, to illustrate written surveys of each of these subdivisions of the city (Hyde, 1967). The wards appear to have been surveyed by William Laybourn and Richard Blome, just before 1700; the first surviving edition of the plans was published by Strype in 1720. Several later editions appeared during the century, most of them copied, and sometimes updated, but no new general survey was done. As the original survey had been carried out at such an early date, the trigonometrical accuracy of these maps is poor. They are drawn at quite large scales, nonetheless, and show details not found on other maps.

The most important London map of the 18th century is undoubtedly Richard

Horwood's 26 in. to the mile plan of 1792-9, which intended to show every house, court, alley and vacant plot. In terms of accuracy and detail it is a considerable improvement on Rocque's map, and remained the best map of London for almost 70 years—until the arrival of the Ordnance Survey 25-inch plans. Revised by Faden in 1807, who added a further eight sheets to show the new East and West India Docks, there were third and fourth editions in 1813 and 1819. Taken together, the four editions span a period of rapid urban development, and are of immense value to any student of London's topography over this 20-year period. Horwood went on to survey Liverpool in 1803, but died there, in poverty—like so many other cartographers.

At about this time, a somewhat unusual map appeared, which was in essence the first real land utilisation map. Published by Thomas Milne in 1800, it covered London and extended out to Ham, Teddington, Woodford and Bromley. Its scale is 2 in. to the mile and it shows 17 different types of land use, including arable, meadow, pasture, market gardens, woods, marshes and parks. It indicates too whether land was enclosed or common (Bull, 1956; Wallis, 1981; Glanville, 1972 gives a colour reproduction of part of the map).

Cartographers mapping London had to cope with the increasingly rapid outward expansion of the built-up area, which often stretched beyond the edge of existing maps, thus making them difficult to use as originals for new editions. Regent's Park, begun in 1812 but not completed until 1838, is an example. Some maps depicted speculative developments taken from plans which were, in fact, never carried out; it is a common failing on maps of this period to show buildings (and other features such as canals and railways) which were planned but never built. In the centre of London there were problems too—as when Regent Street was carved out of an area already cluttered with detail on the existing maps; Faden's final edition of Horwood, however, managed to include this alteration to the street plan.

The first quarter of the 19th century saw many reissues of old maps, but from about 1825 cartographers such as Cruchley, Outhett, Greenwood and Wyld started producing new plans. Often they boasted of the careful triangulation of their surveys. The town surveyors had been slow to recognise the importance of triangulation, even though it had been known about for hundreds of years. The temptation to conduct a simple series of traverse surveys along the streets had been too much for most surveyors; if they thought about the matter at all they would probably have hoped that the large number of intersecting traverses in any town survey would have given the map a firm enough foundation.

A final point to be made about London maps concerns their sheer quantity. Before 1650 Howgego lists only nine, but 34 were produced by 1700, 57 in the first half of the 18th century, 120 in the second half, and no less than 203 between 1800 and 1850. Moreover, there were now maps of all conceivable types—a change brought about by the appearance of the large scale Ordnance Survey plans in the 1850s; from then onwards, the private surveyors turned to more specialised types of maps.

Other Towns

To list every map of each town in the country would be an Herculean task; the only attempts so far to do this have been made by West (1983, pp.150-65) and Armitage (1994). Compared to London, most towns have very few maps from before 1800; for the eight towns in the first volume of Lobel's *Historic Towns* there are only 16 maps for this period, although the generally more prestigious towns in the second volume are better served. (Volume 1 includes Banbury, Caernarfon, Glasgow, Gloucester, Hereford, Nottingham, Reading and Salisbury; volume 2 covers Bristol, Cambridge, Coventry and

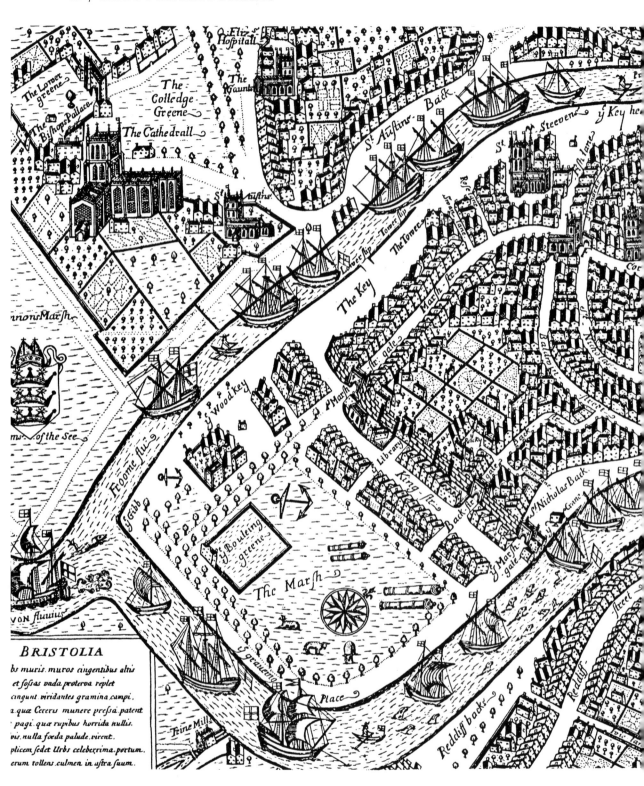

Eliz
Hospitall
The Gaunte
The Lower
greene
The Colledge
Greene
The Bishops Pallace
The Cathedrall
St Aüstins Back
St Steevens
ÿ Key he
Key
Ball lane
Cor
St Aüstins
St Aüstins
Rerc
Corchip
Tower slip
The Tower
The Key
Maftle ftr
nnonsMarsh
ÿ Woodkey
Marfh
Marfh
Library
Marfh
Maryfh gate
Redcliff gate
St Nicholas Back
ms of the See
Froome flu
ÿ Gibb
ÿ Bouleing
greene
King ftr
Back ftr
Redcliff back
Grone
St Marfh
gate
von fluuius
The Marsh
Redcliff backs
Reddiff Street
Teine Mills
grauern
Place

BRISTOLIA

bs muris. muros cingentibus altis
et foſſas vnda proterva replet
cingunt viridantes gramina campi.
a. quæ Cereris munere preſſa patent
pagi. quæ rupibus horrida nullis.
vis. nulla fœda palude virent.
plicem ſedet Urbs celeberrima. portum.
erum tollens culmen in uſtra ſuum.

Norwich.) In fact, most English towns have no more than a couple of maps dating from before 1800.

The number of town plans increased in the middle of the 17th century. A few of the plans have always been singled out as being of special value; these include Ogilby's Ipswich (1674), Loggan's Oxford (1675) and Cambridge (1688), Cleer's Norwich (1696) and Kip's Gloucester (c.1710). Millerd's Bristol (1673) was revised at least four times by 1730, and the revisions give a detailed picture of the growth of the town during that period (Fig. 4.5).

We have already noted the importance of Ogilby in the mapping of London, but nationally he is best remembered for his 1675 *Britannia*, a depiction of the main roads of the country (see Chapter Five). On these road maps each of the major towns through which the roads pass is depicted 'ichnographically, according to their Form and Extent' (i.e. in simple plan form) although smaller places are still depicted pictorially. If no other late 17th-century plan exists, then Ogilby's plans may be useful, but it should be borne in mind that he may have copied an earlier map, and thus his depiction may not relate to the 1670s—and, in any case, his maps are at a scale of one inch to one mile, and thus are unable to show much detail.

Sometimes valuable maps turn up in odd places—as when several tattered plans of Preston and Lancaster, made in 1684, were found in Towneley Hall, in Burnley. These sketch plans had clearly been precisely surveyed, and K.H. Docton (1957) was able to produce accurate maps from them, complete with most of the householders' names. Such detail is rare for a northern town at this early date.

4.5 *Millerd: Bristol, 1673. The town and the harbour awash with ships are depicted pictorially on a surveyed ground plan.*

The 18th century saw many more town plans—partly due to the spate of Georgian rebuilding. However, this rule does not always hold true; Cambridge, for example, has more maps dating from each of the preceding two centuries, while Ludlow has none at all from before 1800. Surveying towns was, after all, an expensive business and it required a substantial number of well-off people to purchase the end product. Thus towns in decline or with little manufacturing industry had poor maps—or none at all; Lobel accurately says that one can confidently judge the economic prosperity of a town by the quality of its maps. A few examples might include Gilmore's Bath (1731) (Fig. 4.6), Downing's Bury St Edmunds (1740), Bradford's Coventry (1750), Taylor's Hereford (1757), Hanson's Birmingham (1778) and Hochstetter's Norwich (1789). John Rocque published large plans of Bristol, Exeter and Shrewsbury, as well as London, in the 1740s, and in the 1760s Andrew Dury issued a collection of small plans (typically measuring 5½ in. × 4½ in.) based on Rocque's surveys of 11 provincial English towns (Fordham, A., 1965) (Fig. 4.7). Manuscript town plans also continued to be made, sometimes in the form of estate maps, emphasising a particular individual's property (Fig. 4.8).

Parallel to the development of town plans was the persistence of the 'prospect' or perspective view which had preceded the town plan proper. Perhaps best known are those of Samuel and Nathaniel Buck, done in the early 18th century—in all they published 83 views of the towns of England and Wales, many of which add to our knowledge of their development (Hyde, 1994). Even the bird's eye view made a reappearance with the advent of the balloon—which allowed such a view to be seen for the first time. Most 'prospects' are views and not plans, and therefore lie within the history of the picture—perhaps between the painting and the photograph.

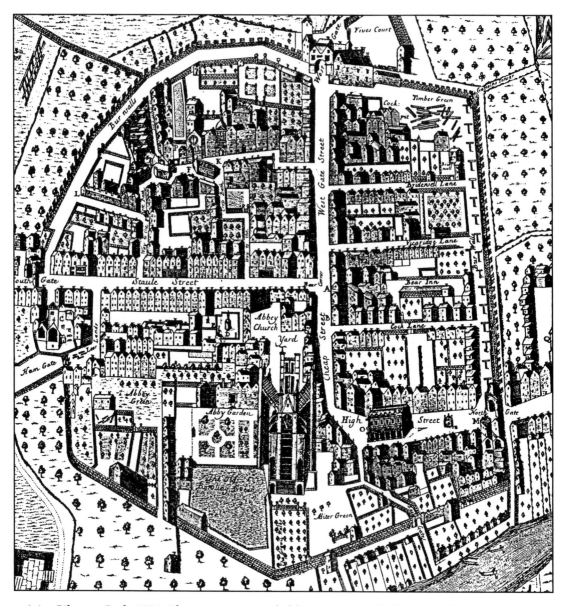

4.6 *Gilmore: Bath, 1731. The map is surrounded by pictures of the houses of the chief citizens, antiquarian detail and a list of the inns.*

The new county maps of the late 18th century sometimes included plans of the principal towns. For example, Donn's Devon (1765) has plans of Exeter and Plymouth, whilst Jefferys' Yorkshire (1771-2) includes Hull, Leeds, Pontefract, Ripon, Scarborough, Sheffield and York. Before using them it is important to find out who carried out these town surveys, when, and whether they were copied. On Jefferys' map, Sheffield was based partly on an existing plan whereas the other six were both original and accurate (Fig. 4.9).

Another problem with such inset maps is that a common reason for their inclusion was to fill up an empty corner of the map. Thus the publisher might have simply resorted to

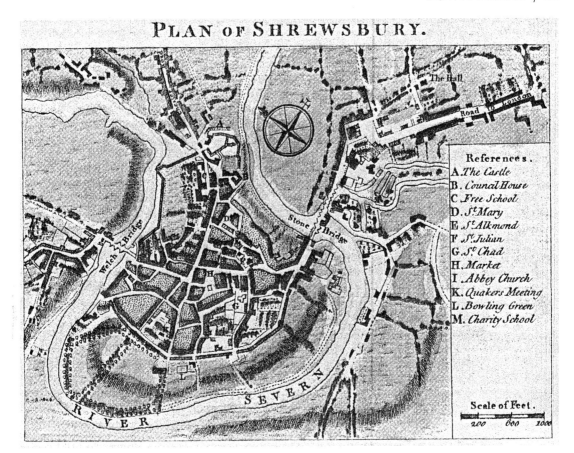

PLAN OF SHREWSBURY.

References.
A. The Castle
B. Counal House
C. Free School
D. St Mary
E. St Alkmond
F. St Julian
G. St Chad
H. Market
I. Abbey Church
K. Quakers Meeting
L. Bowling Green
M. Charity School

Scale of Feet.
200   600   1000

4.7 *Rocque and Dury: Shrewsbury, 1764. Dury published reduced versions of Rocque's surveys.*

4.8 *Lewis: Carmarthen, 1786. A manuscript street map, showing in particular the property of John Vaughan. The extract shows the area east of the castle.*

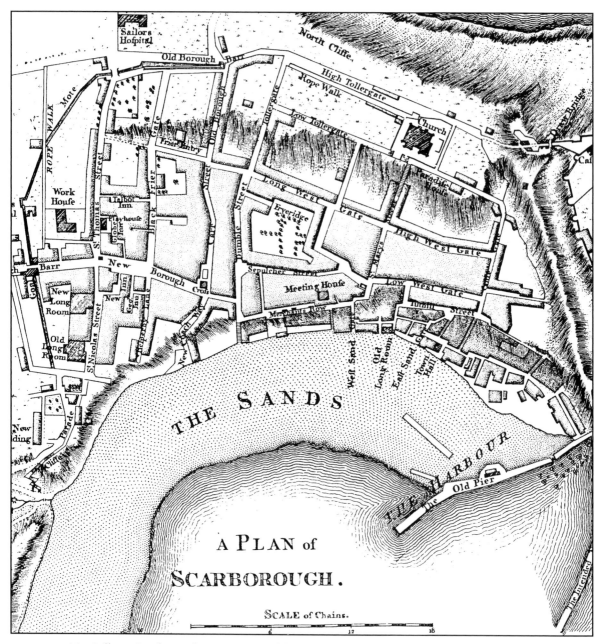

4.9 *Jefferys: Scarborough, 1771-2. One of the seven town plans shown on the county map of Yorkshire.*

copying an old and out of date town plan. Prior's Leicestershire (1779), for example, uses a map of the county town made in 1722. Nevertheless, many of these inset plans are detailed and valuable, especially if the date of the survey can be ascertained (Smith, 1992).

The growth of the great industrial towns was reflected in an increasing number of maps. West (1983) gives a detailed description of the mapping of the new industrial areas between Dudley and Birmingham, whilst Bonser and Nichols' (1960) catalogue of Leeds maps depicts the rapid spread of this town. The growth of Manchester and Salford is also shown graphically in maps (Lee, 1957). The earliest map of Manchester was drawn in about 1670, but only survives in later copied versions; it shows a very small town, with a dozen or so streets, extending no more than half a mile in any direction from Christ Church (Fig. 4.10). Although the Buck brothers drew a prospect in 1728 (and there was another by Whitworth in c.1734) the next maps were not drawn until the 1740s when there was a manuscript map of Salford, and the first detailed plans published by Casson and Berry (Fig. 4.11). There were by then 160 streets with 6,000 houses, and the latter plan, first published in 1741, was reissued and updated four times in 15 years, so rapidly was the built-up area expanding.

By the end of the 18th century, however, Manchester and Salford had grown so much that a new map was needed, and William Green, who had worked with Yates on his Lancashire map, began surveying in 1787. He had still not finished in 1791, however, when Laurent, a French cartographer, visited him to find out how advanced his work was—and probably obtained survey information from him. He stayed in Manchester for only a month, but returned late in 1793 with proof copies of his own map, some four months before Green was able to reach the same stage. Thus Laurent stole the market. Although Laurent included a map of the route to London, his map is less than one-tenth the size of Green's plan. The latter, comprising nine sheets at a scale of 30 in. to the mile, is much more detailed, and is undoubtedly a first-rate piece of work; for example he names the owners of land at the edge of the town—which was still undeveloped—and also indicates the proposed lines of the Ashton, Bolton and Bury, and Rochdale canals. Laurent's map, on the other hand, is more generalised, and although at first glance it seems to look more 'professional' this is because it had been engraved by John Cary—one of the leading London publishers (Fig. 4.12).

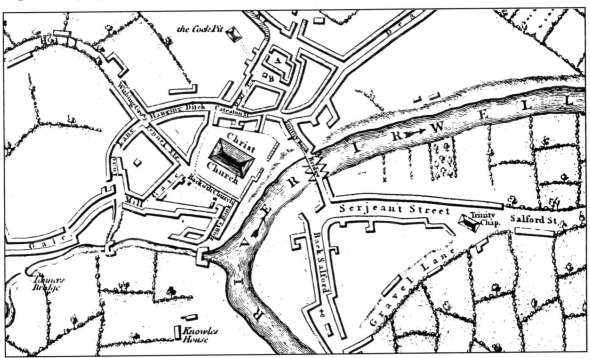

4.10 *Manchester and Salford in 1670, as engraved by Cary on Laurent's map of 1793.*

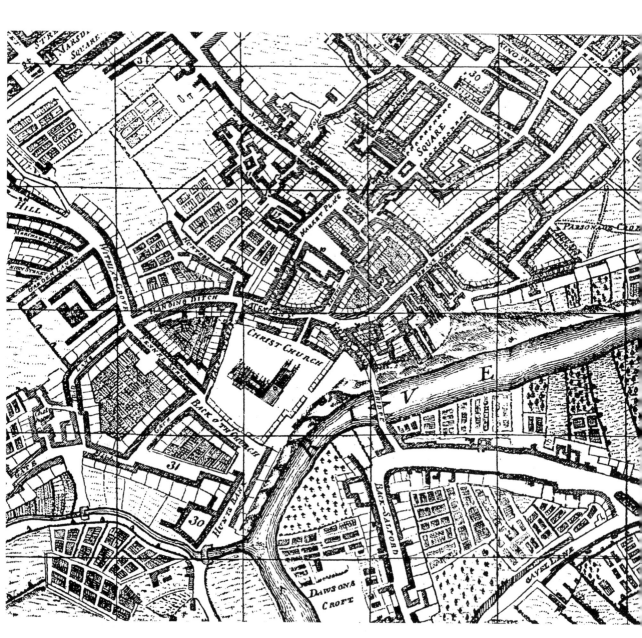

4.11 *Casson and Berry: Manchester and Salford, 1746. The rapid growth of the town since the 1670s is readily apparent.*

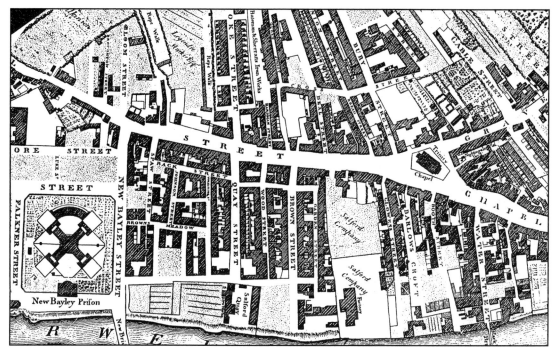

4.12 *Salford on the 1793-4 maps by Green (above) and Laurent (below). Laurent's map looks more professional, but in fact contains less detail than that by Green. Laurent's map is shown upside-down for ease of comparison.*

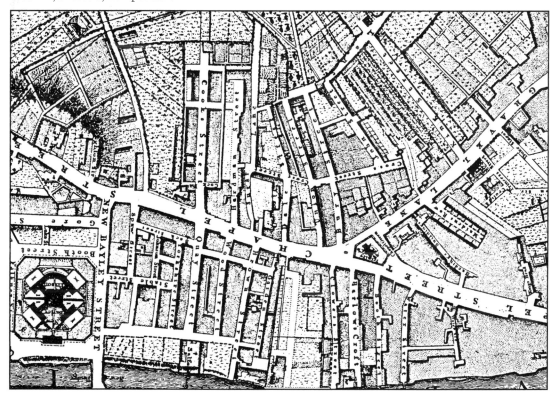

In the first half of the 19th century a succession of plans appeared, some based on original survey, some on earlier plans. An interesting series of directory maps extends from 1804 right through to 1883, published by Pigot and then by Slater who took over his business (Fig. 4.13). In the period up to 1843, 20 maps were produced by Pigot, seven of which were reprints, with nothing more than the date altered. The only long period between revised versions was from 1836 to 1843, the year of Pigot's death. On the other hand, the 1824 Directory states that 'Market Street and Cannon Street appear on the Plan as if the intended improvements had been completed'. Apart from Pigot's series, other notable maps included those by Johnson (1819), Swire (in Baines' *Directory*, 1824) and Thornton (1831).

The explosion of map-making in Manchester in the early 19th century reflects clearly the changes which were going on in all the major industrial towns of the country, and many other places can boast a large array of maps. Rapid growth, the rebuilding of central areas, plus the arrival of the railways, all meant that maps had to be updated more often, and that there was always a demand for new maps. Lee lists only a handful of maps of Manchester for the 18th century, but the first half of the 19th century saw the publication of over a dozen. The number of completely new surveys was less, as many were revised or updated editions of earlier maps. Some maps show areas which were only just being laid out, depicting the alignments of the new streets, and from these we can learn a great deal about the development of the 19th-century town.

If we consider all maps and plans rather than just those of a town as a whole, then the amount of evidence available is even more

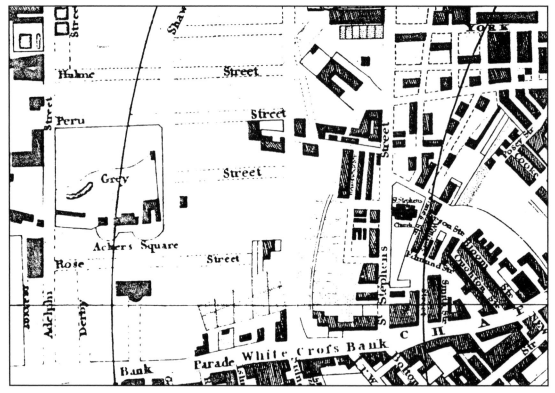

4.13 *Pigot: Manchester and Salford, 1824. One of Pigot's* Directory *maps showing planned streets near the centre of Salford.*

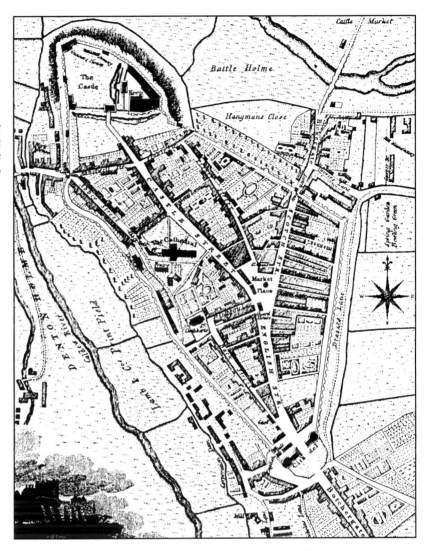

4.14 *Cole and Roper: Carlisle, 1810. Although newly engraved, this plan is very similar to one published in 1794.*

startling. There are only 29 maps and plans of Leeds before 1800, but the first half of the 19th century saw 90 produced, and the second half a further 249 (Bonser and Nichols, 1961). This is complemented by a profusion of other kinds of data—not least the national census, first taken in 1801, and yielding considerable detail from 1841 onwards.

Town plans were published not only in large sheets but in book form too. Town histories, gazetteers, directories and guide books often contained maps—usually copied but occasionally newly surveyed. Commercial directories in particular became increasingly common during the century; they are listed in Norton (1950), West (1983) and Shaw & Tipper (1989), and discussed in Shaw (1982). A few included specially surveyed plans: for example, the maps in Baines' Yorkshire and Lancashire directories (1822-5) and the plans of Manchester by Pigot (1804-43). Some, however, reprinted old maps (often without acknowledgement) and then failed to update them as the town changed and grew. For some larger towns, directories appeared annually, but the maps (if present at all) were altered less frequently. The maps are often missing from library copies.

A total of 294 English and Welsh town plans were issued by the Reform Bill Commissioners to show the new electoral boundaries embodied in the bill of 1832 (Hyde, 1975a). Most were derived from Ordnance Survey plans (whether published or still in manuscript). For those areas of northern England which were yet to be surveyed (principally the fifty or so English towns north of Macclesfield) other existing plans had to be used. In a few cases, special surveys were commissioned for the purpose.

The plans of some towns south of Macclesfield were also based on non-O.S. data: Aldeburgh, Bury St Edmunds, Cambridge, Haverfordwest, Holyhead, Holywell,

Huntingdon, London, Ludlow, Machynlleth, St Albans, Southampton, Stoke, Stroud, Sudbury, Taunton and Wenlock. Lieutenant Dawson of the Ordnance Survey (later important in the tithe survey) was in charge of map production. Boundary information was gleaned from a large number of sources, including existing county maps, town plans, enclosure and estate maps, parish perambulation records, charters and even verbal evidence. The plans were usually made at quite a small scale—the majority at one or two inches to the mile, although 16 were at larger scales. They are undecorated, functional maps, clearly produced for a specific purpose in a very short period of time (about 18 months). They were reprinted in atlas form by Hansard after the Reform Bill had been passed. A later series of 180 plans at 4 in. to the

4.15 *Wood, Ulverston, 1832. This large scale plan (26 inches to the mile) shows detail of the town and a large area around.*

mile was published in 1837 in the *Report of the Municipal Corporation Boundaries Commission* (these maps also show ward boundaries). A popular version of the plans appeared in 1840 as Samuel Lewis' *Representative History of England*.

Collections of town plans continued to appear. The most famous was in Cole and Roper's *British Atlas* (1810), which had 56 county maps, a chart of navigable rivers and canals, and 21 town plans, including maps of Carlisle, Liverpool, Manchester and Salford, and Newcastle and Gateshead—towns not previously included in such collections (Fig. 4.14). Many of the plans, however, including Manchester, were already over ten years old, and were derived from even older surveys (Cole & Roper, 1970).

Many good quality original town plans were being produced in the early 19th century by itinerant surveyors such as John Wood, who travelled around the north and west of the country in the 1820s and 1830s (Fig. 4.15). A good selection of 19th-century town plans by Cole and Roper, Moule, Wood, Tallis and others has been published by Baynton-Williams (1992). Finally, it is important to remember that some tithe maps (c.1840) included urban areas (see Chapter Three).

The heyday of the private cartographer of town plans was brought to an end, just as it had been for county map-makers, by the arrival of the Ordnance Survey, which began publishing town plans on very large scales in the 1840s. Thereafter, private plans tended to be based on the Ordnance maps, and concentrated on depicting specialised aspects of the town.

Specialised Town Plans

A wide variety of plans exists depicting particular features of a town. Some show the town in its entirety, while others cover only part of it—right down to plans of individual buildings. Many allow small scale features of the town to be studied in detail. They fall into six fairly distinct groups: land ownership maps; parish maps; improvement and planning maps; railway maps; medical and social maps; and insurance maps.

Land ownership maps

We have already noted the early London estate plans drawn by Ralph Treswell soon after 1600, and there are many others, increasing in number right through to the 19th century. Some were better than others: those drawn by J. Ward for the Goldsmiths' Company in the 1690s were clear and colourful but grossly inaccurate, and the company had to commission new plans in the middle of the next century (Glanville, 1972).

There is a reasonable chance of maps drawn for urban landowners surviving, particularly if the landowner was the Church or a corporate body, whether a guild, a company or a municipal corporation. The archives of many such bodies have now been transferred to local record offices, but if they have not, then the records of the present and previous landowners may need to be checked. This will be a complicated task for any large town, where a major search in the various record offices and repositories is required. On the other hand, anyone wanting to do research on towns which were largely owned by a single family (such as Whitehaven in Cumbria) should try to track down that family's archives and the records of their municipal authorities in order to obtain a complete set of 'official' maps. Unfortunately, in the case of less important individuals, maps of their landholdings are less likely to have survived; even if they exist, they may be unknown, lying forgotten in some attic or solicitor's office. If their existence is known, it may yet be difficult to gain access to them, but one should still not be deterred from trying to find such maps.

Many land ownership plans are simply the urban equivalent of the rural estate plans described in the previous chapter. They were drawn for the same reasons (i.e. survey, sale or lease) and present many of the same problems. Some of the early 19th-century plans of Leeds were drawn in connection with the sale of land, often divided into building lots. Bonser and Nichols (1960) list a dozen such plans for the 1820s alone. Sale plans were often added to the particulars of the property concerned; and they become increasingly common from the 1820s onwards. They can show considerable detail, though only of the area to be sold. The 12 Leeds plans from the 1820s vary in scale between 11 and 66 yards to the inch (i.e. 1:396 to 1:2376). Sale plans were sometimes derived from existing estate plans, but later they were copied from tithe or Ordnance Survey maps. A number were also specially drawn. Some record offices have substantial collections of these plans.

Towards the end of the 19th century, various attempts were made to produce a map of London showing land ownership; the story is given in full by Hyde (1975, pp.40-3) but the bare bones are as follows. Frank Banfield was commissioned to investigate the problems of 'landlordism' in London, but was amazed to find how difficult it was to discover who owned what; as a result, he produced a first attempt at an ownership map in 1888. The idea evidently caught on, and some copies of existing maps were coloured in to show the major estates—though getting precise information from the landlords was extremely difficult. John Lloyd continued the task in the early 1890s until the new London County Council took over, producing its *Ground Plan of London*, completed in 1910 and updated until 1914. This covered 114 square miles with 35,000 estates, using the Ordnance Survey 25-inch plan as a base, with some areas redrawn at the 5-foot scale. Allied with this map was the *Annual Map of London*, intended to keep the Ordnance Survey map up to date; it appeared in 1903, 1905 and 1908.

Ownership plans of this type are of great value. They can be used to trace patterns of ownership and development, especially in London. Such maps do not exist for most other towns, though it may well be possible to reconstruct land ownership patterns for them, especially if there were only a few landowners. It can be amazingly difficult to find out who owns a piece of land today, let alone for any time in the past.

Parish maps

These depict the area within a parish's boundary, and sometimes land ownership as well. Many such maps were produced in the form of a single manuscript copy, intended to be kept for use by the parochial authorities, but a few were printed—usually by the wealthier parishes or by those with a rich patron. Glanville (1972, pl.37) reprints a map of Islington made by the Bakers in 1793 which contains an inset map of the whole parish, while Smith (1985, p.57) has a plan of the same parish, surveyed in 1805-6 and updated to 1831. One of the more famous cartographers specialising in parish maps was Thomas Starling, who also published a plan of Islington in 1822; Glanville reprints part of his map of St Mary, Kensington (pl.45). Some parishes have perambulation plans, which give details only of the parish boundaries. Harley (1972) notes a plan of St Paul's parish in Canterbury dating from c.1550, and another—of the urban glebe lands in Guildford in 1617—belonging to the parsonage of Shalford (which lies only a mile to the south of Guildford).

Perhaps the most numerous—yet least well known—parish maps were those drawn for rating purposes in the years around 1840. The rating system of England and Wales until 1836 can only be described as chaotic; each parish made its own arrangements, and the inequalities both within and between parishes led

4.16 *Tress and Chambers: St Andrew by the Wardrobe, 1838. A parochial assessment map.*

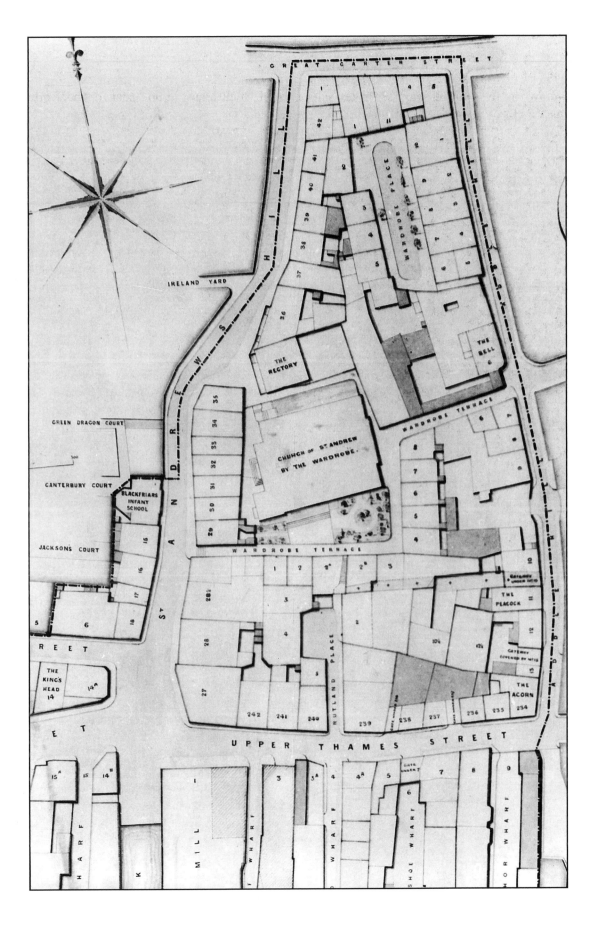

Parliament in this 'Age of Reform' to pass the Act to Regulate Parochial Assessments in that year (Hyde, 1976). All rates were now to be levied on the annual value of property. The Poor Law Commissioners were allowed to 'order a survey to be done, with or without a Map or Plan' if a new valuation was needed. It is an unusual coincidence that the Commutation of Tithes Act was passed in the same year; both acts required much large scale mapping to be undertaken, with similar though not identical cartographic needs. Certainly, Dawson's proposed standards for the tithe surveys were not dismissed by the surveyors of these rating maps (see Chapter Three).

Parishes did not have to undertake a new survey if an adequate one already existed. If a parish did need a survey, then the Poor Law Commissioners would suggest that the Tithe Commissioners were consulted about a suitable surveyor, and that if the tithes of that parish had not been commuted a map could be made to serve both purposes.

The surveys proceeded apace, and by 1843 about 4,000 parishes (out of some 15,000) had been valued, many with accompanying maps. Dawson, writing in 1853, said that 1,267 maps had been made under the Act, but this may be an over-estimate. Indeed, one is left puzzling as to quite where all the necessary surveyors had suddenly come from, especially as this was also the era of Parliamentary railway plans, tithe maps, and the Ordnance Survey. Edwin Chadwick was the driving force behind the Poor Law legislation—he had created the Poor Law Unions in 1832—and he now tried to set standards for the maps, hoping, as Dawson had with the tithe maps, that they would be reliable cadastral surveys, suitable for legal use. His hopes were soon to be frustrated, for by 1840 he was already complaining that less than half the maps were up to Dawson's 'first-class' standards. Nevertheless, this is a far higher proportion than the 12 per cent achieved by the tithe maps themselves.

The Parochial Assessment maps were accompanied by a reference book detailing the valuations; they were first checked locally and then sent to the Poor Law Commissioners who passed them to Dawson in the Tithe Office (also in Somerset House). Once the survey and maps had been approved, they were returned to the parish to be used for rating purposes. Some of the maps are very fine indeed; Hyde (1976) notes Philip Hardwick's survey of the parish of St Edmund the King as being the most detailed surviving plan in London, and those done by Richard Tress as bringing the city parish map which 'had evolved over the past 100 years … to a pitch of near perfection.' (Fig 4.16).

It was perhaps easier for a small city parish to produce a map; its inhabitants would be richer and the area to be surveyed smaller than in a country parish (the total perimeter of many London parishes was less than half a mile). Where city parish maps were made, and survive, they are usually invaluable cartographic sources, and indeed have been described by Hyde as 'the most dependable maps of the period'. They are more useful than tithe maps in their coverage of urban areas because they cover a whole parish and not only the areas where tithes were to be commuted.

These maps have been almost entirely ignored, for reasons which are not hard to understand. First, only about a quarter of parishes were ever surveyed and many of these did not produce a map. Second, only a single manuscript copy was usually made, and this was intended to be a working copy for use by the parish. There was no production in triplicate as with the tithe maps, and only a few parishes printed their maps. Third, there was no legal requirement to preserve the map; they were intended to be kept and used in the vestry. In fact, only the maps for London have been studied in any detail; a manuscript catalogue of these exists in the Guildhall Library. There is no national list, and those that have survived elsewhere need to be tracked down. Some may

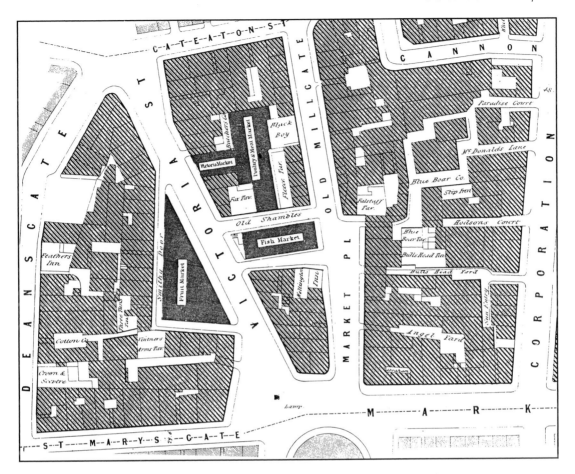

4.17 *Map of Exchange and Collegiate Church Wards, Manchester, 1850. Surveyed by Richard Thornton, published by Joseph Adshead. This large scale plan (80 inches to the mile) is not a copy of large scale Ordnance Survey maps available at that date, and provides extra detail.*

be in local history libraries or record offices, but others may be lying forgotten and gathering dust in the darker corners of parish churches. A few may still hang on the vestry wall. The first step towards finding one of these maps would be to read through the vestry minutes and the Board of Guardian minutes of a parish to find references (if any) to a survey and map.

Ward maps are closely related to ownership and parish maps, usually depicting a particular ward at a large scale. The early London examples have already been noted, but many other large towns produced them (Fig. 4.17). There are numerous other 'official' maps, and one example will have to suffice, namely maps drawn to show the location of enumeration districts for the various censuses (Fig. 4.18).

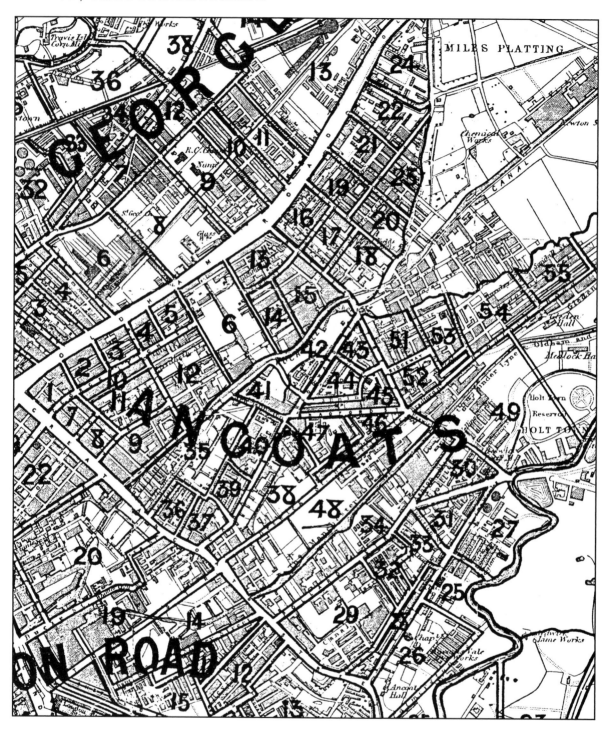

▲ **4.18** *A map of enumeration district in Manchester for the 1871 census, superimposed on a 'Sanitary Map of the City of Manchester'.*

4.19 *Laurent: Manchester, 1793. This map shows numerous planned streets due to be laid out on either side of Oxford Street close to the River Medlock.* ➤

Improvement and planning maps

Most of the larger towns of Britain were extensively altered during the 19th century. Over three-quarters of the City of London was rebuilt during the second half of the century, and even quiet country towns like Ludlow were added to, though here the alterations tended to take the form of new developments at the edge of the town. Such improvements might have included redevelopment of a town centre, the creation of new roads, parks, harbours and public buildings, the clearance of slums, and above all the construction of the railways which cut swathes into most sizeable towns. Perhaps the most famous single improvement scheme was the creation of Regent Street by John Nash, intended to link Charing Cross to Portland Place and Regent's Park, first planned in 1813 (Smith, 1985, p.70).

Such developments required maps and plans to be made—for the developers, the builders and the local council, for sale to the general public, and sometimes for the granting of Parliamentary approval. Parliament first required plans for canal schemes in 1792-4. This requirement was slowly extended to other public utility schemes, and to railways by 1837; the House of Lords' series begins in 1792, and the Commons' series in 1818 (Bond, 1964). From 1837 a Parliamentary standing order also required the deposit of sealed duplicates with the Clerk of the Peace; these are now generally known as 'deposited plans', and usually come under the heading of 'Quarter Sessions Records' in the

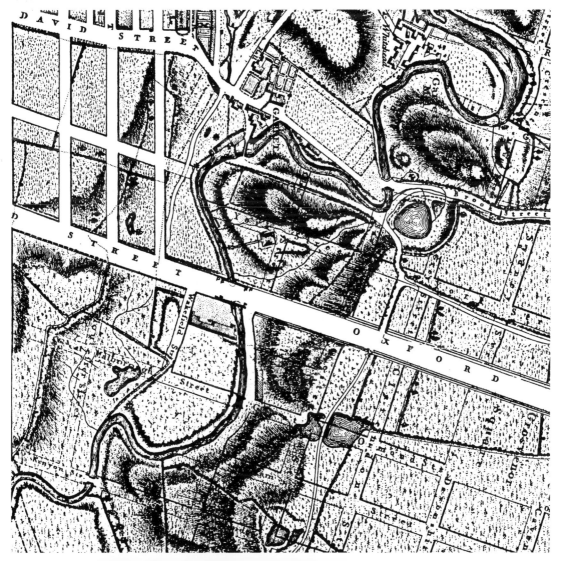

local record office. We shall come across these plans again in the next chapter, where they are described more fully.

One curious cartographic result of this activity was that proposed schemes were often drawn on new maps as if they had been completed. Thus, as Harley (1972, p.17) says, such maps should be 'treated cautiously as evidence of *actual* change; an over-enthusiasm to keep up to date tempted cartographers to anticipate housing developments, which may, in the end, have turned out differently'. As we shall see in the next chapter this did not only apply to housing, but to all improvements, and to canals and railways in particular. However, some cartographers drew in proposed developments only as dotted or dashed lines superimposed on the existing townscape (Fig. 4.19).

Quite apart from such obvious changes to the outward appearance of the town, a whole host of plans was drawn up for the provision of water, sewerage, electricity, gas (including street lighting) and drainage. Later plans of this type were usually based on existing (often O.S.) maps, but earlier ones were sometimes specially drawn and may show detail other than that which was strictly pertinent to the map.

Once again, London has the best array of improvement maps, and it will serve as a guide to what may exist elsewhere (Hyde, 1975, pp.25-6). Special maps showing the areas to be served by competing water and gas companies were drawn, and a few were published for more general use. Moreover, the gas companies had to keep an updated map of their mains with the local Clerk of the Peace.

The provision of sewers at this time was a serious problem—both in medical terms (as we shall see later) and cartographically for, in order to plan the new sewerage systems, maps needed accurate levels. Until the early 19th century, only the canal engineers had needed to bother about precise levelling, but now their skills were required for a very different type of canal. The first London sewer map was drawn by Richard Kelsey in 1844, but it gave neither levels nor directions of flow; this was rectified by William Haywood. Eventually a new survey was carried out by the Ordnance Survey. This was an outline plan only, at the scale of 5 feet to the inch, onto which the existing sewers could be plotted; it was completed by 1851. With this detailed information, the new sewer network could be planned accurately.

An even larger scale manuscript map of the central areas of Westminster and Kensington was also prepared—at a scale of 10 feet to the mile—in order to show the extra detail needed for house drains. The 5-foot scale was thought inadequate for detailed sanitary planning. This experiment probably influenced the decision to publish later O.S. town plans at this larger scale (see Chapter Six).

Several 'popular' sewerage maps were printed for public delectation, the best of which was probably Mylne's 'Map of the Contours of London and its Environs showing the Districts of the Metropolitan Local Management Act and Lines of the Principal Sewers' (1856); a later map also took special care to indicate 'those places where noxious vapours are emitted'!

Such was the overall rate of improvements in London that cartographers had great difficulty in keeping pace with them; several firms such as James Wyld and C. Smith began to reprint their existing maps with the improvements superimposed. But the most important maps were those produced by Edward Stanford, who adapted his 'Library Map of London' (Fig. 4.20), which had first appeared in 1862 (partly based on the O.S. maps) to become a quasi-official map, both for the Metropolitan Board of Works and for depicting plans laid before Parliament. As each sheet cost only two shillings, the map was also clearly aimed at a larger market, enabling ordinary citizens to see how the intended improvements might affect them and their property. Improvements were usually printed in red and further details added when the map was reprinted annually. By 1870 Smith and Wyld had ceased producing such maps, leaving Stanford alone in the business.

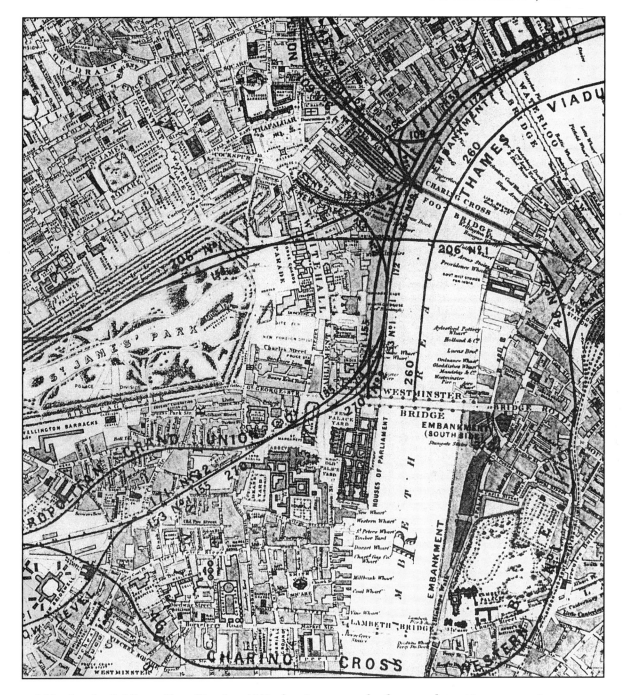

4.20 *Stanford's Library Map of London, 1862, showing proposed railways and street improvements.*

Urban railway plans

Above all it was the railways which had the biggest single impact on 19th-century towns. The railways themselves are dealt with in the next chapter, but their impact on town plans is discussed briefly here.

From the 1830s onwards the new railways carved their way into many British towns. In the larger towns, they were unable to reach the centres because of the high land values and the unwillingness of landowners to sell land with good property on it. Areas of lower-class housing proved less of a barrier, and landowners of such areas positively welcomed the railways. Thus it was that the main lines entering London from the north all terminated over a mile and a half from Charing Cross, while the original Manchester terminus of the line to Liverpool was three-quarters of a mile from the city centre. London eventually overcame the problem of peripheral termini with the underground lines, whilst Manchester's later lines march around the edge of the city on massive arches, which originally still had some housing beneath them.

The railway developers needed plans not only for the construction of the lines themselves but also for the diversion of roads and sewers, and the building of bridges and embankments. Plans showing property were more important later, as the railways acquired land and became major urban landowners in their own right. The Great Western Railway, for example, maintained large scale plans (at 40 feet to the inch) showing its lands, buildings, and sometimes parts of the surrounding area too. Such was the upheaval caused by railway development that, after 1853, the companies had to produce formal 'demolition statements', illustrated by large scale plans, if they wished to demolish more than 30 houses in any one parish (Dyos, 1957-8).

The cartographic record of all this activity is usually very clear—with town plans dated before and after the building of various lines

(but beware cartographers who showed planned lines *as if* they had been built!). We also have various editions of the large scale Ordnance maps, plus the maps accompanying the Acts of Parliament (Fig. 4.21), the construction plans (where they survive), the demolition statement plans, and, for London, the improvement maps described above (Fig. 4.20). Apart from searching the usual local record office and Parliamentary archives, the British Transport Commission's former archives may also be of use; these are now in the Public Record Office.

Later in this period, special urban railway guides were produced, such as Macauley's 'Metropolitan Railway Map', which first appeared in 1859, showing lines up to 15 miles from London. Indeed there were so many railways in and around London by the 1860s that several maps and guides appeared; they are described by Hyde (1975, pp.18-21).

If railways had the greatest single impact on the 19th-century landscape, we must not forget the other transport schemes ranging from the canals of the years around 1800 through to more modern means of transport such as the underground railways, tramways and the trolley bus or omnibus systems. All have maps depicting at least their networks, even if they don't always illustrate their construction.

Medical and social maps

The mid-19th century saw novelists writing about the acute social conditions of the time, and some of the more public-spirited members of the Establishment showed a deep concern for these matters; this interest is reflected in a wide variety of maps. Because of the rapid and continuing growth of the towns, most of these 'social' maps are of urban areas, where conditions were at their most acute. The original impetus for the production of these maps may well have been provided by the arrival of Asiatic cholera in the 1830s; this prompted several doctors and surveyors to produce 'cholera plans' showing the distribution of deaths from the

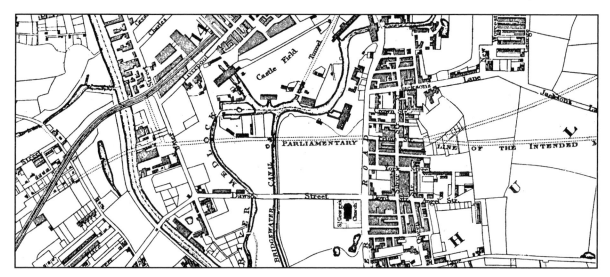

▲4.21 *Davies: Manchester, 1833. The map shows the proposed railway line leaving the existing line from Liverpool; no railway was ever built along this route.*

▽4.22 *Fowler's Cholera Plan of Leeds, 1833. The shaded areas show the districts affected by cholera; on the original they were coloured in red.*

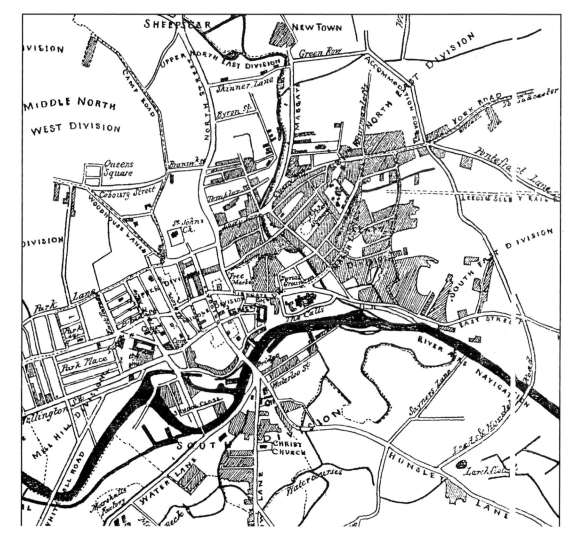

disease. The first was drawn up by Charles Fowler to illustrate the outbreak of the disease in Leeds in 1833 (Fig. 4.22), and was followed by others of Exeter, London and Oxford—the last of these being a series of maps (Fig. 4.23) by H.W. Acland depicting the ravages of the disease in 1832, 1849 and 1854 (Gilbert, 1958). The most famous of these maps was drawn up in 1855 by Dr. John Snow for an outbreak of cholera in Soho in 1854; on this he also marked the water pumps, and was able to demonstrate clearly that the disease was water-borne.

This concern with the spread of diseases led to the Public Health Act of 1848 which set up local Boards of Health whose brief was to ensure proper drainage and sewage systems. In order to achieve this, a large scale plan was needed. The scales adopted at first were 5 feet to the mile (1:1056) or 10 feet to the mile (1:528), but after about 1855 it was usually 1:500. About

170 local Boards of Health were set up under this Act, and about thirty had plans drawn by the Ordnance Survey; others used private surveyors, a third group used existing plans and the remainder had no maps at all. The reason for this inconsistency was that the Act had made the use of maps optional. In Warwickshire, for example, Coventry, Rugby, Stratford, and Warwick had plans surveyed by the O.S. while those for Leamington and Nuneaton were done privately (Fig. 4.24).

The value of such plans was noted in Birmingham, whose street commissioners promoted their own 10-foot survey (Harley, 1982). Many areas instigated private surveys, either by choice or because the area concerned was on the outskirts of a town and thus not covered by the existing large scale Ordnance maps. Around Liverpool, Smith (1985) notes maps of Garston, Toxteth, Wavertree, West Derby and

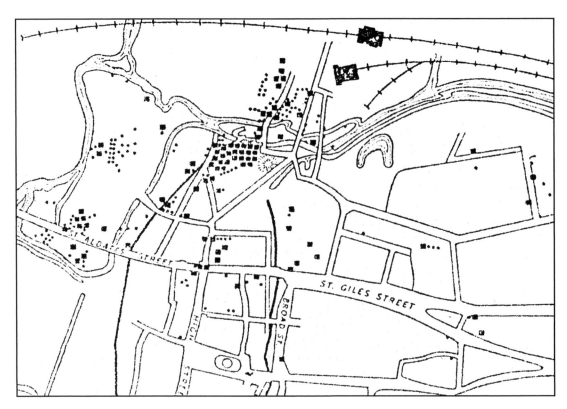

4.23   *Acland's map of the distribution of choleraic diarrhoea in Oxford in 1854.*

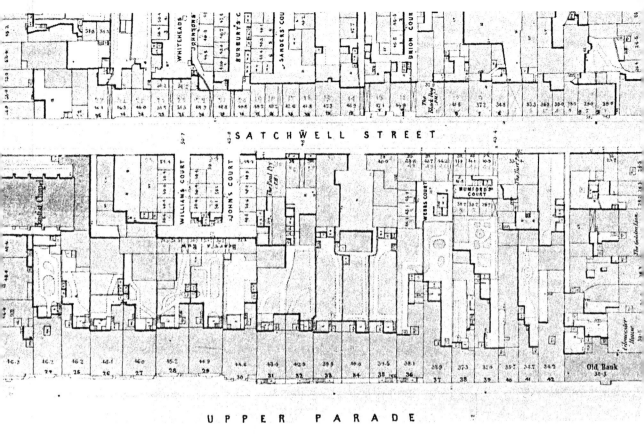

4.24 *Leamington Priors Board of Health Plan (1:528) surveyed by J.L. Alexander in 1852.*

Wallasey surveyed in 1854-6. These maps are important as the precursors of the Ordnance Survey's own large scale printed maps (see Chapter Six). They were drawn to a standard specification (rather like the tithe maps) and although they remained in manuscript, they were sometimes copied and used in other ways, notably in the planning of improvements.

Disease maps continued to be published throughout the century, often alongside maps depicting poverty, social status, housing conditions or crime, showing, on purpose or by accident, the close relationship between these variables. An early example was the 'Ecclesiastical and Social' map of Liverpool drawn by the Reverend Abraham Hume in 1858, which differentiated between 'Pauper Streets', 'Semi-Pauper Streets' and 'Streets of Crime and Immorality'. The best known social maps, though, are those produced by Henry Mayhew in 1862, and those of Charles Booth after 1889.

Henry Mayhew used the criminal statistics for 1857 to construct a series of social maps, following an already well-established tradition which had begun in France in the 1830s (Smith, 1985a). Joseph Fletcher (1849) had already published a dozen maps, covering such subjects as ignorance, crime, improvident marriages and bastardy. Mayhew, however, went much further, producing maps concerning rape, carnal abuse, bigamy, brothel-keeping, abduction, paedophilic assault and abortion. They are poorly devised and drawn, and in truth say little about their subject matter. Although his maps present the statistics on a county basis, he clearly believed that the growing towns, and London in particular, were the centres of depravity among the lower classes. His statistics were evidently not detailed enough to allow him to produce social maps of London (or any other city) but this lack of data was to be rectified in a grand manner by Charles Booth at the end of the century.

Booth conducted a vast survey of social conditions, and it appeared in various forms over 15 years (C. Booth, 1889, 1891, 1892-7; Fried and Elman, 1969; Hyde, 1975). (Note that this is not William Booth of the Salvation Army, though both he and Charles Booth were interested in poverty and social problems at much the same time.) Booth's maps depicted areas of different social character, using a seven-colour code, ranging from black and dark blue (depicting semi-criminal and very poor areas), through light blue and purple (standard poverty and mixed areas) to pink, red and yellow (working-class comfort, well-to-do, wealthy). Beatrice Webb, who helped with the survey, described these maps as 'perhaps the most impressive achievement, and certainly the most picturesque outcome of the whole enquiry'.

Booth's sources included the police, School Board visitors, parish officials, clergy and charity workers, as well as his own investigators and secretaries. The information was first plotted by hand on the O.S. 25-inch plans, while for publication Stanford's 6-inch Library Map was used, with the colours over-printed. For his second publication, Booth extended the area covered, and also updated those previously surveyed, so that it is possible to observe some changes in the social patterns depicted; for example, certain streets in Limehouse changed from purple to black in only a few years. Booth's poverty maps have a high reputation for accuracy and clarity, but it should be remembered that his information was very subjective in character. His maps have been unfairly criticised for using the purple shading for 'mixed' streets too frequently (for about one-third of the population) but this was simply because poverty and well-being *were* intermixed in many streets. Stanford published a number of Booth's maps separately, in particular a map showing churches, schools and public houses in an area of 24 square miles between Regent Street and Poplar which, as Booth wrote later, was intended 'to give the ordinary reader at a glance the impression of the ubiquitous and manifold character of the three most important social influences'.

An interest in the demon drink was not uncommon among Victorians, who often saw drinking as a working-class vice. It was the tee-total lobby which took the lead in this, usually linking alcohol directly to all forms of moral and social failure. The first recorded 'drink map' of London was apparently drawn in about 1859 by the National Temperance League (no copy survives), but it was followed by others. One entitled 'The Modern Plague of London' (Hyde, 1978) showed each public house as a red spot on the face of London. Its incomplete information was taken from Kelly's directory (the map did not include licensed hotels or grocers, for example). Booth's map, already mentioned, was rather less partisan. The London drink maps have provided basic data for a study of pubs in the Victorian city (Harrison, 1976). Other towns had drink maps—including Liverpool, Newcastle, Oxford, York, King's Lynn, Great Yarmouth and Norwich; in the latter case, there was a series of maps by Ratcliff showing a drop in the number of licensed premises from 655 in 1878 to 615 in 1903. More striking than the slight drop is the massive *total* of such establishments, far greater than the number of licensed premises today.

Religion and schooling were the other two important social influences noted by Booth, and these were both represented in map form. Religious maps were either drawn for the Church's own administrative purposes, or were maps of the location of particular religious groups, whether Methodists, Catholics or Jews. Often the maps were aimed *against* the religious group concerned, trying to show how numerous and thus how dangerous or insidious the group was. For example, in 1871 the *Royal Standard* published a 'Map showing the Romish Establishments in London, and the

Public Institutions to which Romish Priests have obtained access'. Not all examples were as bigoted as this: Abraham Hume, for example, depicted the origin, spread and distribution of the different religions in Liverpool, while George Arkell mapped the Jewish community of East London in 1899.

The most important set of 'school maps' was that done in 1877 by Stanford for the School Board of London. These maps showed the location of existing schools, deficiencies

in school places, and where new schools ought to be built. The scale was 6 inches to the mile and the maps were updated in 1881, 1886, 1892 and 1902 (Fig. 4.25). The maps give a clear picture of improvements in educational provision in London at the end of the 19th century, but there are problems with them—principally because the different editions were not precisely dated, and in any case were being continuously revised (Hyde, 1975, pp.38-9).

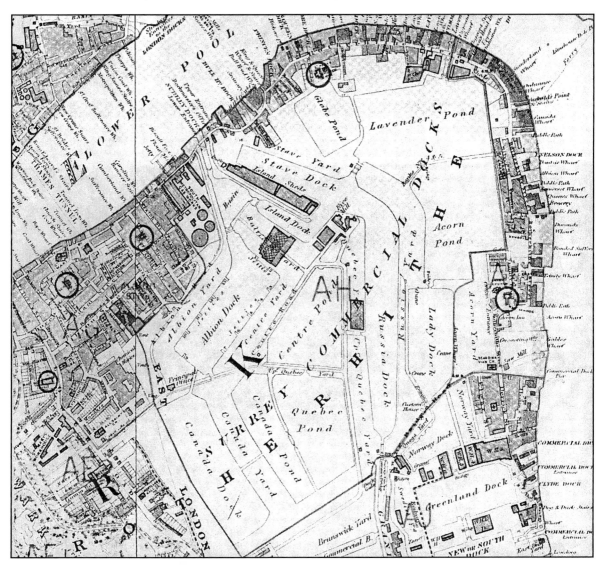

4.25   *One of Stanford's maps, overprinted for the School Board of London.*

Insurance plans

Until recently, the very existence of this type of map was barely known. Insurance plans were introduced to local historians only in 1975 (Aspinall), and it was not until 1984 that a full description of them appeared (Rowley, G.). Much of what follows is based on this latter work, and anyone wishing to know the full complications of these maps must refer to it. Fire insurance plans for specific insurance companies were first drawn in the 18th century (Hyde, 1970-3), but from 1885 until 1968 the business was undertaken principally by the firm of Chas. E. Goad Ltd. Their maps covered over 50 urban areas and industrial districts, showing warehouses, railways, ports and canals in England and Wales. They were updated, often every five or six years, thus allowing us to see changes in the areas depicted. One problem with the method of updating is that the company often reprinted only individual blocks or parts of a plan, and then pasted these onto the original, thus obscuring earlier details, and resulting in a map of two (or more) different dates. However, copies of a map in each of its states can usually be found somewhere, either in the British Library, the Guildhall or County Hall Libraries in London, Manchester Central Reference Library, in other local libraries, in Goad's own collections or in the archives of insurance companies.

The Goad company wished to keep its plans as secret as possible, in order to preserve their value, especially in view of the high and

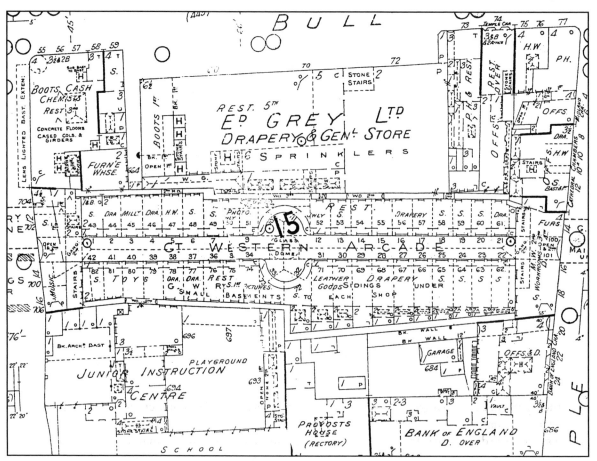

4.26 *Goad Insurance Plan of the Great Western Arcade, Birmingham, 1934.*

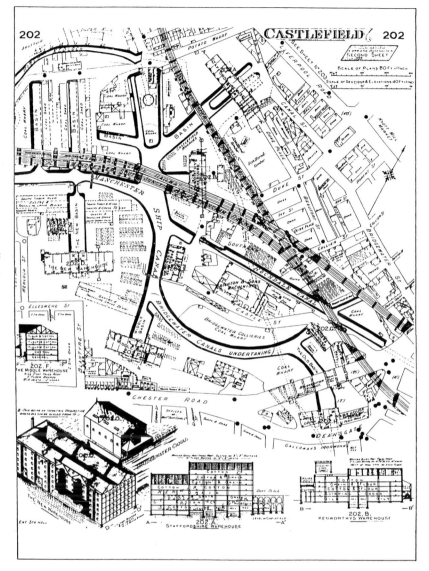

4.27 *Goad Insurance Plan of Castlefield, Manchester, 1889.*

continually rising re-surveying costs. Thus the maps were not sold, but rather leased to insurance companies, who were in effect subscribers, helping to pay for the surveying and production costs. The net result is that it can be very difficult to track down a copy of a particular revision date for a particular town and, even then, parts of the plan might not have been revised for that date.

Despite these difficulties, these large scale plans not only show buildings, with their construction details, heights and type of use, but also give incidental information such as street widths and names, rights of way, property boundaries, communications, boilers, engines, and hydrants, and other details of importance to insurance companies. The maps use a large range of conventional signs, and abbreviations such as D (dwelling), S (shop), PH (public house), GAR (garage), TENS (tenements), TAI (tailors) and OFFS (offices). The maps were coloured to indicate different building materials and thus different fire risks. The scale used was usually 40 feet to the inch (1:480), though other scales

(30, 80, 100 and 200 feet to the inch) were used in very special circumstances (Figs. 4.26, 4.27). In addition there were 'Key Plans' at much smaller scales.

As sources of data for industrial, commercial and urban change since the 1880s in the main towns they can hardly be bettered, and they are equally valuable to transport and architectural historians. Because of the precise depiction of each property it is a relatively simple matter to use these maps alongside written material such as directory, census or rating lists. One big advantage they have over the large scale Ordnance maps of the period is that they show property numbers. Of course, the maps usually only covered the main commercial districts of each town, though adjacent residential areas are often included, especially where certain trades had spread out into them. Aspinall suggests that, in the case of Sheffield, the plans covered about one-tenth of the city area.

Rowley gives a list of plans produced, although copies of the plans at each stage may not now exist. The company itself published a list of its remaining stock (Goad, 1984). The list of areas covered is as follows: Bath, Batley, Birmingham, Bradford, Brighton, Bristol, Canterbury, Cardiff, Chatham, Chelmsford, Colchester, Coventry, Dewsbury, Dover, Exeter, Gloucester, Goole, Grimsby, Halifax, Huddersfield, Hull, Ipswich, Kidderminster, King's Lynn, Leeds (and Leeds Carriers), Leicester, Lincoln, Liverpool, London, Long Eaton, Luton, Maidstone, Manchester (and Manchester Carriers), Marylebone, Newcastle, Newport, Northampton, Norwich, Nottingham, Plymouth, Reading, Sheffield, Southampton, Sunderland, Thames Valley, the River Tyne and Hartlepool Docks, and Yarmouth. A further 13 towns have a key map only, a full survey not having been undertaken. Most towns are covered in one volume, but London requires 22 volumes, Manchester seven and Liverpool six (Rowley, 1984, pp.48-9). Most

were begun before 1900 and all, except for Marylebone and Shoreditch, had been started by 1912. The 'Carriers' volumes for Manchester and Leeds cover canal and railway warehouses up to 30 miles from each of these cities; the Manchester volume, for example, includes details of Burnley, Preston, Blackburn, Oldham and Rochdale.

Where to find town plans

The location of certain special maps has already been discussed but we must now look at where to find the great mass of town plans. West's *Town Records* (1983, pp.150-65) makes an attempt to list the maps available of each town. His list is admittedly incomplete and selective: a vast list of maps is given for Dudley, hardly a town of the first rank, which is the subject of his chapter on town plans. The most recent list is by Armitage (1994). The obvious starting place in any search for town plans is the local history library, municipal library or record office; many have good collections of town plans, at least for the town in which they are situated and sometimes for other places nearby or in the same county. University libraries, and others, may have collections, as may some archaeological societies. There is also a whole host of other institutions to investigate (mostly in London), listed in *Record Repositories in Great Britain* and in Foster (1989) and Chibnall (1995). These list all the main collections, and can be used in conjunction with Emmison and Smith (1980). Three major repositories contain maps from far and wide: the Map Library in the British Library, the Public Record Office, and the Map Room of the Royal Geographical Society.

There are three principal problems involved in finding town plans: first, to find out what maps were originally drawn; second, to determine which repositories may have maps of the town in which you are interested, and, third, to find out what each repository actually does contain, given the often poor standard of cataloguing and indexing. Harley (1972, p.9) summed up the situation rather pessimistically: 'for the local historian there may be no easy end to the systematic search for these valuable documents'. Specialised town plans in particular may be hidden away in all sorts of places. Improvement Plans may be filed under 'Quarter Sessions Records' or 'Deposited Plans', while Sale Plans might be under 'Estate Plans' (or vice versa). And, of course, manuscript maps are often kept and indexed entirely separately. Lateral thinking is frequently required to solve some of these problems!

A few towns have printed carto-bibliographies; those by Howgego (1978) and Hyde (1975) for London have already been noted. These deal only with *printed* maps, however, although a few manuscript maps are mentioned in their introductions. Other towns with such listings include Bristol (Pritchard, 1928), Chichester (Butler, 1972), Manchester (Lee, 1957), Leeds (Bonser and Nichols, 1960), Norwich (Chubb and Stephen, 1928), Portsmouth (Hodson, 1978) and Southampton

(Welch, 1964), plus the towns of Berkshire (Burden, 1992) and Bedfordshire in 5 volumes including county maps as well (Chambers, 1983). Tooley began to list town plans on a county-by-county basis (Tooley, 1978-87) and this has been continued by Rodger (1989-95). One of the sad features of many carto-bibliographies is that they only reproduce a few, and sometimes *none* of the maps, being more concerned with tracking down and listing every last edition and reprint, rather than showing us what the maps actually look like. The production of full, detailed and illustrated bibliographies of town plans is a fruitful area for further research; much yet remains to be done. Anyone seeking a model need look no further than the volume on Leeds (Bonsor and Nichols, 1960), which has a useful introduction, bibliographical notes and an index to supplement the catalogue; most gratifying of all, a dozen of the maps are reproduced at the end of the volume. But it deals only with printed maps; local historians are interested in *all* the maps surveyed and drawn of a particular place—whether or not they have been printed is rather irrelevant.

Chapter Five

TRANSPORT MAPS

The previous two chapters have concentrated on maps of the countryside and the town respectively. Roads, canals and railways often appear in these maps, but there are also specific types of plan devoted to each form of transport. In this chapter we shall be concerned principally with transport maps, but will also examine the depiction of routes on other types of map. As coastal trading is a part of the transport system, a brief consideration of sea charts and their rather limited uses in local historical studies will also be given.

Road Maps

The need for road maps scarcely has to be demonstrated. They are but one part of an array of publications designed to help the traveller, from written itineraries through to county maps and even national maps which depict little else other than major roads and the towns which they connect. In our mapless Middle Ages, the written itinerary was commonly used, one example giving the distances from Titchfield Abbey to all the other Premonstratensian houses scattered across the country (Dickens, 1938). The earliest road-book, though concerned only with a single route, was drawn by Matthew Paris in about 1250 to illustrate the pilgrim route to Rome; for England it shows the road from London to Dover. Pilgrims going on very infrequent journeys needed a guide book, whereas merchants travelling frequently from town to town did not.

Medieval maps showing roads (Matthew Paris, Gough) were discussed at the end of Chapter One; in many ways they stand quite apart from the rest of our cartographic history which, as we have seen, begins in the mid-16th century. The modern road map was not developed for another hundred years after that. In the meantime, travellers had to use written itineraries, or road-books (Fordham, 1914, 1924). Early examples of these are found in Grafton's and Holinshed's respective *Chronicles of Englande* (1570; 1577), and roads continued to be detailed in this written form for many years. Perhaps the most interesting example is John Norden's *An Intended Guyde for English Travailers* (1625), in which he introduced the triangular distance table which is still in use today. Meanwhile, Saxton had produced his county maps without showing roads, and, although Norden did include them, his maps did not have a wide circulation and the idea did not catch on.

When the first detailed cartographic depiction of English and Welsh roads did finally appear, just a hundred years after Saxton's maps, it is hardly surprising that it was in a form resembling a written itinerary. John Ogilby's *Britannia*, published in 1675, was at first sight just the latest in a line of descriptions of the kingdom (the most famous of which had been by Camden). But Ogilby's volume was different in that it intended to illustrate England and Wales 'By a Geographical and Historical DESCRIPTION of the Principal Roads thereof. Actually Admeasured and Delineated in a Century of Whole-Sheet *Copper-Sculps*. Accommodated with the Ichnography of the several Cities and Capital towns' (Ogilby, 1675). Two hundred pages of text were interleaved with a hundred road maps, based on surveys carried out over the previous six years. There had been nothing like it before (either in detail or presentation), and it was to be another hundred years before another full road survey was to be undertaken.

The device which Ogilby used was to depict each route in a series of scrolls, working across every page from bottom left to top right (MacEachran & Johnson, 1987). Each scroll has its own compass rose to indicate changes of direction (Fig. 5.1). Roads are shown by solid lines where enclosed, and by dotted lines where they cross open country; down the centre of the roads are dots marking each quarter-mile or furlong. These maps were the first to use the statute mile, popularising the scale of one inch to one mile. Numerous features on or near the roads, such as bridges, rivers, villages, castles, woods, churches and beacons, are indicated, all intended to help the traveller on his way. Steep hills are shown pictorially, with a hill indicating an ascent, and an upside-down hill showing a descent. The evidence of roads is, however, greater than just the routes depicted in detail; alternatives are given (often described as 'worst' ways), and there are numerous indications of side routes leaving the main routes. The total road network shown is thus quite substantial, even in a remote area like Cumbria (Fig. 5.2).

Larger towns are shown in plan form, and these rough outlines, although only at the one-inch scale, can give useful (and sometimes the *only*) evidence of the extent of some towns at this date. Ogilby's maps depict much more than just roads; for example, they have been used to estimate regional variations in the proportion of open and enclosed land,

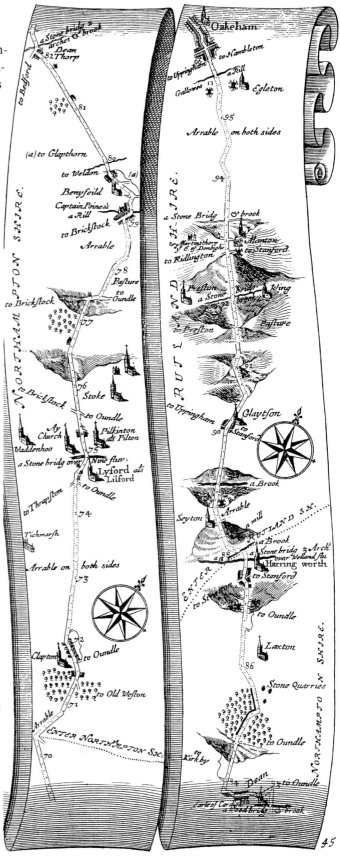

5.1 *Ogilby: Britannia, 1675. Two strips showing the road from Clapton to Oakham, also illustrating land use (arable, pasture and woodland).*

by measuring whether the roads are shown by dotted or solid lines. A detailed county-by-county study of Ogilby's roads can be seen in Bagley and Hodgkiss (1985, pp.30-6) and a more biographical study in Van Eerde (1976).

Like Saxton's, Ogilby's work was to be copied by many later publishers, who made only minor changes. John Senex, for example, published his version of Ogilby's maps in 1719, 'now improved, very much corrected, and made portable'; that is, he reduced Ogilby's folio volume to oblong quarto size (8 in. × 10 in.). Emanuel Bowen went even further—to octavo (8 in. × 5 in.)—in his *Britannia Depicta* of 1720 (Bower, 1970). This last volume also claimed to be an improved version of Ogilby's work: it reduced the scale by half, and John Owen supplied a text which was engraved alongside or around the strip maps, together with local coats of arms. In addition, small county maps were interspersed in appropriate places. Both Senex and Bowen were much reprinted during the next 50 years or so.

In the meantime, various county maps had been printed with the addition of roads from about 1676, though the first complete set was not accomplished until 1695, when Robert Morden drew maps to illustrate the latest edition of Camden's *Britannia* (Morden, 1695). The maps themselves were still largely based on Saxton, but evidently other road surveys had been undertaken, as Morden's routes are not always the same as those of Ogilby (Fig. 5.2).

During the 18th century a whole series of road-books and county maps showing roads appeared. Notable publishers of these included Daniel Paterson and William Owen (Fordham, 1925), while most London map publishers such as Jefferys, Kitchin and Rocque also ventured into the production of road maps. One problem was that these and other London mapmakers were, as we have seen before, primarily interested in selling maps, and thus they copied from each other, with little or no attempt to check the accuracy of the roads they were

∧5.2 *Routes shown by Ogilby, 1675 (above) and Morden, 1695 (opposite) in Cumbria. Notice the large number of side routes indicated by Ogilby, and the different routes shown by Morden.*

5.3 *Bowen and Kitchin: 'New Map of … Cumberland and Westmorland', 1769. The infamous, non-existent mountain road from the Three Shire Stones to 'Enerdale' can be seen ➤ here.*

showing. The information available in the second half of the century came from a variety of sources, including Ogilby—now a hundred years out of date! What can perhaps best be described as 'cartographic inertia' ruled the day; put simply, once something was on a map, it tended to remain there, whether right or wrong. The classic example of this is on Bowen and Kitchin's 'New Map of the Counties of Cumberland and Westmorland' (1769), said to be a copy of a 1749-55 map and also very similar to Bowles and Sayer's 'New Map' of 1760 (Hindle, 1984, pp.83-96). This set of maps has

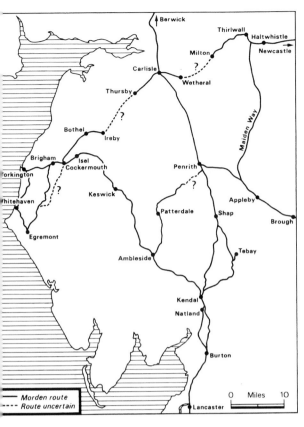

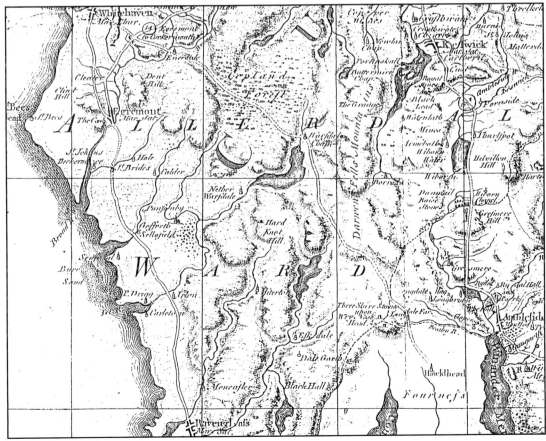

since become infamous for showing a road running straight across some of the highest ground in England—from the top of Wrynose Pass to Wasdale Head, and then on to Ennerdale (Fig. 5.3). This nonexistent (and impossible) road reappeared on Kitchin's map of Cumberland (1777), in his *Traveller's Guide* of 1783, in Paterson's *British Itinerary* (1785) and even in Cary's *New Itinerary* (1798), even though his previous *Traveller's Companion* (1790) had omitted the road. One can only pity any traveller unfortunate enough to rely on the products of the London map trade in these remote areas. The map publishers had not even taken the trouble to check their roads against those shown on Donald's large scale county map, published in 1774. Eventually, however, the detailed county mapping done at this time (see Chapter Two), which usually depicted the main roads very well, did start to be used by the hack publishers of road maps in London.

5.4 *Cary: 'New Itiner-ary', 1802 (2nd edition).* *The only map in Cary's* *new written description* *of the roads is this* *general key map.*

The county maps drawn between 1760 and 1840 give an indispensable depiction of roads during this period; the arrival of reasonably accurate maps coincided with the virtual completion of the turnpike road system (see below). Even in such remote counties as Cumberland and Westmorland, 'turnpike mania' was over by 1767, just before Donald and Jefferys surveyed and published their county maps (Hindle, 1984, pp.140-54) (Fig.2.13). Most of the county maps show turnpikes specifically as well as the mileages along them.

The demand for road maps continued to grow, principally as a result of the vast growth of coach travel from the 1780s until the arrival of the railways after 1830. The maps thus began to show coaching inns more prominently, while reducing the depiction of the countryside.

The most important improvement was to come in 1798 with the publication of John Cary's *New Itinerary*, with information derived 'From an Actual Admeasurement made by Command of His Majesty's Postmaster

General'. His 'information on roads may be viewed with above-average confidence' (Harley, 1972, p.44). Cary had been in the road map business since 1782 but had managed to obtain official support to undertake a new perambulation of over 9,000 miles of roads (Fig. 5.4). His new information was, of course, copied by others (first by Paterson as early as 1799). Details of many of the various editions of many road-books can be found in Fordham (1914, 1924).

Road-books varied from written descriptions, through strip maps, to small county maps showing little else but roads. Paterson's *British Itinerary* (1785), for example, included both written descriptions (copied from earlier sources) and strip maps which Paterson had surveyed himself (Fig. 5.5). On the other hand, Cary's *Traveller's Companion* was a set of small county maps showing little apart from the roads. The diverse nature of maps showing roads means that some are likely to be catalogued and shelved as books; this is not at all unreasonable, but it is to be hoped that those which contain maps are cross-referenced in the map section of each library's catalogue.

The production of road maps continued in the 19th and 20th centuries in the hands of firms such as Laurie and Whittle, and later George Philip and Son. Environs and cycling maps in turn gave way to maps for the motor car (Nicholson, 1983). In the early 19th century, the later county maps and then the Ordnance Survey provide detailed depictions of roads; most subsequent road maps were not original, but were derived from these more general surveys.

Searching for road maps for a particular area can be difficult; the only national lists published are by Fordham (1924, 1927), although Chubb (1927) is also a useful source. At least one (old) county has its own list (Powell, 1978-9). This is another area for local research.

A second main group of road maps concerned the building, diverting and turnpiking

of roads. In 1555, each parish had been made responsible for the roads passing through it, for they were starting to deteriorate, especially with the rapid growth of internal trade under the Tudors. There are increasingly numerous references to difficult and impassable roads

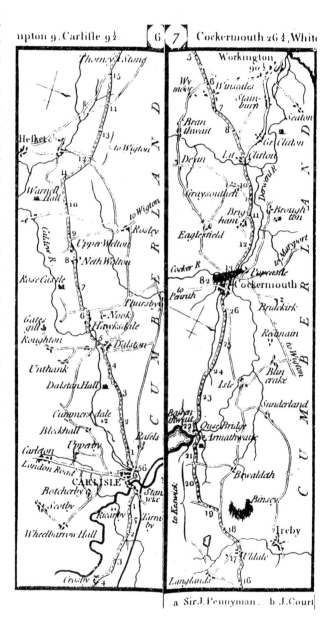

5.5 *Paterson: 'British Itinerary', 1785. One of Paterson's own surveys of the road from Carlisle to Workington via Bassenthwaite.*

after this period, and it became clear to those with an interest in trade that something had to be done. The eventual solution was the creation of *turnpike* roads; local landowners and traders would present a bill to Parliament to allow them to improve a certain section of road and to charge a toll for all traffic using that road. These were not new roads, but existing ones made better; they established the principle that travellers should pay for the upkeep of roads. The first turnpike was a section of the Great North Road in Hertford and Huntingdon in 1663; the second was not until 1695, but by 1730 there were 3,200 km (2,000 miles) of turnpikes and, after the 'turnpike mania' of the 1750s and 1760s, they totalled over 24,000 km (15,000 miles) (Albert, 1972; Pawson, 1977; Hindle, 1993). Some turnpike acts were never carried out, and some proposals or alterations never completed—yet the planning maps may survive.

Road improvements were just one class of more general improvements. After 1773 any two Justices of the Peace had the power to require a map to be drawn of any diversion or closure of highways; if there was no objection, the order and the accompanying map were confirmed by the Quarter Sessions. The resulting enrolled copy should now be in the record office. For example, the Sussex records list several late 18th-century plans, including one of a 'new intended road from Howicks to North-Heath' (Fernhurst) drawn in 1790. It is at a scale of 20 inches to the mile, and shows the existing and proposed roads, together with the lengths, rises and falls of each. Adjacent owners' lands are shown, as well as other details such as the house of 'Pratt, ye Smith' (Steer, 1968).

These maps became much more numerous after 1800, and their accuracy and detail also improved. The main reason for this is that the great series of Parliamentary 'deposited plans' began at this time. This series included plans for numerous types of public works; not only roads and bridges, but also for railways, tramways, canals and navigations, harbours, lighting, water supplies and drainage (Bond, 1964). These plans and sections, and their accompanying books of reference, had to be submitted with any private canal bill presented to Parliament after 1794, and this stipulation was subsequently extended to the other public schemes named above. There is no complete set, but the British Library, House of Commons, House of Lords, Bodleian Library, Cambridge University and Southampton University have collections. The duplicates which had to be deposited with the local Clerk of the Peace can usually now be found in local record offices.

The plans vary a good deal in both scale and content; at first, scales of as little as 2 inches to the mile were used, but in 1807 the minimum scale was raised to 4 inches to the mile, with buildings plotted at up to 44 inches to the mile. Most are manuscript maps, often using several different colours, but some were printed; later, Ordnance Survey maps were used as base plans, with appropriate additions. Such maps give details not found elsewhere, and the accompanying books of reference give even more information about ownership, as well as descriptions of each plot of land affected. The earlier, specially drawn, maps may show much more than just the scheme in hand, often depicting an area up to a quarter of a mile on either side, perhaps including the names of adjacent landowners, other roads, field names, tenants and even details of land use (such as 'road through arable') and woodland. Later maps, based on the Ordnance Survey, may give details of periods between successive revisions of the base map, and will also supplement what the base map already shows. Bond says that 'the whole series is clearly of outstanding importance'. (Figs. 5.6 and 5.7.)

Other plans occur in the records of the Turnpike Trusts themselves, usually concerning improvement or diversion of particular sections of road; these were especially common in the early years of the 19th century, when engineers such as Telford and McAdam were engaged in road rebuilding. West (1997, pp.225-7) gives two lists of printed material concerning local turnpike studies. When the turnpikes were dissolved due to competition from the railways, usually in the 1870s, new road maps were sometimes drawn, and the county authorities which took over responsibility for the roads should now have a century-long cartographic record.

Another source of information on 19th-century roads is the enclosure map (Chapter Three). Enclosure often involved a complete reorganisation of the landscape, and thus many present-day roads may be only 150 years old. As we have seen, it is sometimes possible to reconstruct

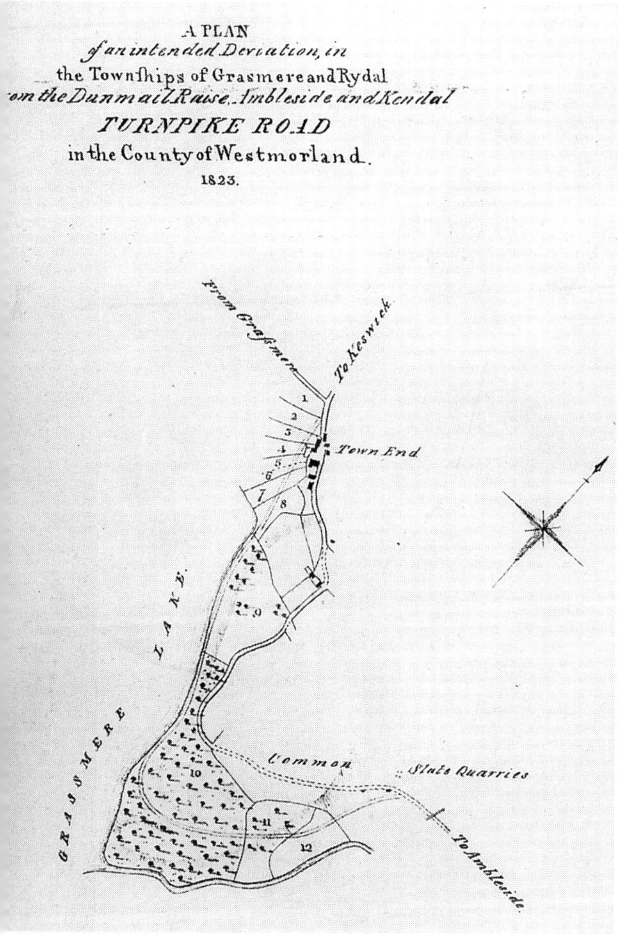

◂ **5.6** *A plan of 1823 for diverting the turnpike between Grasmere and Rydal. Both the new and the old roads still exist. Wordsworth's Dove Cottage is at Town End.*

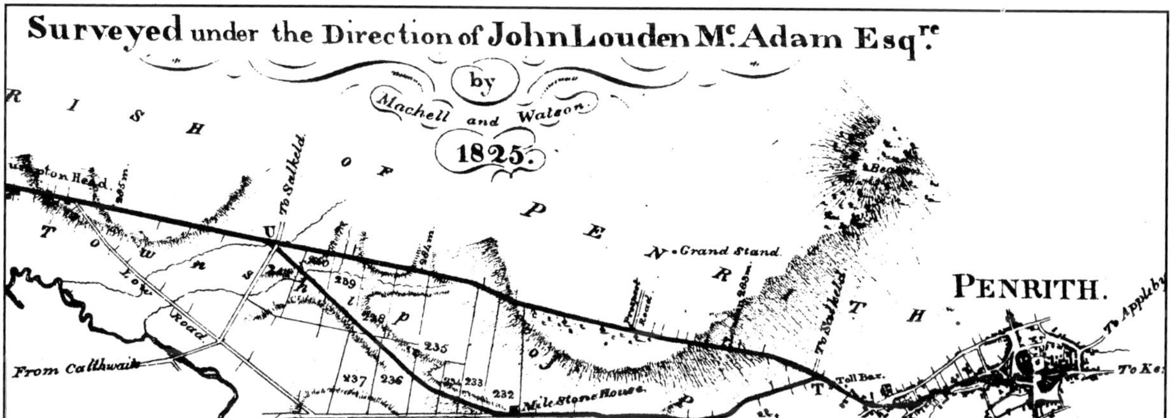

5.7 *A plan of proposed deviations in the turnpike from Penrith to Carlisle, surveyed for John McAdam in 1825. Here a short new road (running across 10 numbered fields) would avoid the steep climb out of Penrith.* ▾

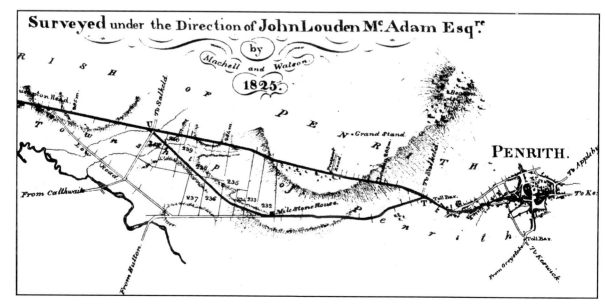

the pre-enclosure landscape, and occasionally a pre-enclosure survey survives; it is, however, surprising how little has been written about enclosure roads or the old roads they replaced.

There are, of course, other types of road maps; Bonser and Nichols (1960) reprint a map of 1822 which compares the three turnpike routes between Leeds and Doncaster, including several intended diversions. The present author unearthed an unusual map in the Cavendish records at the Lancashire Record Office; it was drawn in 1839, and shows roads diverted, stopped up or given up on the Holker Hall estate since about 1780 (Hindle, 1984, pp.166-7). It is in no way an 'official' map, but

simply a depiction of what had happened—several diversions being made due to the expansion of the park around the hall (Fig. 5.8). Another special type of road map depicts tram and bus route networks—essentially the equivalent of railway line maps.

Virtually every class of map depicts some roads, and anyone interested in the roads of an area has a large task in hand, especially if interested in the 19th century; for here there is an embarrassment of riches. Roads are, however, a surprisingly under-researched topic at any scale (from local to national), for any period (apart from Roman) and for any particular type of road.

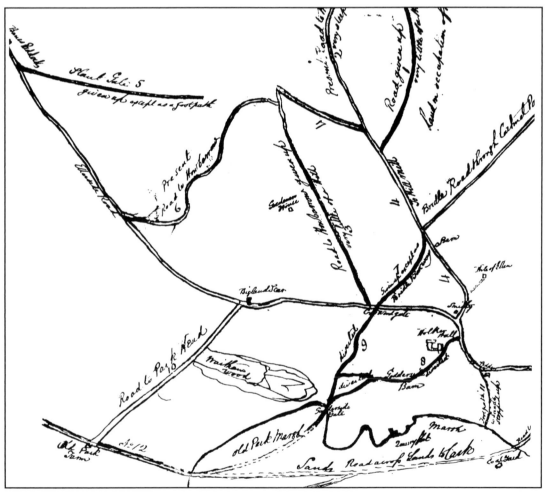

5.8 *'Sketch of Roads diverted stopped up or given up about Holker Hall within the last 60 Years' (1839).*

Canal maps

The development of canals in England, culminating in the 'canal mania' of the 1790s, needs little explanation here. The increasing industrialisation of the country required the movement of heavy cargoes (particularly coal) by water, and canals were simply an extension of the existing river routes; for our purposes there is no real distinction between them. Both allowed goods to be transported between the major industrial centres; whether the route was a river (often including sections of canal) or a totally new canal is largely irrelevant.

The history of inland navigation is well covered by the extensive series of books edited by Charles Hadfield (published by David and Charles) both on individual canals and the various regions of the country. From these, and from numerous other works, you can find out the history of the canals (including some which were proposed but never built), and river navigations. It is surprising how little canal plans have been used in the literature of canal history, even for illustration. This section will look in turn at river navigation and canal plans, and then at the depiction of canals on other types of maps.

Most British rivers had been continuously navigated since medieval times, but it was not really until the 18th century, with the upswing in industrial growth, that any improvements to the waterways were made (Willan, 1936). Very few plans survive for this early period, though Bull (1958) has noted two particularly early examples: maps of the lower Lea valley, dating from Elizabethan times, both wholly or partially drawn by Lord Burghley. In Yorkshire we know that the River Aire had been accurately measured by John Hadley in 1697, in connection with the bill for the Aire and Calder navigation (passed in 1699 and opened in 1704), but no map survives (Hadfield, 1972-3). In their list of maps of Leeds, Bonser and Nichols (1960) list only one surviving map of its waterways, drawn in 1712, at a scale of 3.6 inches to the mile and published as an insert on an environs map. They list 10 more maps of waterways, but these all date from after 1772, and depict new canals.

In Sussex, there are a number of plans concerning the improvement of the Arun Navigation in the last 18 years of the 18th century; most are in the Petworth House Archives. Drawn up for the improvement of the Arun and Rother rivers, plus various schemes to build new canals to Horsham, Petworth and through to the River Wey, their scales vary from 4 inches to 40 inches to the mile. These maps show locks, mills and bridges, as well as fields, farms and owners—especially important where a new cut was to be made.

Although the first canal with locks dates from as far back as 1566 (the Exeter Canal), it was the Sankey and Bridgewater Canals of 1755 and 1759-62 respectively which really set the process of canal building in motion. One fascination of the early canal plans lies in their recording of the way surveyors saw the countryside, and thus which routes they proposed. Quite how they planned their routes without the aid of contoured maps has never been fully explained; a detailed study of their plans would no doubt be very illuminating.

From the period after 1794, we have of course the series of deposited plans (already noted in the previous section) (Hadfield, 1955-6). It is worth repeating that it was the canal mania which prompted Parliament to insist on these plans; 30 new canals were authorised in 1793-4 alone, compared to only three in 1789-90. Not only do we have the original plans, but also those drawn up for any later bill altering the canal's route. In the years of competition from the railways, if a canal was bought out in order to build a railway along the same route, plans again had to be deposited by the company involved. Of course, some canal schemes presented to Parliament were never built, but their plans survive. Each plan is accompanied by a schedule of property to be bought, and together these can give information on land use and ownership; in addition the map may show roads, footpaths, fields, rivers, inns, and so on (Fig. 5.9). Some include sections, tables of distances, tidal ranges, costs, and even drawings for tunnels and bridges. Because canals were built primarily for industrial reasons, their maps can be a vital source for the study of early industry, showing the coal pits, ironworks, mills, towns and markets to be served by the proposed (or existing) canal. On a few maps, larger scale inset plans show especially important areas, such as towns or private estates. A few canals were built without an Act of Parliament—perhaps where all the landowners along the route were in favour of the plan; for these no Parliamentary plans exist.

The canal companies themselves sometimes had to prepare accurate plans for their own construction or maintenance purposes, and these may survive in their records (often taken over by railway companies), now sometimes to be found in record offices (Fig. 5.10). Other canal maps include those printed as part of a prospectus by the canal's promoters, and, once built, some companies printed maps of their canals for their shareholders and others. Good collections of these can be found in the Map Library of the British Library, and in the British Transport Historical Records (now in the Public Record Office). Canal maps also sometimes appeared in periodicals; Brindley and Whitworth's 1770 plan of the proposed canal from Stockton to Winston (Durham) was reproduced in the *Gentleman's Magazine* in 1772. John Cary published a collection of canal plans entitled *Inland Navigation* in 1795. The most famous and reliable of this genre are the maps of George Bradshaw (c.1830) which were

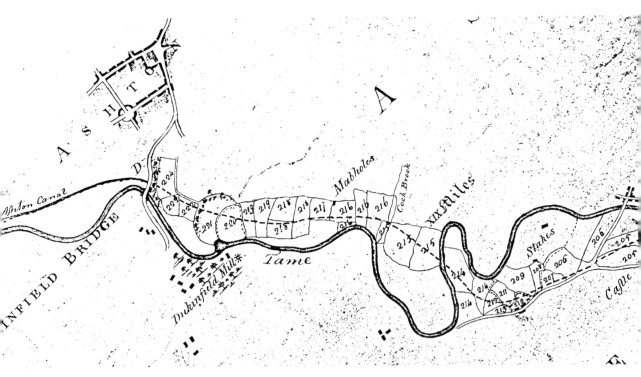

5.9 *Map of proposed canal between Huddersfield and Ashton-under-Lyne, N. Brown, 1793. The proposed route is shown as a dashed line, leading from the Ashton Canal up the valley of the River Tame.*

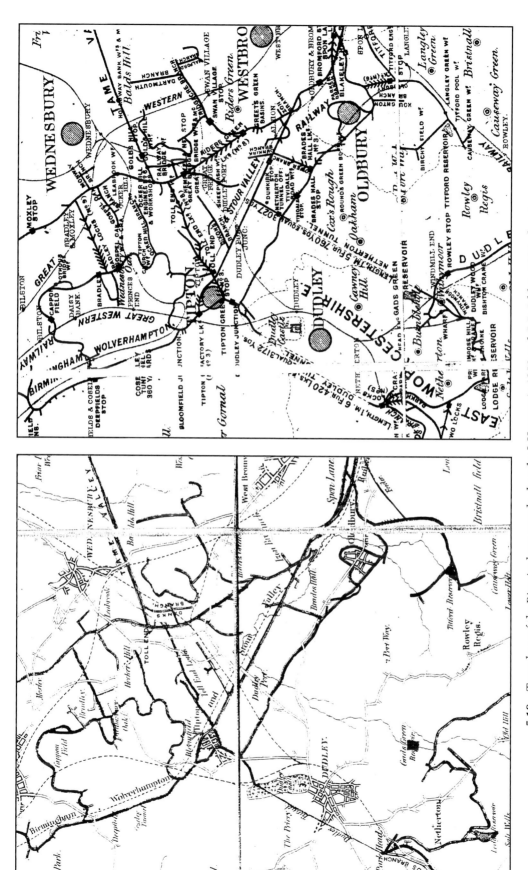

5.10 *Two plans of the Birmingham canals, done by J. Hancox in 1850 and G.R. Jebb in 1886, showing the changes in the network between these dates.*

later to include railways as well. Such secondary maps are not always reliable; Stockdale's map of the Lancaster Canal (1795) shows a route very different from that which was eventually built (Fig. 5.11).

Canals, of course, appeared on other maps, notably on county maps. Most of the first good quality 18th-century county surveys, however, were being done before or at the same time as the canals were appearing. Naturally, the cartographer wanted to be up to date, and thus he might sometimes use a canal company's plans as a source—this was fine, unless the canal route was changed (as it often was) or the canal itself never built. Jefferys' county map of Yorkshire of 1771 shows a canal below Leeds, based on proposals put forward by John Longbottom (Fig. 5.12). No canal was built on this line; instead, most of the Aire Navigation was retained, although in 1778 a new cut was made from Haddesley to the Ouse at Selby. William Yates' map of Staffordshire (surveyed between 1769 and 1775) shows the full length of the Trent and Mersey Canal, which was not finally completed until 1775. On the other hand, he also shows part of a proposed canal from Newport (Shropshire) to Stafford which was never built. This line was deleted by Wm. Faden in his edition of the map in 1799, but he too tempted fate by showing the whole of the Caldon Canal, which had been approved in 1777, but was not completed until 1811 (Phillips, 1984). A more spectacular error was on John Cary's *New Map of Lancashire* (1806) which showed a canal across the Rossendale hills, linking existing canals at Bury and Church (Accrington); approved in 1794, it was never built. The presence or absence of a canal

5.11 *Stockdale: Lancaster Canal, 1795. Most of the canal was not built along the route shown, and the central section (from Preston to Whittle) was never built (it was replaced by a tramway).*

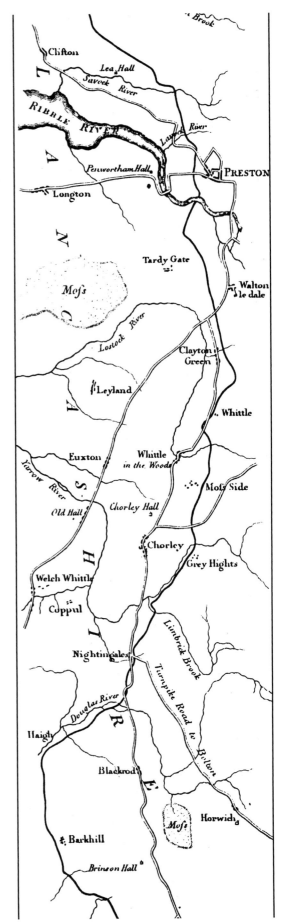

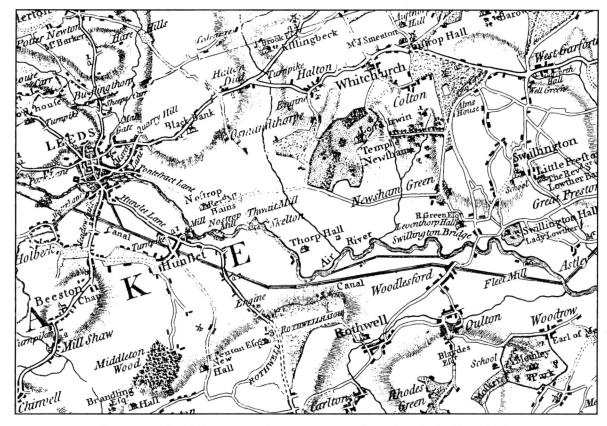

5.12   *Jefferys' map of Yorkshire, 1771, showing a projected canal as if it had been built.*

on an undated map should thus never be used to help date it. Another example of the problems of using maps as evidence (this time of the Somerset Coal Canal) can be seen in Torrens (1974). The later county maps produced by Greenwood and his competitors are generally more reliable; by then the canal system was nearing completion and the 'mania' was over. Most canals had tramways or waggonways linking them to coal mines or other industrial sites; these often appear on the better county maps and Ordnance Survey maps, and are sometimes the sole documentary evidence for their existence.

A basic guide to finding canal maps would be to begin with the relevant canal's history, then look for other histories of the local area in order to find out the routes, engineers and surveyors of each canal—and then to search out maps in local collections, under the canal's, the surveyor's and the engineer's names; also, any maps for major towns or industrial sites along the route would be useful. A good library or record office will have its canal maps listed separately (see Public Record Office, 1967; British Museum, 1967, in which English canal maps are listed together).

Only one county record office appears to have published its own lists of canal plans (Shropshire—see Bibliography) although several others (including Cambridge, Stafford, Sheffield and the Central Library in Manchester) indicate canal maps separately in their indexing systems. A few repositories have special collections of canal maps: for example, Derby's Local Studies Library has nearly 40 maps and plans in the Derby Canal Company records, dating from 1790. If a deposited plan does not reside locally, then recourse may have to be made to the House of Lords Record Office. Finally, other types of maps should be checked—principally county maps, but also estate, parish, enclosure or tithe maps of places along the route, not forgetting town plans for the urban sections of canal (especially important for Birmingham which had a vast network of canals) and port, harbour or dock plans (see for example, Bristol, in Williams, 1962). Finally, the Ordnance Survey maps show canals, and successive editions of the 6-inch and 25-inch plans can be most useful (Chapter Six). But, above all, the large scale O.S. town plans of the second half of the 19th century give an amazing amount of detail, those drawn in mid-century usually depicting the canal network at the height of its development. For example, the 5-foot plan of Manchester (1850) shows in great detail the various arms and basins around the junction of the Rochdale and Ashton canals (Fig. 5.13).

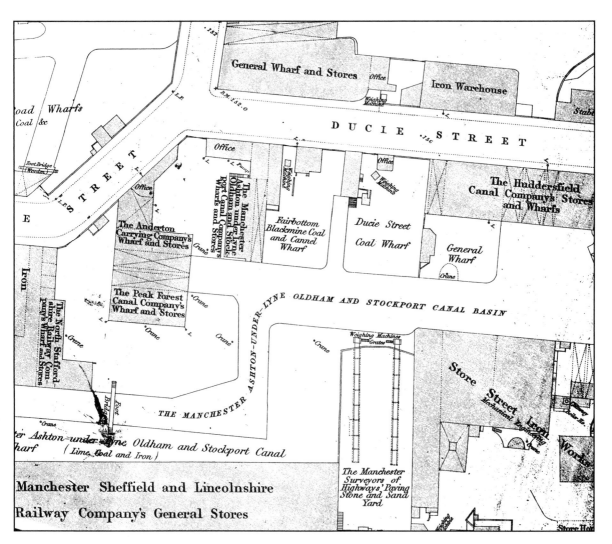

5.13 *The five-foot (1:1056) plan of Manchester (1850), shows great detail of the wharves and warehouses around the junction of the Ashton and Rochdale canals.*

Coastal charts

Coastal charts overlap with the plans of the lower reaches of river navigations, and can include considerable lengths of river. It is sometimes difficult to decide precisely where a river becomes an estuary and where an estuary becomes coastal water; thus coastal charts are included here. By definition, such charts are of only limited use, and are most valuable when they cover the more deeply indented estuaries. These maps are primarily concerned with safe navigation, and usually only show inland detail where it is of assistance for fixing a vessel's position. Harley (1972) devotes 12 pages to these charts, and the reader is directed both there and to Robinson (1962). A few general observations will suffice for our purposes.

The first maritime charts date from Tudor times and their production has continued right through to the present day. It is often difficult to ascertain when an individual chart was surveyed (as opposed to published) by the early private publishers. There are also the usual problems of finding a particular chart for a specific area. These difficulties are much reduced by the appearance of official Admiralty Charts in 1795, and their catalogues from 1825. For some periods, notably for the 1680s, these charts provide the best coastal detail available in an age when land-based cartography was poor. In particular, the charts of Greenvile Collins, produced in this decade, were of a high standard. Murdoch Mackenzie in the 1770s was the first to use on-shore triangulation for his maps of the west coast of Britain and, because of this, he depicts some inland detail at scales of up to one inch to one mile.

Harley notes three basic types of information on these maps which may be of use to the local historian: first, the site and detail of coastal fortifications against invasion; second, the depiction of harbours and docks (Tudor examples are often in bird's eye view), and third, changes to coastlines, sand banks, mud flats, dunes and marshes. He concludes that coastal charts may 'help to locate a decayed haven, a parish eroded by the sea, a chapel engulfed by sand, or to fix the site of a lighthouse once crucial to navigation'. (Harley, 1972, p.62.)

Despite Harley's advocacy of coastal charts, they are in fact of limited use, but they should not be totally ignored by anyone studying an area bounded by the coast or an estuary (see for example Clark, 1960, for the Exe estuary; Lynam, 1936, for part of the Wash; and Carr, 1962, for three sites in Devon, Somerset and Suffolk).

Railway maps

It is hardly necessary to go into the history of the growth of railways, so much having already been written on this topic. In the 19th century, railways were part of the continuing effort to find ways of transporting heavy or bulky cargoes easily, in exactly the same way that the canals had been forty years earlier, but this time using a faster mode of transport, and one without major water supply or control problems. Railways did not suddenly appear in 1825 with the Stockton and Darlington line or in 1830 with the Liverpool-Manchester line. Waggonways and plateways had existed for many years, from as early as the mid-17th century, especially in coalmining and industrial areas. The first line to be approved by Parliament was that from Middleton to Leeds in 1758, worked at first by horse traction, and then by steam after 1812. Some of these early routes are shown on county or local maps. Horse-drawn tramways or mineral lines were especially common in the north-east, where a well developed network connected the collieries to the staithes of the Tyne and Wear; the longest line was over four miles in length. John Gibson's colliery map of 1788 shows these private tramways clearly.

It was the invention and improvement of self-propelled steam locomotives which eventually made long distance railways a financial and practical possibility. Just as with the canals in the 1790s, there was another period of manic development, principally in 1836-7 and 1845-7, which by 1848 had created a rail network of some 7,400 km (4,600 miles).

The railways had a great impact on the whole country, in both urban and rural areas. Here we will deal with specific railway maps as well as the more general depiction of railways on county and Ordnance Survey maps. The particular impact of the railways on towns, and the specific types of maps which show this, have already been dealt with in Chapter Four.

Basic historical descriptions of the development of railways include Dyos and Aldcroft (1969), Simmons (1968), Turnock (1982), and Freeman and Aldcroft (1985), plus the series of regional histories edited by Thomas and Patmore (published by David and Charles, 1960-83). The major bibliographic source is Ottley (1983, 1988), although this gives references only up to 1980. Some counties have published lists of all the railway proposal acts of their area—for example, Oxford (1983) and Hertford (Hodson, 1974, pp.61-5), while Lancashire is very fortunate in having a full railway bibliography, including references to some 300 maps and plans (Turner, P.M., 1981).

For the study of railways, *deposited plans* are a prime source of information; these had been established for over 40 years when the railway mania began. What has already been said about them in connection with the study of roads and canals applies again here and the main points need only a brief reiteration.

First, plans were drawn up for any new railway proposal, and had to be deposited locally with the Clerk of the Peace, as well as with Parliament; the local copy should now be in the Record Office. Second, plans exist for some railways which were never built; these plans may still be of interest for their depiction of the proposed route, showing detail of the countryside up to a quarter of a mile on either side of the proposed line, at a scale of 4 inches to the mile, or greater. Third, although their prime aim was to indicate the route, major engineering works and, above all, land ownership, these plans also show much else in the landscape, from fields and roads to villages and industrial sites. Fourth, they were accompanied by a book of reference giving further details. Fifth, they can usually be regarded as accurate cadastral plans, for they were to be the basis of legislation concerning land ownership. Finally, they may also contain inset larger scale plans of urban areas, as well as longitudinal sections, which were compulsory after 1838 (Figs. 5.14, 5.15, 5.16).

These plans have been little studied; it would, for example, be interesting to know how the line of each railway was first chosen (in the absence of any existing maps showing contours or detailed elevations), then how the survey was done, and in particular to what extent existing estate, enclosure or tithe maps were used to save time and expense. Matters were made easier, of course, by the appearance of the larger scale (6-inch) Ordnance Survey sheets as the century progressed, but the survey was relatively slow, beginning with Lancashire and Yorkshire in the 1840s and not finally covering the whole of England and Wales until 1888. Despite the best intentions, some of the plans were not as good as they might have been, especially during the period of railway mania when so many plans were being surveyed, not only for proposed railways, but also for the tithe surveys; the net result was a shortage of good surveyors and a consequent decline in map quality. It was not unknown for plans to be rejected, often because any objectors to the line would study the plans very closely in order to find any inaccuracies which could help their case; the map had to be accurate because legal decisions were to be made on the basis of what was shown. The sheer number of these plans is enormous; over a thousand were lodged in 1844 and 1845 alone.

After obtaining Parliamentary approval, the railway engineers then set about the task of pre-

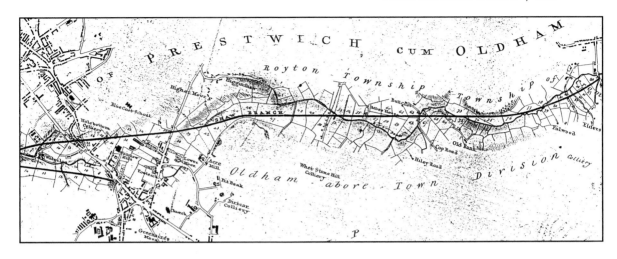

5.14 *Plan of an intended railway from Oldham to Manchester, 1830, giving much detail of the adjacent area.*

5.15 *Plan of proposed railway or tram-road from Bolton to Leigh: G. Stephenson, 1824. A large scale plan showing the proposed line through the town to the canal.*

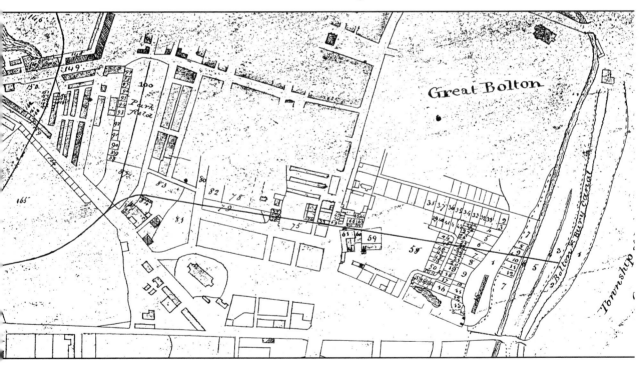

paring detailed engineering plans, often using existing Ordnance and tithe survey maps or any other large scale plans available. Meanwhile, the companies issued prospectuses, in order to attract more capital; these usually contained a small scale map of the route. The prospectus maps were often copied from existing county maps, with the new railway line added and sometimes other information such as town populations, the location of industrial sites and the distances covered by rival companies; other than this, these maps give little or no local detail.

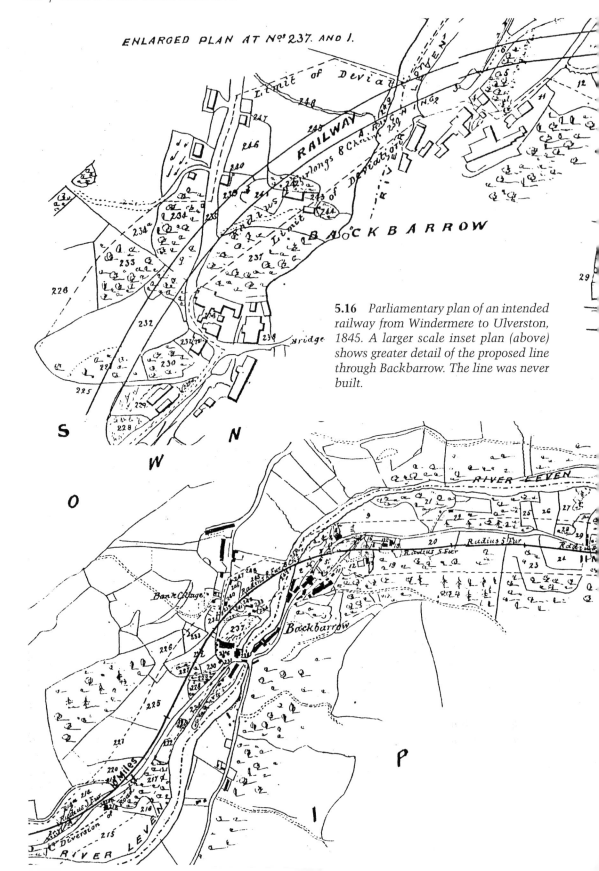

5.16 *Parliamentary plan of an intended railway from Windermere to Ulverston, 1845. A larger scale inset plan (above) shows greater detail of the proposed line through Backbarrow. The line was never built.*

A useful starting point for studying these plans is Simmons (1953-4); in the same journal, Wardle (1955-6) looks at the records held in the Public Record Office, and Johnson (1953-4) describes those then kept by the British Transport Commission, which have now joined those in the Public Record Office. Between them these writers note a grandiose but abortive system for west Kent, a tinted plan of the parish of Paddington in 1828, a map of the proposed (Caledonian) West Cumberland, Furness and Morecambe Bay Railway showing a line across the Bay and Dudden (*sic*) Sands (1838), as well as two maps of a proposed railway in the Forest of Dean dated 1801 and 1802.

Simmons makes two very pertinent points: first, that maps may now be geographically far removed from the place to which they refer—he cites Exeter City Library which has five boxes of documents relating to the Mersey

Railway Company between 1893 and 1897; second, he points out that information on railways may lie in 'non-railway' collections in particular, in family and estate papers concerning negotiations for the sale of land or any other dealings with the railway companies (Fig. 5.17). Much railway history has been written only from the point of view of the companies, but landowners also played a large part in it.

Many, if not most, local libraries and record offices list their railway maps separately—or at least under the heading of 'deposited plans'. Several have substantial holdings of railway maps and a few have published hand-lists of their holdings, including Cheshire (1953), Oxford (1983) and Shropshire (1902, 1969, 1978). (See Bibliography, under county name.) A number of special collections exist, such as the Clinker and Garnett collections in Brunel University Library (see Bibliography); there

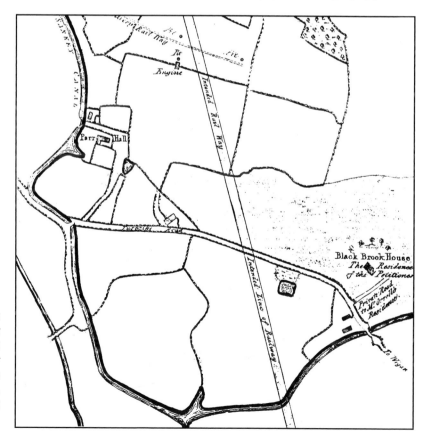

5.17 *Plan of part of the estate of C. Orrell in Parr (Lancashire) showing a turnpike, the Sankey canal, a colliery and its rail link to the canal, and the line of an intended railway.*

must be other similar collections elsewhere whose existence is little known.

After the deposited plans, there are two other important map types for the local railway historian to study. The first includes various maps specifically drawn of railways, while the second includes maps which show railways as part of the whole landscape.

Of specialised railway maps, the best known are those of John Airey, published from 1867 to 1894. Airey worked in the Distances Section of the Mileage Department of the Railway Clearing House, responsible for calculating the mileage done by trains of one company over the tracks of another. The House had

published its own plans in 1853, intended for use in goods depots and by the railway companies, but Airey later decided to make them more widely available in book form. Entitled *Railway Junction Diagrams*, this work ran to seven editions (Garnett, 1984), until eventually, in 1895, the House took over its publication. Some areas were too congested to fit Airey's original page size, and thus he began publishing sheet maps of areas such as Manchester, London and South Wales. It is quite rare to find these books or maps in mint condition; they were working maps, often updated by those using them. They show little other than railways (and canals), and though

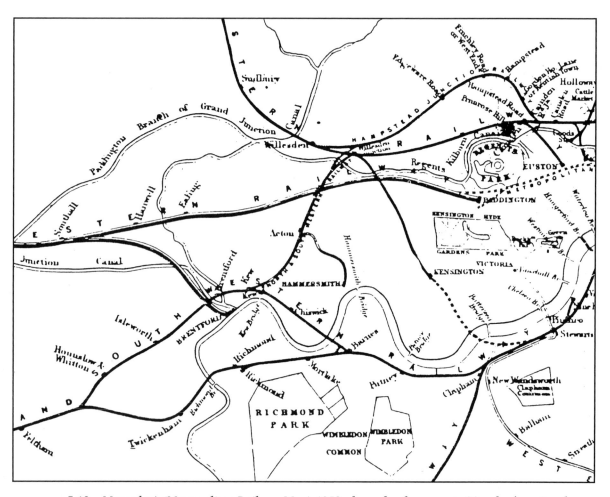

5.18 *Macaulay's 'Metropolitan Railway Map', 1859, showed railways up to 20 miles from London.*

they are not all drawn precisely to scale, exact distances *are* given.

Of more general maps we may note those of Bradshaw (1830 onwards) and Macaulay (from 1851) (Fig. 5.18). Bradshaw's first proper railway map was published in 1839 (the earlier ones dealt primarily with canals), and his maps were always regarded as among the best. Publishers like Cruchley and Collins simply added railways to existing plates or, worse, just overprinted the lines onto existing maps. Cruchley, for example, was still using Cary's county maps of 1801 as base maps in the 1870s! Complete railway atlases appeared (for example, that published by Cassell in *c*.1867) as did amended versions of regional or environs maps (for example, Mogg's 'Forty-five miles around London ... showing all the Railways' published in *c*.1847). There were also handbooks and timetables which were occasionally illustrated (for example, one published by Mogg in 1840), as well as guides to particular lines, pocket-maps, and the Metropolitan 'District Railway Map' which sold almost half a million copies. All these are secondary cartographic sources, but they may give some useful information (Smith, 1985, pp.100-3).

Finally, the Ordnance Survey maps also depicted railways; the Old Series one-inch maps had railways added to them in successive printings throughout the century. In many areas, the original surveying was completed before any railways had been built, and thus the earliest editions (like those reprinted by H. Margary) are largely devoid of railways. The so-called 'first editions' published by David and Charles are usually later editions with the railways added. In the north of England, however, some of the railways were in place before the Ordnance surveyors arrived. Although the detail on the O.S. sheets was altered, the date at the bottom of the sheet remained the same until the 1860s; Simmons (1968, p.258) notes an O.S. map of West Somerset showing railways up to about 1850, but which still bears the date 1809. This leads us on to consider the topic of Ordnance Survey maps in the final chapter.

Chapter Six

ORDNANCE SURVEY MAPS

IT IS FITTING to end this book by dealing with the maps of the Ordnance Survey. So many of the other types of maps already discussed were supplanted by the Ordnance Survey's products; the one-inch map replaced commercial county maps, while larger scale plans were used as the base maps for estate plans, various types of town plans and deposited railway plans, to give but three examples. Thus these 'official' cartographic publications follow on in direct succession to many of the types of maps already discussed. During the 19th century, the Survey slowly began to produce the definitive maps, leaving private cartographers either to adapt them for special purposes, or to produce specialist types of maps—such as cycling and road maps, fire insurance plans and tourist maps.

The basic handbook on the uses of early Ordnance maps was written by Brian Harley (1964); it remains a useful text but has now been superseded by Oliver (1993). The history of the Ordnance Survey has been detailed by Seymour (1980) and Owen & Pilbeam (1992). Harley's 'descriptive manual' (1975) also contains some historical detail. This chapter will give a brief résumé of the history of the Ordnance Survey, and will then deal with each scale of maps in turn, starting with the 1-inch, then the 6-inch and 25-inch and finally the large scale town plans. A brief note of maps at other scales will also be given.

The origins of the Ordnance Survey can be traced back to the military need for maps in the second half of the 18th century, combined with the great explosion of county cartography at the time. Britain had lagged behind many

other countries in Europe in terms of military topographic surveying, but it was the arrival of the Jacobite army in 1745 (which reached as far as Derby before turning back) that led to the realisation by the English commanders that their maps of Britain, and in particular of Scotland, were woefully inadequate; this is one of the most important episodes leading to the creation of the Ordnance Survey (Skelton, 1962; Close, 1969; Hodson, 1987, 1991b). In 1747-55, William Roy surveyed the whole of the mainland of Scotland at a scale of 1 inch to 1,000 yards; he was to become the most significant figure in the early history of the Survey. The Scottish survey remains in manuscript in the British Library, and, surprisingly, has never been published in facsimile (O'Donoghue, 1977; Whittington and Gibson, 1986).

The large scale county maps beginning to be produced at this time did not show relief well (if at all), and, as this was of vital interest to the army, various proposals for a new national survey were made (the first in 1766). County maps were produced independently of each other, with different levels of detail, at different scales, and were difficult to fit together. So entrenched was the notion of the county map that it took the new survey some time to move away from it and ignore county boundaries. By 1800, before a single Ordnance Survey sheet had been published, there were detailed maps of all kinds—of counties, estates, towns, roads and canals. Indeed the Survey was born out of a need for a consistent official survey which was able to benefit from the cartographic improvements of the previous 40 years. Equally, it would be true to say that the production of private county maps certainly held up the start of the Ordnance Survey. The Survey, as its name suggests, began life as a component of the Army, run by the Board of Ordnance until 1855; it was closely linked to the Artillery and the Engineers, branches of the service which also required scientific and mathematical expertise. It should always be borne in mind that the earlier maps of the Survey were executed partly for military purposes, during the period of the Napoleonic Wars, with the possible threat of invasion.

The Trigonometrical (later termed Ordnance) Survey is customarily taken as having begun in 1791, with the aim of producing a military survey of the country. It continued the triangulation work begun in 1784, and extended the isolated military surveys carried out at about the same time. The triangulation was virtually completed by 1824. The guiding lights in this were William Mudge, and then Thomas Colby, who between them took the Survey through 50 years (1798-1847). The Ordnance Survey rapidly developed into a publisher of maps—as commercial as any in the long-established London map trade.

Our interest lies in the topographic output of the Survey, which began in 1801 with the 1-inch map of Kent (actually published by Faden). The topographic survey for the 1-inch continued (though its progress was slowed after 1820 by Colby's insistence on older unpublished plans being revised to meet new standards) and in 1824 the Survey began work on a 6-inch map of Ireland, completed in 1846, in 1,875 large sheets. The more detailed mapping of Ireland inspired demands for something similar in Britain, so in September 1841 surveying on a 6-inch scale began in Lancashire and Yorkshire. By this time, Dawson's plans of 1836-7 for an accurate cadastral survey, at 26½ inches to the mile (3 chains to the inch) had degenerated into the Tithe Survey (see Chapter Three). The intense discussions about which scale to adopt which went on through most of the 1850s

are often referred to as the 'Battle of the Scales'. The 25-inch survey was authorised in July 1854, and henceforth this scale was generally taken as standard, except for waste and mountainous areas, where the 6-inch survey scale was retained; elsewhere the 6-inch and 1-inch maps were prepared by reduction from the 25-inch plans. Further complications were to come—notably the large scale town plans at the 5-foot scale (from 1843), 10-foot scale (from 1850) and 1:500 scale (from 1855).

The battle was finally resolved in 1863; the 1-inch survey was to be completed, while the whole country was to be mapped at 6 inches and 25 inches to the mile (as begun in 1856) with the towns at 1:500 (very close to the 10-foot scale). With all this activity it is hardly surprising that the 1-inch survey was not complete until 1873. But many problems remained: the 1-inch sheets for southern England were by then half a century old, and most had only been partially revised, so much of the detail was long out of date. The Duke of Wellington even suggested that the work at this scale could be left to private mapmakers! Such criticism continued intermittently until the end of the century, especially as the Survey came to concentrate so much on its 25-inch surveys.

One-inch maps

The Old Series
One inch to the mile was the original scale of Ordnance Survey maps, a scale which had been widely used by private county map-makers for half a century before the first Ordnance map appeared (Hodson, 1991a). The earliest Ordnance maps at this scale, known as the 'Old Series', have been reprinted by Harry Margary (see Bibliography) in book form, with introductory essays by J.B. Harley and others. These are very different from the so-called 'First Edition' maps published by David and Charles, which are usually later reprints with railways and other detail added. There is a basic problem

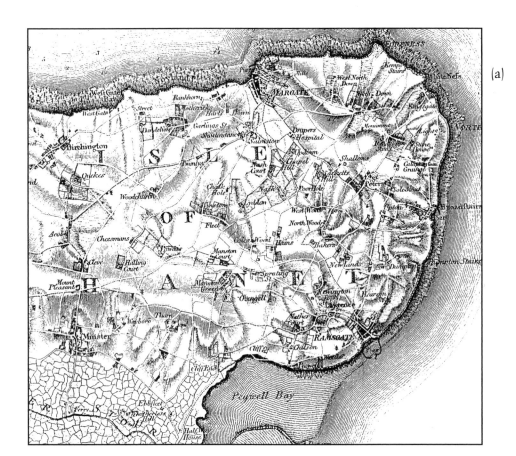

(a)

(b)

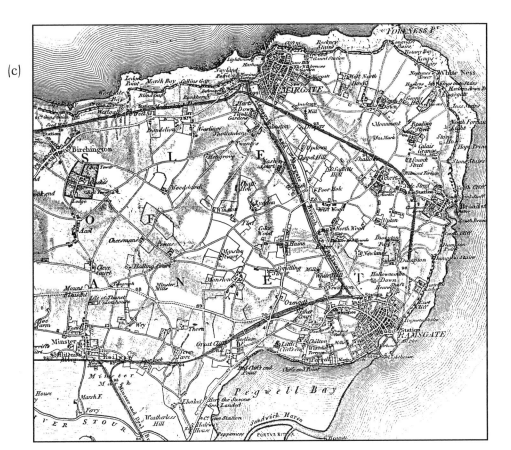

(c)

6.1 *Three editions of the 1-inch map of Kent: (a) as published by Faden in 1801; (b) as published by the Ordnance Survey in 1819 and (c) 1891. Note the changes in style as well as in detail.*

about using the word 'edition' in relation to 1-inch maps; this is because periodic revisions were made to the plates, especially of the Old Series. These maps were being partly revised for up to 80 years in some parts of the country, before a wholesale revision (i.e. a new 'edition' in the proper sense of the term) was issued. To avoid this problem it is better to use the word 'series' which will encompass the various revised reprints (referred to as different 'states' of the map) done from time to time.

The first survey work for the 1-inch was begun near Plymouth in 1784, but work really started in earnest in Kent in 1797, and the first map (of Kent) was published privately by William Faden in 1801 (Fig. 6.1a). Although in effect the first product of the Ordnance Survey

(bearing Mudge's name prominently in its title) it was actually little more than another county map, its depiction of the countryside stopping at the county borders. It was not even the first map to make use of the trigonometrical work of the Survey; this had already been used in Gream's completion of Yeakell and Gardner's map of Sussex (1795).

After the appearance of the Kent map, the Ordnance Survey took two clear decisions: first, to publish its own maps, and second, to ignore county boundaries by creating an official national numbered series (Fig. 6.2). Thus the first 'standard' Ordnance Survey sheets are the four sheets for Essex, published in 1805; Kent had been re-issued in this new format by 1819 (Fig. 6.1b). By that time two separate 'editions' of Kent had appeared, both based on the same field survey. The actual date of survey does not appear on Old Series maps, and it is important to ascertain it. This can be done with reference to the original field drawings, most of which

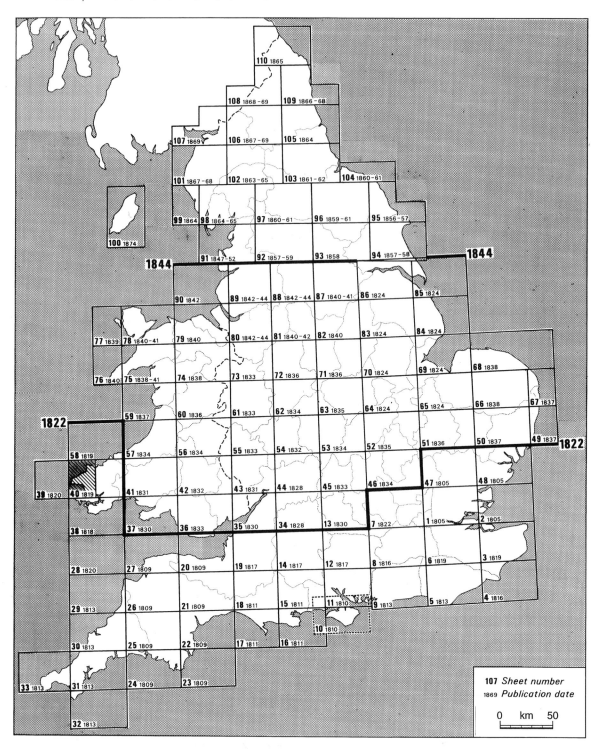

▲ **6.2** *Old Series One-Inch sheets: dates of publication (after J.B. Harley with revisions by Richard Oliver).*

6.3 *Field survey dates for sheets 1, 2, 3 and 6 of the Old Series One-Inch (after J.B. Harley and Y. O'Donoghue: Margary edition, Vol.1).* ➤

have been deposited in the British Library's Map Library (Hodson, 1989). There can sometimes be a ten- or twenty-year gap between the date of survey and the date of publication. Moreover, the field surveys were done at different scales in different areas, usually at 2 inches but also at 3 inches or 6 inches to the mile (Fig. 6.3). The 6-inch was restricted to parts of Kent, the Isle of Wight, and the area around Plymouth. These field drawings are valuable for the much greater detail which they give (Fig. 6.4). They are coloured to show pasture (green), arable (brown), water (blue), settlement (red) and roads (ochre). Because of their scale, they show details such as field boundaries which it was not possible to include on the published maps.

Some of the early 2-inch field surveys were later found to be of poor quality, and between 1825 and 1835 much re-surveying work was done, principally in a broad swathe from Pembrokeshire to the Wash (mainly sheets 13, 34-46, 51-57, 61-65, 69-70, and 83-86).

The Old Series eventually extended to 110 sheets by the time the last sheet (the Isle of Man) was published in 1873-4. The first 90 sheets, published by 1844, form a distinct group; they were surveyed mostly at the 2-inch scale, whereas the later maps had all of their field surveys done at 6-inch (from 1840) or at 25-inch (from 1854). Therefore, sheets 91-110 (i.e. north of the Preston-Hull Line) are more accurate than the earlier sheets.

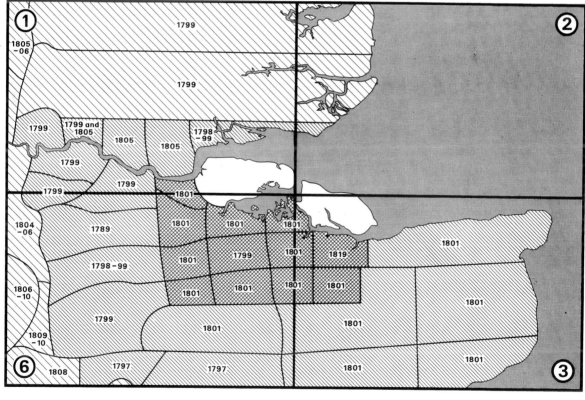

SCALE OF MAPPING

2 inches to 1 mile (1:31,680)

3 inches to 1 mile (1:21,120)

6 inches to 1 mile (1:10,560)

No surviving drawings

② Original sheet numbers

0   km   20

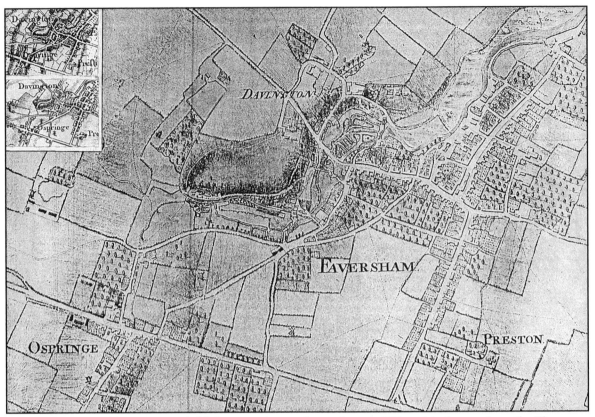

6.4 *Ordnance survey field drawing of Faversham, Kent, c.1789 at 6 inches to the mile. The two insets show how the same area appeared in the published 1-inch maps (upper by Faden, lower by O.S.).*

The various reprints of the Old Series 1-inch have meant that individual examples of these maps (especially sheets 1-90) can be difficult to date. A few sheets were entirely re-engraved in the 1830s and 1840s (sheets 1, 2, 33, 38, 40, 48, and 58) but in most cases only minor additions and corrections were made to the copper plates, the most frequent additions being of railways; parish boundaries were added progressively between 1849 and 1867. (Booth, J.R.S., 1980.) If the appropriate Margary volume is not to hand, then a few clues may help to date a map:

Adjacent sheet numbers given – from 1837
'Printed from an Electrotype' – from 1847
Latitude and longitude shown – from 1856 (not reliable until 1865)

Electrotype date given – from 1862
Dated railway insertion – from 1882

Revision was usually done either to make a smooth join of sheets published several years apart, or in connection with the addition of railways (urban detail was sometimes revised at the same time). Maps showing areas of rapid urban or industrial growth went through more revisions not only because the areas were changing, but also because of greater demand.

Such complications can be seen in the fourth volume of Margary's edition of the maps, which includes 28 pages of information about the various states of the 12 sheets covered in that volume. Sheet 7, for example, covering the area from London in its south-eastern corner to Princes Risborough in the north-west, originally surveyed between 1805 and 1822, and first published in 1822, has no less than 29 different identifiable states: railways are first shown on state 10, but it is not until state 18 that a new date is added (1862). Its final state bears the words 'railways inserted to May 1891'. Anyone wishing to delve further into the detailed carto-bibliography of the Old Series is referred to the essay by J.B. Manterfield in the Margary edition (Volume 4) where further detail and references are given. The changes which occurred in the map of north-east Kent by 1891 can be seen in Fig. 6.1c.

The detail shown on these Old Series 1-inch maps varies a little, depending on when the survey was done and on the original field survey scale. These maps are more accurate than other maps of their period—though sheets 1-90 are probably the least accurate ever published by the Ordnance Survey. In rural areas, large houses and their gardens stand out, and most farms are named; field boundaries are not shown (though they may be correctly depicted on the field surveys which in turn should be compared with available estate, enclosure or tithe maps). Roads and canals are shown more precisely than, for example, on the contemporary Greenwood county maps but, above all, there is some attempt to show relief, at first by the use of hachures, and then by contours. Most of the northern sheets (91-110) were in fact published in two versions—either hill-shaded with contours or outline-with-contours— sometimes up to five years apart. For the first time, the ups and downs of the landscape start to appear on maps, though not always with great accuracy, especially in the areas surveyed in the ten or fifteen years of hurried survey work before 1825. Towns are shown with their complete street layouts, and different styles of lettering are used for different sizes of town. A few conventional signs were used—for windmills, churches, woodland and orchards, for example, although there was no key. Again, reference should be made to the Margary

edition in which the cartographic symbols and conventions are illustrated. A good deal of archaeological information is shown on the maps (Phillips, C.W., 1980), and after 1820 the survey also established a system for the full and correct rendering of place names (Harley, 1971).

The later one-inch maps

The subsequent history of the 1-inch can be dealt with quite briefly as, by the time these maps appeared, larger scale maps, of much greater use, had also been published. Richard Oliver has supplied details of the survey and publication dates of the later editions, all of which he classes as part of the 'New Series' (see also Oliver, 1982). (See Table on p.122.)

All these O.S. maps were available in several formats, the most important development being the introduction of colour versions in the 1890s. Specific district maps were produced from 1887 onwards (Cook & McIntosh, 1991). The steady introduction of contours from 1847 had been a major innovation of the New Series; they were shown at first by finely dotted lines and then by more prominent dot-dash lines, with various vertical intervals; spot heights were also shown. Parish boundaries were another innovation, depicted by dots which are unfortunately easily mistaken for contours or footpaths.

Survey and revision dates are usually given on maps after 1891 (except from 1935 to 1945). As these maps were derived directly from the 6-inch and 25-inch plans, the table (pp.126-7) which gives their survey dates also applies to the New Series 1-inch maps. One complication is that the survey date given on any of these maps is probably that on which the manuscript plans were certified as ready for publication; the field survey could easily have been carried out up to three years earlier. The gap between the stated date of survey and the date of publication is usually well under ten years, but it can vary between one and 30 years.

One-Inch Series/Edition	Survey	Publication	Sheets	Notes
OLD	1784-1869	(1801) 1805-74	110	(a)
NEW/1st	1841-93	(1847) 1874-96	348	(b)
			(69 + 279)	
NEW/2nd	1893-8	1895-9	346	(b)
NEW/3rd (small sheets)	1901-12	1903-13	347	(b)
NEW/3rd (large sheets)	1901-12	1906-13	152	
NEW/4th	1909-10	1911-12	7	(c)
NEW/(3rd National Revision), 'Popular Edition'	1912-23	1918-26	146	
NEW/5th	1928-38	1931-9	38	(d)
NEW/ War Revision, 1940	1913-40	1940-1	146	
NEW/ Second War Revision, 1940	1913-42	1940-3	128	(e)
NEW/6th or New Popular Edition (1)	1913-46	1940-7	114	
(2)	1946-8	1947-50	21	(f)
NEW/ Seventh Series	1947-58	1952-61	115	(g)
'Seventh Series' (revised)	1958-71	1960-73	115	

Notes:

(a) Many sheets published as quarter-sheets after 1831. Sheets 91-110 were renumbered as sheets 1-73 of NEW/1st in 1881-2.

(b) Sheets were numbered 1 to 360, but a few were combined in coastal areas.

(c) Abandoned: covers East Kent only.

(d) Abandoned: covers southern England roughly up to a line from Cheltenham to Luton, but omits east Kent and east Sussex.

(e) Abandoned incomplete: south-west England, parts of Wales and Midlands not published.

(f) Partial revision only; covers London and south-east England; abandoned.

(g) This incorporated revision which was also used for the 6-inch provisional edition on National Grid sheetlines, and for the 1:25,000 provisional edition.

The various editions and revisions of the 1-inch map present a valuable record of the changing landscape of the 19th century. Whether one's interest lies in roads or railways, windmills or woodlands, the evidence, if used correctly, is there. Even if you are only drawing a general map to locate the places mentioned in a text, it is important to use a contemporary plan as a base map; it would be foolish to use a modern Ordnance map to illustrate a study of a particular parish in 1850; the 1-inch (or 6-inch) map of that date is needed. The first edition of the 25-inch plan may be better still, perhaps yielding new information about features in the landscape long since gone. The later 1-inch maps are of limited use; you are better served by the 25-inch and 6-inch plans from which the 1-inch was derived. The 1-inch was finally abandoned in favour of the metric 1:50,000 in 1974-6 (Harley, 1975).

6-inch and 25-inch maps

The introduction of larger scale maps was a slow process, to which some reference has already been made. It was complicated by the Irish survey (1825-42) which produced maps at the 6-inch scale, by Dawson's proposals for a national cadastral survey, by the wishes of commercial surveyors not to have national large scale maps, and by the perennial desire of the government to avoid spending money. This whole story, culminating in the 'Battle of the Scales', can be read in Seymour (1980) and in Owen & Pilbeam (1992).

The first cartographic outcome of the process was a set of 6-inch maps of Lancashire and Yorkshire, surveyed and published between 1841 and 1854; these were produced by surveyors who had spent the previous years working at that scale in Ireland. These maps (Fig. 6.5) give us a valuable and detailed picture of these two rapidly industrialising counties ten or twenty years earlier than might otherwise have been the case (Whitaker, 1933, 1938). This group of maps is quite distinct from the First Edition 6-inch set which later covered the whole country.

The 25-inch scale (in fact 25.344 inches to the mile—a metric scale of 1:2500) was adopted progressively between 1854 and 1863; it was finally agreed that the whole country, except for uncultivated areas, should be published at this scale, with the 6-inch maps made by reduction from it; the uncultivated areas would be surveyed and published at the 6-inch scale only. Surveying at the 25-inch scale began in County Durham in 1854, and within five years work was under way in a total of eight widely scattered counties—including some areas of military importance in southern England, where the decision to survey at this scale had not yet been made. By 1863 the four northernmost counties of England (Durham, Westmorland, Northumberland and Cumberland) had been mapped. Between 1863 and 1888 the whole of England and Wales south of

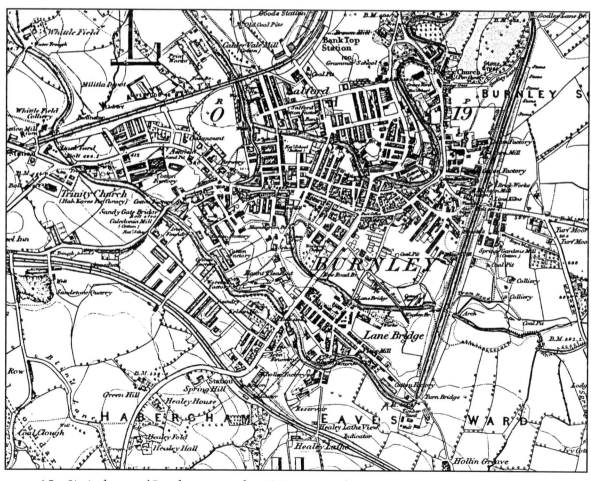

6.5 *Six-inch map of Burnley, surveyed in 1844, contoured in 1847 and published in 1848.*

Lancashire and Yorkshire was surveyed. After 1868 there was a tendency to survey mining areas first, while a few towns were surveyed in advance of the surrounding countryside in return for paying part of the cost. Finally, between 1888 and 1893 the 25-inch mapping was completed by the re-surveying of Lancashire and Yorkshire (see Table overleaf).

The Ordnance Survey published a *Catalogue* of its maps from 1862 to 1924, and these books provide a useful index to the 6-inch and 25-inch plans (Oliver, 1991a). In addition, county index maps appeared at ¼-inch scale. These maps were not part of a national series as they were compiled county by county; the plans of some counties (up to 1873) were even published in parish map format, despite this leaving large blank areas on some sheets. This complicated system survived until the introduction of the National Grid after the Second World War.

The 6-inch maps were usually published a little later than the 25-inch plans on which most of them were based; both always bear the same survey date. At first, both scales appeared on large sheets (the 25-inch sheets measure 38 in x 25⅓ in.), but from 1882 the 6-inch maps began to appear in quarter-sheet format, which became virtually standard. Early 6-inch quarter-sheets were direct photographic reductions of the 25-inch; the linework is thus very fine and the map crowded with detail; photo reduction was abandoned by 1895. Some 6-inch sheets first appeared without contours but later these were added; the 25-inch had only spot heights (Fig. 6.6). The net result of all this activity was that by 1900 there were about 15,000 6-inch sheets and 51,000 25-inch sheets covering Great Britain. As we have already seen, these surveys were the basis for the 1-inch and smaller scale maps published from 1847 onwards.

6.6 *The original style of the 25-inch and 6-inch plans. The 6-inch reduction is inset top right. (Winterbottom, 1934)*

The whole series was revised between 1891 and 1914, on the principle that such revisions should take place every 20 years. This series is known as the Second Edition, and was followed by the Second Revision (or Third Edition) which began in 1904. This revision was never completed, due to the War and its aftermath, and it was decided that only urban areas should be revised on a 20-year cycle. By 1928 this system was replaced by the continuous revision of areas which were changing rapidly (an 'area' being defined as a 6-inch quarter-sheet containing four 25-inch plans). Usually, however, blocks of 6-inch sheets were revised together, so that what is effectively another revised map (or more than one) may exist for the period 1922-38. Another set of 'Provisional' revisions took place during the Second World War, after which both 6-inch and 25-inch maps were transferred onto the national grid system.

The 25-inch plans were also used as base maps for the valuation of properties under the Finance Act (1909-10). Copies of the plans had hand-drawn annotations of ownership area numbers and boundaries (Kain & Baigent, 1992). The major change since then has been the replacement of the 6-inch by the metric 1:10,000 (the 6-inch was 1:10,560), a process which began in 1969. This can present problems for the local researcher who is trying to make any accurate comparisons with earlier 6-inch maps. The reduction needed of the new 1:10,000 is 5.3 per cent (linear), but it is easier to rely on the last available 6-inch map from the 1970s if there have been no major changes since then in the area concerned.

The detail and accuracy of the 25-inch plans set new standards for cartography in the 19th century. For the first time, the whole of the cultivated and built-up area was depicted at a scale sufficient to show almost every feature of the landscape (Fig. 6.7). Roads are shown at their true scale, as are the buildings, while fields and their boundaries are equally accurately depicted, each field or enclosure being

6-inch and 25-inch maps

	First Edition (date of survey)	Second Edition or First Revision (date of revision)	Third Edition or Second Revision (date of revision)
Bedford	1876-82	1898-1900	1921-4 #
Berks	1866-83	1897-9	1909-12
Buckingham	1867-81	1897-9	1918-33 #
Cambridge	1876-86	1896-1901	1924-6 #
Cheshire	1870-5 P	1896-8	1904-9
Cornwall	†1859-88	1905-7	1912 #
Cumberland	1859-65 P	1897-1900	1922-4 #
Derby	1871-83	1896-1900	1912-21
Devon	†1855-89	1902-5 ⊗	1912 #
Dorset	†1862-89	1900-1	1923-32 #
Durham	1854-7 P	1894-7	1912-19
Essex	1861-76 (P)	1893-6	1911-22
Gloucester	1873-84	1898-1902	1912-22
Hants	1856-75 P	1894-7	1906-10
Hereford	1878-87	1902-4	1924-8 #
Hertford	1863-86	1895-7	1912-23
Huntingdon	1882-7	1899-1901	1924-5 #
Isle of Man	1866-9 P	NR	NR
Kent	1858-73 P	1893-7	1905-10
Lancashire	*1888-93	1904-12	1924-38 #
Leicester	1879-86	1899-1902	1927-30 #
Lincoln	1883-8	1898-1906	1914-32 #
London	1862-72	1891-5	1912-14
Middlesex	1862-71 P	1891-5	1910-13
Norfolk	1879-86	1900-6	1925-7 #
Northants	1880-7	1898-1900	1923-8 #
Northumberland	1856-64 P	1894-7	1912-22
Nottingham	1876-85	1897-9	1912-19
Oxford	1872-80	1897-9	1910-21
Rutland	1883-4	1899-1903	1928 #
Shropshire	1873-84	1899-1902	1924-6 #
Somerset	1882-8	1900-3	1927-30 #
Stafford	†1875-86	1897-1902	1912-23
Suffolk	1876-85	1900-4	1924-6 #
Surrey	1861-71 (P)	1891-6	1910-13
Sussex	1869-75	1895-8	1907-10
Warwick	1880-8	1898-1904	1912-23 #
Westmorland	1856-60 P	1896-8	1910-13
Wilts	1873-85	1898-1900	1921-4
Worcester	1880-8	1898-1904	1921-6 #
Yorkshire	*1888-93	1901-14	1913-39 #

	First Edition (date of survey)	Second Edition or First Revision (date of revision)	Third Edition or Second Revision (date of revision)
Anglesey	1886-7	1899	1913-23
Brecknock	1874-88	1903-4	1913-16 #
Caernarvon	1885-8	1898-1900	1910-14
Cardigan	1885-8	1900-4	NR
Carmarthen	1875-87	1903-6	1913 #
Denbigh	1870-5 P	1897-9	1909-12
Flint	1869-72 P	1897-9	1909-11
Glamorgan	1867-78 P	1896-9	1913-16
Merioneth	1873-88	1899-1900	1913-14 #
Monmouth	1875-81 P	1898-1900	1915-20
Montgomery	1874-87	1900-1	NR
Pembroke	†1860-88 P	1904-6	NR
Radnor	1883-8	1901-4	1926-7 #

Notes:

First Edition:	*	Originally surveyed and published at six-inch scale only, 1841-54
	†	Limited areas surveyed for military purposes, c.1858-63
	P	Published as Parish maps
	(P)	Part of county published as Parish maps
Second Edition:	⊗	Around Plymouth there are two second Editions (1893 and 1904-5)
Third Edition:	#	Incomplete: part revision only.
	NR	No revision started.

Source: Harley (1964), Oliver (1991)

numbered. The maps were accompanied by reference books (*Parish Area Books* from 1855-72; *Books of Reference* from 1873-86) of which some 5,000 exist. These show not only the area of each land unit, but also its use, indicating various types of woodland, moorland, marsh and pasture, plus arable, orchards and other forms of cultivation (Harley, 1979). The reference books tend to coincide with those 25-inch maps published as parish maps; thus the main problem is that they do not cover the whole country—in fact only about one-quarter of England and Wales (roughly, those counties indicated by the letter P in the above table). Other problems include the fact that land use details were no longer given after 1879-80, that wholly uncultivated areas were not published at this scale, that information available relates to a period stretching across 25 years, and that we do not know what instructions were given to the surveyors. Overall, therefore, the quality of the data cannot be ascertained. Nevertheless, the information can be used locally, especially if it can be tied in with other sources (for example, the tithe survey). Even after the reference books were discontinued, the surveyors still continued to collect land use data, but

6.7 (overleaf) *Twenty-five-inch plans of Great Lever, Bolton, showing the great changes between the 1893 (left) and 1937 (right) editions. For rapidly changing areas a whole series of these maps may exist.*

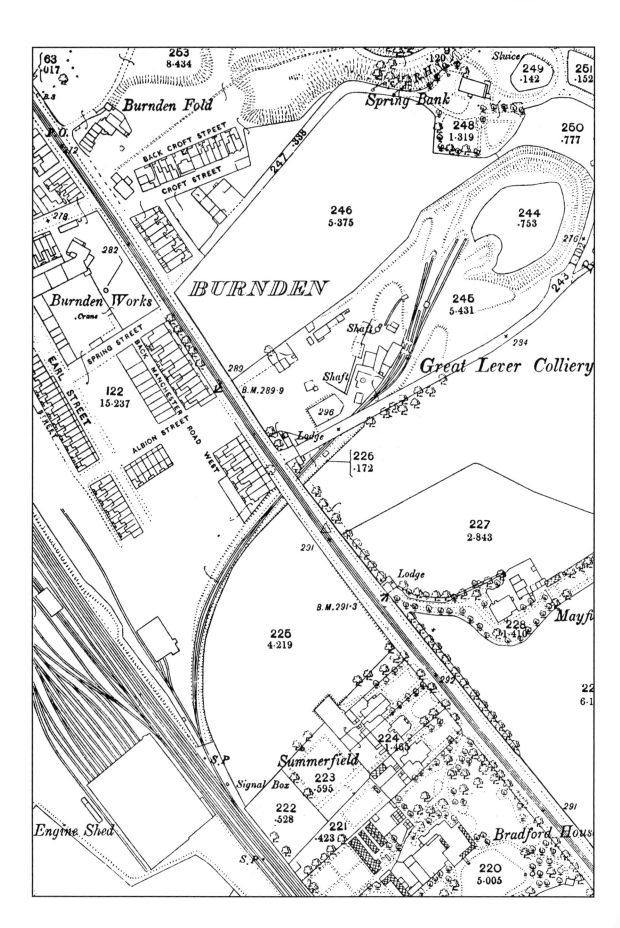

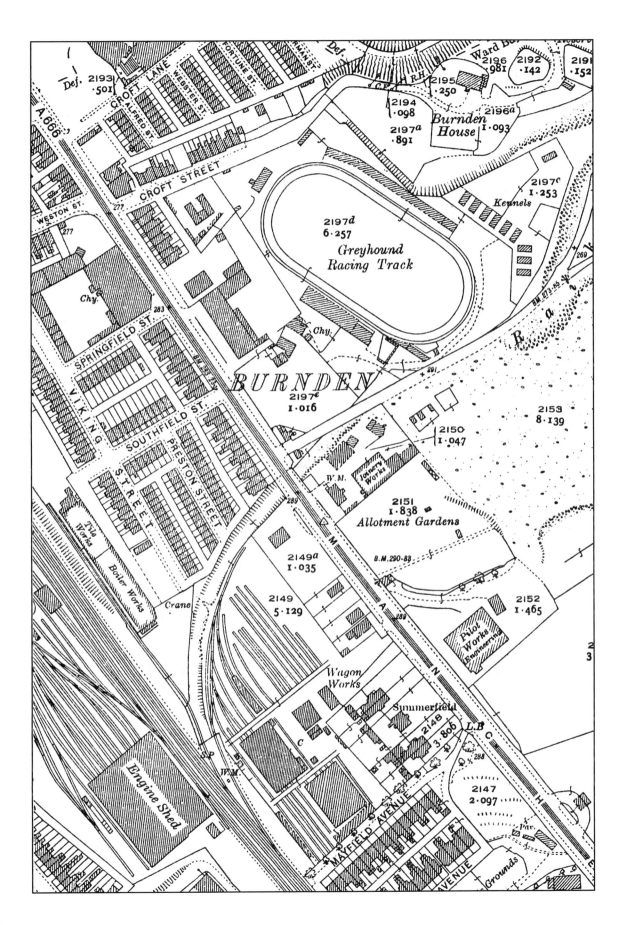

in a progressively simpler form (principally of woodland), shown merely by conventional signs. The acreage was now inserted on the map itself, underneath the reference number. It needs pointing out that these maps are not cadastral plans; they are not concerned with property boundaries, but with the physical details of the landscape—such as walls and hedges.

The maps had little or no colour. The First Edition 25-inch plans could be had hand-coloured, however; brick and stone buildings were coloured carmine, while wood or iron buildings were coloured grey; the 6-inch had printed colour contours after 1909. A special series of revised town plans was produced at the 6-inch scale in the 1920s, with yellow roads, red buildings, green parks, purple boundaries and tramways and blue water. The towns for which these were published were Cambridge, Canterbury, Cheltenham, Colchester, Gloucester, Hull, Ipswich, Keighley, Leeds, Leicester, Lincoln, Northampton, Nottingham, Oxford, Portsmouth, Southampton, Southend, South Shields, Wolverhampton and York.

Other features of the 25-inch maps included their archaeological detail (Phillips, C.W., 1980), the marking of civil and ecclesiastical boundaries (Booth, J.R.S., 1980), and many minor place names (including a few field names until 1888). The Second Edition has slightly less detail overall; 'in 1892 the showing of individual trees in hedgerows, gates in fields, paths and flowerbeds in even quite small gardens, and bay windows was discontinued' (Harley, 1964, p.26).

The 6-inch map was derived from the 25-inch in a variety of ways, either by being photographed down or completely redrawn. The numbers and acreages of plots were omitted, boundaries were removed in congested areas, buildings were shown in a more generalised manner in heavily built-up areas and true scale was abandoned for railways (they are shown conventionally) and even for some roads in towns.

For the purposes of local research, either scale may be of use—it depends simply on the size of the area involved and the detail required. In these terms, the two scales are very different; the 25-inch map in fact requires almost 18 times the space to show the same geographical area as a 6-inch map. They give a detailed record reaching back between 100 and 145 years; in the case of the 25-inch plans, this is a survey of great accuracy and detail. Even if the maps are being used only as illustrations, then it is, once again, important to use a contemporary map and not a modern one.

Alan Godfrey has reprinted slightly reduced versions of early 25-inch plans, plus a few five-foot plans. His 1998 list has about 1,000 sheets of parts of towns throughout Britain. Most of his reproductions have historical notes and local directory extracts on the reverse. (Alan Godfrey Maps, 12 The Off Quay Building, Foundry Lane, Newcastle, NE6 1LH.)

Maps at the scale of 50 inches to the mile (1:1250) were produced for a few special areas from 1911—but only by photographic enlargement of the 25-inch maps.

Large scale town plans

The introduction of these plans was originally due to the imitation in northern England of a practice which had begun during the surveying of Ireland; the 5 foot to 1 mile (1:1056) scale was convenient for checking complex detail in towns during survey operations. However, the production of such plans acquired an added justification with the growing concern in the 1840s about improved urban sanitation to combat Asiatic cholera and other diseases (see Chapter Four) (Smith, 1994). In Lancashire and Yorkshire this scale was adopted for towns with populations of more than 4,000; elsewhere only a few towns were surveyed at this scale. Surveying was carried out as part of the 6-inch mapping of the surrounding area. Winterbotham (1934) says that St Helens was the first

English town to be surveyed at 1:1056, but it has become clear that surveys of Manchester and Leeds were in hand as early as 1843. But probably because of the 'Battle of the Scales', the survey dates given on the maps of Manchester are wrongly given as between 1848 and 1850. The most obvious giveaway is that Manchester's Royal Exchange is shown as it was before its rebuilding in 1845. By 1850 some 40 town plans were published or in progress, and the total at this scale finally reached 60 (Figs. 5.13 and 6.8). Southampton was surveyed at this scale as a training exercise in 1845-6; the manuscript survey remains in the City Record Office. A few towns had their 1:1056 fully revised later—for example Liverpool and Middlesbrough.

Town plans at 1:1056 (5 feet to one mile) 1844-54 (Oliver, 1993)

Accrington, Ashton-under-Lyne, Bacup, Barnsley, Beverley, Bingley, Blackburn, Bolton, Bradford, Bridlington, Burnley, Bury, Chorley, Clitheroe, Colne, Darlington, Dewsbury, Doncaster, Fleetwood, Halifax, Haslingden, Heywood, Howden, Huddersfield, Keighley, Kingston upon Hull, Knaresborough, Lancaster, Leeds, Liverpool, London, Malton, Manchester, Middlesborough, Middleton, Oldham, Ormskirk, Pontefract, Prescot, Preston, Ripon, Rochdale, Rotherham, St Helens, Salford, Scarborough, Selby, Sheffield, Skipton, Southampton, Stalybridge, Stockport, Todmorden, Ulverston, Wakefield, Warrington, Whitby, Wigan, Windsor, York.

In addition there were plans at this scale of Brentford and Kingston upon Thames in 1865-70.

As we have already seen (Chapter Four), London was surveyed at this scale by the Ordnance Survey between 1847-52 (at London's own expense), in order to provide a suitable map for the planning and construction of new sewers. The maps left details blank within blocks of buildings. This was thus a 'block', 'outline'

or 'skeleton' survey, known as the Old Series, comprising some 487 sheets. It was completed by the O.S. in 1862-72 and revised in 1893-5. It was again revised in 1906-23 and extended further out into Surrey, Middlesex and Kent. The Land Registry made its own revised series in 1906-23 and this was merged with the O.S. series in 1931. Thus the London 1:1056 plans stand apart from those of other towns. (The Old Series 1:1056 survey of London was also published at 6-inch and 12-inch scale.)

For the purposes of sanitary engineering, the 5-foot scale was found to be too small, and from 1850 various towns paid for surveys at the 10-foot scale (1:528) at the instigation of the Board of Health. Over thirty were done by the Ordnance Survey, others by private surveyors. Some remained in manuscript, and were handed over to the Local Board of Health, whilst others were printed (Fig. 4.24). In Warwickshire, for example, five towns were surveyed (four by the O.S.), but none was ever published—they remain only in manuscript (Harley, 1982).

Town Plans at 1:528 (10 feet to one mile), 1850-7 (surveyed and published by the O.S.) (Oliver, 1993)

Alnwick, Ashby-de-la-Zouch, Barnard Castle, Berwick-upon-Tweed, Bishop Auckland, Braintree, Burslem, Cardiff, Chelmsford, Coventry, Dartford, Derby, Gloucester, Hitchin, Kingston upon Hull, Knighton, Margate, Merthyr Tydfil, Nantwich, Newcastle-under-Lyme, North Shields, Rugby, Sandgate, Sheerness, South Shields, Stockton-on-Tees, Stratford-upon-Avon, Sunderland, Torquay, Tynemouth, Uxbridge, Ware, Warwick, Woolwich, Worthing.

In addition there were plans at this scale of Hornsey and Plumstead in 1893-4.

Finally, in 1855, the Treasury decided to sanction the nationwide large scale mapping of towns, and the 'metric 10-foot' scale of 1:500 was chosen (it is, in fact, about 127 inches to

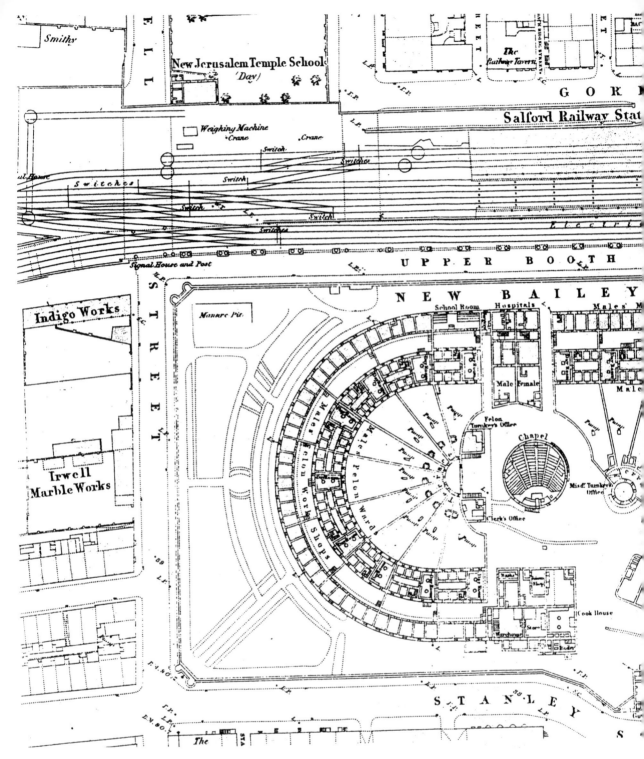

6.8 *Five-foot plan (1:1056) showing Salford Railway station and the internal layout of the New Bailey Prison.*

the mile but complements the 25-inch maps which are also metric—1:2500). The criterion for a town's inclusion in this scale of survey was again a population of over 4,000; almost 400 English and Welsh towns were surveyed

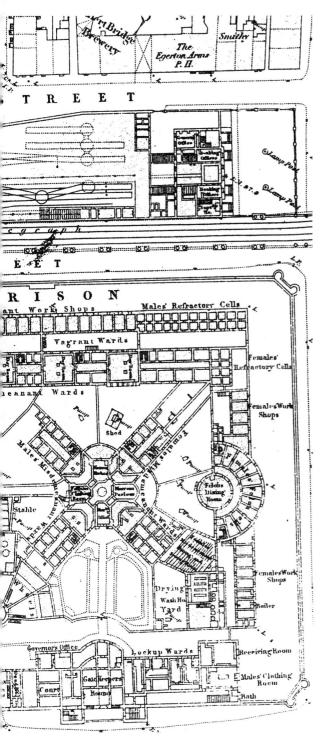

Town Plans at 1:500, 1855-95 (Oliver, 1993)

Towns in **bold** had a revised 1:500 edition (some partial only), 1872-1910

Aberdare, Abergavenny, **Aberystwyth**, Abingdon, Accrington, Aldershot, Altrincham, Andover, Appleby, Ashford, Atherstone, Atherton, Aylesbury.

Bacup, Banbury, Bangor, Barnsley, Barnstaple, **Barrow-in-Furness**, Basingstoke, Bath, Batley, Beccles, Bedford, Belper, Berkhamsted, Bideford, Biggleswade, Bingley, Birkenhead, Birmingham, Birstall, Bishops Stortford, Blackburn, Blackpool, Blyth, Bodmin, Bolton, Bootle, Boston, Bournemouth, Bradford, Bradford on Avon, Braintree, Brecon, Brentwood, Bridgnorth, Bridgwater, Bridlington, Bridport, Brierley Hill, Brighouse, Brighton, Bristol, Brixham, Bromsgrove, Buckingham, Burnley, Burslem, Burton-on-Trent, Bury, Bury St Edmunds, Buxton.

Caernarfon, Camborne, **Cambridge**, Canterbury, **Cardiff**, **Carlisle**, Carmarthen, Castleford, Chatham, Cheltenham, Chertsey, Chester, Chesterfield, Chesterton, Chichester, Chippenham, Chorley, Christchurch, Cirencester, Clayton-le-Moors, Cleckheaton, Clevedon, Cockermouth, Colchester, Colne, Congleton, **Coventry**, Cowes, Crediton, Crewe, Crewkerne, Croydon.

Dalton in Furness, Darlaston, Dartford, Dartmouth, Darwen, Dawlish, Deal, Denbigh, Derby, Devizes, Dewsbury, **Doncaster**, Dorchester, Dorking, Douglas, Dover, Droitwich, Dudley, Dunstable, Durham.

Eastbourne, East Dereham, East Retford, Eccles, Elland, Ely, Evesham, Exeter, Exmouth, Exning.

Falmouth, Farnham, Farnworth, Farsley, Faversham, Fleetwood, Folkestone, Frome.

Gainsborough, Garston, **Gateshead**, Glossop, Godmanchester, Goole, **Gosport**, Grantham, Gravesend, Great Driffield, Great Harwood, Great Yarmouth, **Grimsby**, Guildford.

Halifax, Halstead, **Hanley**, Harrogate, **Hartlepool**, Harwich, Haslingden, Hastings, Haverfordwest, Hebden Bridge, Heckmondwyke, Hemel Hemp-

and published by 1895. Twenty-one towns revised their 1:500 plans, several at their own expense after the Ordnance Survey had ceased to publish at this scale. Some of these revisions covered only newly built-up areas.

stead, Henley-on-Thames, Hereford, Hertford, Hexham, Heywood, High Wycombe, Hinckley, Hindley, Holyhead, Holywell, Horncastle, Horsham, Horwich, Hucknall Torkard, Huddersfield, Huntingdon, Hyde.

Idle, Ilfracombe, Ilkeston, Ilkley, Ipswich, Jarrow.

Keighley, Kendal, Kettering, Kidderminster, Kidsgrove, Kings Lynn, Kingston upon Hull, Knaresborough, Knottingley.

Lancaster, Leamington, **Leeds,** Leek, Leicester, Leigh, Leighton Buzzard, Leominster, Lewes, Lichfield, Lincoln, Liskeard, Littleborough, Liverpool, Llandudno, Long Eaton, **Longton**, Loughborough, Lowestoft, Ludlow, Luton, Lymington, Lytham.

Macclesfield, Maidenhead, Maidstone, Maldon, Malton, Malvern, Manchester, Mansfield, March, Maryport, Melton Mowbray, Middlesbrough, Middleton, Mirfield, Mold, Monmouth, Morecambe, Morley, Morpeth, Mossley.

Neath, Nelson, Newark-on-Trent, Newbury, Newcastle under Lyme, **Newcastle upon Tyne**, Newmarket, Newport (IoW), Newport (Mon), Newton Abbot, Newtown, Northampton, North Shields, Northwich, Norwich, Nottingham, Nuneaton.

Oldbury, **Oldham**, Ormskirk, Oswestry, Otley, Oxford.

Padiham, Pembroke, Penrith, Penzance, Peterborough, Petersfield, Petworth, Plumstead, **Plymouth**, Pontefract, Pontypool, Poole, **Portsmouth**, Prescot, Preston, Pudsey.

Radcliffe, Ramsbottom, Ramsey, Ravensthorpe, Rawtenstall, Reading, Redditch, Redhill, Redruth, Reigate, Rhyl, Richmond (Yorks), Ripon, Rishton, **Rochdale, Rochester,** Romford, Romsey, Rotherham, Royton, Rugby, Runcorn, Ryde, Rye.

Saffron Walden, St Albans, St Austell, St Helens, St Ives, Salford, Salisbury, Saltaire, Sandwich, Scarborough, Selby, Sevenoaks, **Sheffield**, Shepton Mallet, Sherborne, Shipley, Shrewsbury, Skipton, Sleaford, Slough, Smethwick, Southampton, Southport, South Shields, Sowerby Bridge, Spalding, Stafford, Stamford, Stanningley,

Stockton-on-Tees, Stoke-on-Trent, Stone, Stourbridge, Stowmarket, Stratford-upon-Avon, Strood, Stroud, Sudbury, Sutton-in-Ashfield, Swansea, Swindon, Swinton.

Tamworth, Taunton, Tavistock, Teignmouth, Tenby, Tewkesbury, Thetford, Todmorden, Tonbridge, Torquay, Totnes, Tring, Trowbridge, Truro, Tunbridge Wells, Tunstall, Tyldesley, Tynemouth, Ulverston.

Wakefield, Wallsend, Walsall, Waltham Abbey, Warminster, Warrington, Warwick, Watford, Wednesbury, Wellingborough, Wellington, Wells, Welshpool, West Bromwich, Weston-super-Mare, Weymouth, Whitby, Whitchurch, Whitehaven, Widnes, Wigan, Wigton, Winchester, Wisbech, Withington, Wokingham, Wolverhampton, Worcester, Workington, Worksop, Worthing, Wrexham.

Yeovil, York.

It should be remembered that many towns previously surveyed and published at 1:1056 (and even a few done at 1:528) were surveyed and published again at 1:500. Thus many towns (particularly in Lancashire and Yorkshire) have two (or even three) of these large scale plans. The best served include Cardiff, Doncaster, Leeds, Rochdale and Sheffield, which had 1:1056 surveys, then 1:500 surveys and finally 1:500 revised surveys. Most towns, however, are covered by only one edition. The coverage is further improved if the 1:528 Board of Health surveys are also included—whether done by the O.S. or not, and whether printed or not. The revised or extended 1:500 plans were not sent to copyright libraries, so they may only survive in local collections. All these large scale plans ceased publication in 1894 (apart from the municipal revisions already noted) and there were no new large scale plans until the 1:1250 (50-inch) series began after the Second World War.

These plans were published on large sheets (up to 40 in × 27 in), which bear the dates of both survey and publication. Because of the enormous scales, and despite the sheet size, the number of sheets required to cover even a modest town was often large. In the 1:500 series, Nottingham required 352 sheets, and a further dozen towns needed more than a hundred sheets. At this scale, each sheet covered an area of only about 525 yards by 350 yards. For each town (at each of the three scales), an index map, usually at 6-inch scale, was published.

The detail included on these maps is immense, with remarkably small details recorded. Each property is clearly shown, and the maps indicate public houses, schools, bakehouses, smithies, breweries and mills, as well as more basic details such as street names and, of course, detailed spot heights so that sewers and

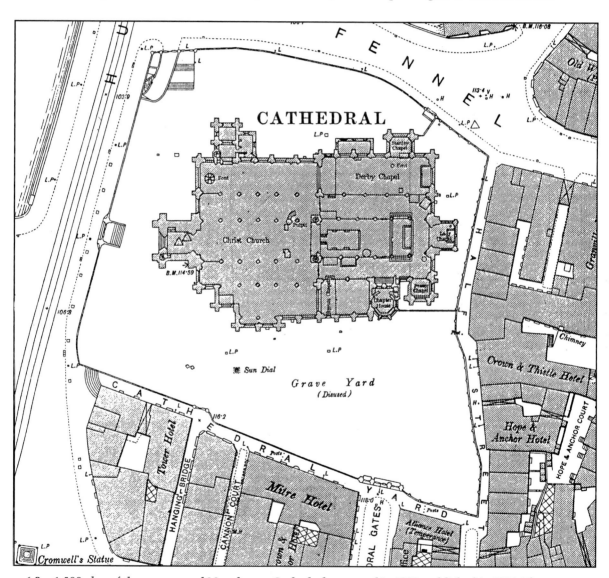

6.9 *1:500 plan of the area around Manchester Cathedral; surveyed in 1888, published in 1891. The enormous scale requires many walls to be depicted by double lines. Note the fine detail such as lampposts (L.P.).*

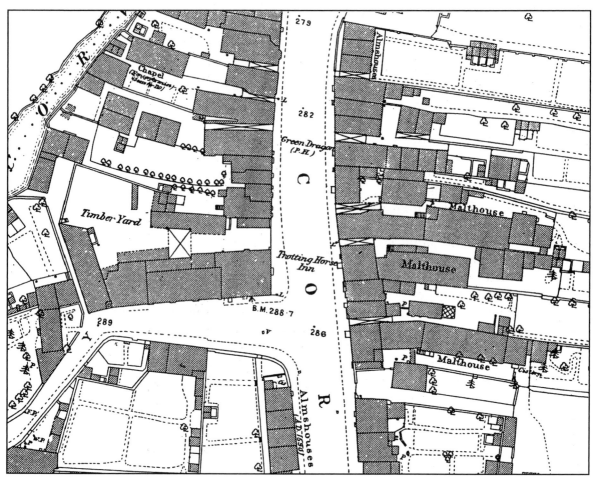

6.10 *1:500 plan of Ludlow, surveyed in 1884, showing precise detail of the house plots in the northern part of the town.*

other works could be planned (Figs. 6.9 and 6.10). The Board of Health plans tend to have more detail. On some plans, the interior layout of certain buildings is given—for example, of prisons and churches, although in the latter case some plans say simply 'seats for 200'. By 1891 the Ordnance Survey's Annual Report was able to claim that the whole of urban Britain had been surveyed at a scale 'sufficiently large to show detail down to the size of a doorstep' (Oliver, 1991b).

By any standards, these large scale plans present a remarkable source for the study of the Victorian town, from London down to quite small country towns. Finally, many of them,

particularly the 1:1056 of northern England, are almost works of art in their own right, representing some of the finest efforts of the Ordnance Survey.

Maps at other scales

The other scales at which the Ordnance Survey has published maps are generally of quite recent date and can be described briefly. More details are to be found in Harley (1975) and Oliver (1993). The small scales in general have little to offer the local historian: they include 1:1,000,000 (about 16 miles to the inch), 1:625,000 (about 10 miles to the inch), quarter-inch (4 miles to the inch) and half-inch (2 miles to the inch). They are all derived from larger scale maps, and their principal use in local studies will be in locating places, as route finding/motoring maps or as base maps for plotting data—they will hardly ever be useful in providing basic data for research.

The first quarter-inch series was begun in 1859 and completed in 1888; it has gone through various revisions and editions since then and is currently in its sixth series. The half-inch began publication in 1903 and later included a number of 'district' maps—of areas such as the Cotswolds and Birmingham; it was abandoned as a national series in 1961.

Of some interest to the historian may be the county administrative maps, published mostly at half-inch scale from the late 1880s. They developed from the county index maps to the 6-inch and 25-inch plans which showed parish boundaries. The earliest administrative maps were at quarter-inch scale, and showed civil parishes and sanitary districts. By 1900, similar maps at half-inch scale were appearing, showing, in addition, poor law unions, rural and urban districts, and boroughs. Since then, they have added river catchment area boundaries and Parliamentary divisions. From 1965 their scale was changed to 1:100,000.

The final series is the 2½-inch or 1:25,000, which was first produced for military use in the First World War, but then covered only the eastern counties. A new series was begun in the 1930s, and it eventually became the Pathfinder series of maps so beloved of walkers today. Produced from the 6-inch maps, these maps are not original in any way, but they do provide what is often a very useful scale for plotting the results of local research—and simply finding places; they are the smallest scale maps to show every field, and they also show rights of way in some detail, which the 6-inch does not.

Ordnance Survey maps exist in a bewildering number of scales, editions, series and dates for most areas and the first problem is to decide which scale or scales are likely to yield information for a particular topic. Research into railways in rural Oxfordshire will require the 1-inch and 6-inch maps, whereas a study of lampposts in Victorian Manchester will need the 1:1056 or 1:500 plans. In 1963, Joan Thirsk in reviewing a volume of the *Victoria County History of Middlesex* noted that 'the Ordnance Survey map has been used with as much care as more conventional historical documents, and the result is most rewarding'. Oliver Rackham's *History of the Countryside* (1986) makes great use of early O.S. maps to depict landscape features such as woodland, fields and roads—some still remaining, others long since gone.

For 1-inch and 6-inch maps the most likely repositories are the local history library or local record office, although the main local library or the local council may also have a good collection. University libraries and geography departments are equally worth checking. In the last resort, though, the precise map you need may be in one of the copyright libraries: the Map Library of the British Library, or the Cambridge or Oxford (Bodleian) University Libraries. The Royal Geographical Society also has a large collection of plans up to 6-inch scale. Ordnance maps over 50 years old may be copied freely but the copying of more recent maps requires a licence from the Ordnance Survey.

Appendix

SCALES

The following table lists the main scales mentioned in the text.

Representative fraction	Inches/mile (M = metric)	Common name	Tithe maps chains/inch	Goad Maps feet/inch
1:253,440	¼	quarter-inch		
1:250,000	M ≏ ¼			
1:126,720	½	half-inch		
1:100,000	M ≏ ¾			
1 :63,360	1			
1:50,000	M ≏ 1¼	one-inch		
1:25,344	2½			
1:25,000	M ≏ 2½	two-and-a-half-inch		
1:10,560	6			
1:10,000	M ≏ 6	six-inch		
1:6336	10		8	
1:3168	20		4	
1:2500	M ≏ 25	twenty-five inch (true 25-inch = 1:2534)		
1:2376	26.7		3	
1:1584	40		2	
1:1250	M ≏ 50	fifty-inch (true 50-inch = 1:1267)		
1:1056	60	five-foot		
1:792	80		1	
1:640				30
1:528	120	ten-foot		
1:500	M ≏ 127			
1:480	132			40
1:240	264			80

138

BIBLIOGRAPHY

A note on the references

References to books are given as follows: Author, (Date), *Title*, (Place). The place of publication is only given if other than London; where a work is published by a particular body this is named. Articles in journals are referred to as follows: Author, (Date), 'Title', *Journal*, **Volume**, Pages.

The following abbreviations are used:

Antiquarian	*Archaeological*	*Association*	*Bulletin*	*Cartographic*
Geographical	*Historical*	*Journal*	*Library*	*Miscellany*
Natural	*Philosophical*	*Proceedings*	*Record*	*Review*
Series	*Society*	*Transactions*	*University*	*NS* = New Series

County names are generally abbreviated.

Accessions to Repositories (Annual) Published by the Royal Commission on Historical Manuscripts: HMSO

Albert, W. (1972) *The Turnpike Road System in England, 1663-1840*

Andrews, J. and Dury, A. (1952) 'Map of Wiltshire, 1773' *Wilts. Arch. and Nat. Hist. Soc. Records Branch*, **8** (facsimile)

Armitage, G. (1990/95) 'County Cartobibliographies of England and Wales: a select list' *The Map Collector*, **52**, 16-24; **73**, 20-3

Armitage, G. (1994) 'Cartobibliographies of city and town plans of England and Wales: a select list' *The Map Collector*, **66**, 42-7; **67**, 33-40

Aspinall, P.J. (1975) 'The use of nineteenth-century fire insurance plans for the urban historian' *Local Historian*, **11/6**, 342-9

Aston, M. (1985) *Interpreting the Landscape*

Aston, M. and Rowley, T. (1974) *Landscape Archaeology*

Bagley, J.J. (1971) *Historical Interpretations* **2** (County Maps and Town Plans, 173-87; Enclosure and Tithe, 200-217)

Bagley, J.J. and Hodgkiss, A.G. (1985) *Lancashire: A History of the County in Early Maps* (Manchester)

Baker, A.R.H. (1962) 'Local history in early estate maps' *Amateur Historian*, **5**, 66-71

Baker, A.R.H. and Harley, J.B. (1973) *Man Made the Land*

Baptist, M. (1967) 'Eighteenth century maps and estate plans of Bromley, Beckenham and Penge' *Archaeologia Cantiana*, **81**, 31-8

Barber, P. and Board, C. (eds) (1993) *Tales from the Map Room*

Barker, F. and Jackson, P. (1990) *The History of London in Maps*

Barker, K. and Kain, R. J. P. (1991) *Maps and History in South-West England* (Exeter)

Batten, K. and Bennett, F. (1996) *The Printed Maps of Devon—County Maps 1575-1837*

Baum, R.K. (1972) *Antique Maps of Leicestershire* (Loughborough)

Baynton-Williams, A. (1992) *Town and City Maps of the British Isles, 1800-1855*

Beech, G. (1985) 'Tithe Maps' *The Map Collector*, **33**, 20-25

Bendall, A. S. (1992) *Maps, Land and Society: a History with a Cartobibliography of Cambridgeshire Estate Maps, c.1600-1836* (Cambridge)

Beresford, M. (1984) *History on the Ground* (little changed from 1957 edition)

Beresford, M.W. and St Joseph, J.K.S. (1979) *Medieval England—An Aerial Survey*

Bergess, W. (1992) *Kent Maps and Plans*

Bond, M. (1964) *The Records of Parliament: A Guide for Genealogists and Local Historians* (Canterbury)

Bonser, K.J. and Nichols, H. (1960) 'Printed maps and plans of Leeds, 1711-1900' *Thoresby Soc.*, **47** (For 1958)

Booth, C. (1889; 1891) *Labour and Life of the People* (2 vols plus appendix volume of maps)

Booth, C. (1892-7) *Life and Labour of the People in London* (9 vols plus maps; 2nd edition in 17 vols, 1902-3)

Booth, J. (1977) *Antique Maps of Wales* (Montacute)

Booth, J. (1979) *Looking at Old Maps*

Booth, J.R.S. (1980) *Public Boundaries and Ordnance Survey, 1840-1980*

Bowen, E. (1970) *Britannia Depicta or Ogilby*

Improved (Newcastle) (originally published in 1720; facsimile with introduction by J.B. Harley)

Bowen, E. and Kitchin, T. (1971) *The Royal English Atlas* (Newton Abbot) (Facsimile of 18th-century county maps with introduction by J.B. Harley)

Bowen, I. (1914) *The great Inclosures of Common Lands in Wales*

Brewer, J.G. (1972) *Enclosures and the Open Fields: A Bibliography* (British Agricultural Hist. Soc.)

British Museum (1928) *Four Maps of Great Britain designed by Matthew Paris about A.D. 1250*

British Museum (1962) *Catalogue of the Manuscript Maps, Charts and Plans* (3 vols, 1844-61). See also various *Catalogues of Additions to Manuscripts*

British Museum (1967) *Catalogue of Printed Maps, Charts and Plans, complete to 1964* (15 vols). See also *Ten Year Supplement, 1965-74* (1978)

Brunel University Library (1986) *Railway Maps and the Railway Clearing House* (a collection of articles connected with the David Garnett collection in the library)

Buckinghamshire Record Office (1961) *Catalogue of Maps*

Buckinghamshire Rec. Soc. (1964) *Buckinghamshire Estate Maps* (facsimiles). See also Elvey (1963)

Bull, G.B.G. (1956) 'Thomas Milne's Land Utilization map of the London area in 1800' *Geog. J.*, **122/1**, 25-30

Bull, G.B.G. (1958), 'Elizabethan maps of the Lower Lea valley' *Geog. J.*, **124/3**, 375-8

Burden, E. (1988-95) *Printed Maps of Berkshire, 1574-1900* [Vol 1: County maps, 1988; Vol 2: Town Plans, 1992; Vol 3: Environs and District Maps, 1995. All since revised]

Butler, D.J. (1972) *The Town Plans of Chichester 1595-1898* (W. Sussex County Council)

Campbell, E.M.J. (1962) 'The beginnings of the characteristic sheet to English maps' *Geog. J.*, **128/4**, 411-15

Cantor, L. (1982) *The English Medieval Landscape*

Carpenter, A.M. (1967) 'The value of the tithe surveys to the study of land ownership and occupancy in the mid-nineteenth century, with special reference to south Hertfordshire' *Hertfordshire Past and Present*, 7, 48-52

Carr, A.P. (1962) 'Cartographic record and historical accuracy' *Geography*, **47**, 135-44

Carroll, R.A. *The Printed Maps of Lincolnshire, 1576-1900* (Lincoln)

Chambers, B. (1964) 'M.J. Armstrong in Norfolk; the progress of an eighteenth century county survey' *Geog J.*, **130**, 427-31

Chambers, B. (1983) 'Printed maps and town plans of Bedfordshire, 1576-1900' *Bedfordshire Hist. Rec. Soc.*, **62**

Chapman, J. (1987) 'The extent and nature of Parliamentary Enclosure' *Agricultural Hist Rev*, **35**, 25-35

Chapman, J. (1992) *A Guide to Parliamentary Enclosures in Wales* (Cardiff)

Cheshire County Council (1953) *Alphabetical List of Deposited Plans at the County Record Office ... regarding Railways ...*

Chibnall, J. (1995) *A Directory of U.K. Map Collections*, Map Curators' Group Publication No.4, The British Cartographic Society

Chubb, T. (1912) 'A descriptive catalogue of printed maps of Wiltshire, 1576-1885' *Wilts. Arch. Soc.*, **37**

Chubb, T. (1927) *The Printed Maps in the Atlases of Great Britain and Ireland: a Bibliography 1579-1870* (reprinted 1966)

Chubb, T. and Stephen, G.H. (1928) *Descriptive List of the Printed Maps of Norfolk, 1574-1916; Descriptive List of Norwich Plans, 1541-1914* (Norwich)

Clark, E.A.G. (1960) *The Ports of the Exe Estuary, 1660-1860*

Close, C. (1969) *The Early Years of the Ordnance Survey* (Newton Abbot) (reprint of 1926, with introduction by J.B. Harley)

Coakley, F.P. (forthcoming) *Printed Maps of the Isle of Man, 1605-1900*

Cole, G. and Roper, J. (1970) *Plans of English Towns, 1810* (Monmouth)

Constable, K.M. (1932) 'The early printed plans of Exeter, 1587-1724' *Trans. Devonshire Assoc.*, **64**, 455-73

Cook, K.S. and McIntosh, R.P. (1991) *One-Inch District and Tourist Maps* (Charles Close Society)

Cowling, G.C. (1959) *A Descriptive List of the Printed Maps of Shropshire, 1577-1900* (Shropshire County Council)

Crone, G.R. (1961) *Early Maps of the British Isles A.D. 1000 - A.D. 1579* (Royal Geog. Soc., London) (a set of reproductions with a commentary)

Crosthwaite, P. (1968) *A Series of Accurate Maps of the Principal Lakes of Cumberland, Westmorland and Lancashire* (Newcastle) (facsimile of c.1790 maps with introduction by W. Rollinson)

Crump, W.B. (1928) 'The genesis of Warburton's map of Yorkshire, 1720' *Thoresby Soc. Miscellanea*, **28**, 385-404

Cubbon, A.M. (1967) *Early Maps of the Isle of Man* (Douglas)

Curwen, J.F. (1918) 'A descriptive Catalogue of the printed maps of Cumberland and Westmorland' *Trans. Cumb. and West. Antiq. and Arch. Soc.*, (NS) **18**

Davies, A. (1987) *The Map of London: From 1746 to the Present Day*

Davies, R. (1982) *Estate Maps of Wales 1600-1836* (Aberystwyth)

Davies, R. (forthcoming) *An Atlas of the Tithe Maps of Wales* (Aberystwyth)

Dickens, B. (1938) 'Premonstratensian Itineraries from a Titchfield Abbey MS at Welbeck' *Proc. Leeds Phil. Soc.*, **4**, 349-61

Dickins, K.W. (1981) *A Catalogue of Manuscript Maps in ... Sussex Archaeological Society* (Lewes)

Dickinson, P.G. (1968) *Maps in the County Record Office, Huntingdon*

Docton, K.H. (1957) 'Lancaster, 1684' *Trans. Hist. Soc. of Lancs. and Cheshire*, **109**, 125-42

Dodd, A.H. (1951) *The Industrial Revolution in North Wales* (2nd edition)

Dyos, H.J. (1957) 'Some social costs of railway building in London' *J. Transport History*, **3**/1, 23-30

Dyos, H.J. and Aldcroft, D.H. (1969) *British Transport: an Economic Survey from the Seventeenth Century to the Twentieth* (Leicester)

Eden, P. (ed.) (1975-79) *Dictionary of Land Surveyors and Local Cartographers of Great Britain and Ireland, 1550-1850* (3 vols plus supplement)

Eden, P. (1983) 'Three Elizabethan estate surveyors: Peter Kempe, Thomas Clerke and Thomas Langdon' in Tyacke (1983), 68-83

Edwards, A.C. and Newton, K.C. (1984) *The Walkers of Hanningfield—Surveyors and Mapmakers Extraordinary*

Elliot, J. (1987) *The City in Maps—Urban Mapping to 1900*

Elvey, E.M. (1963) 'A hand-list of Buckinghamshire estate maps' *Bucks. Rec. Soc.*

Emmison, F.G. (1947) *Catalogue of Maps in the Essex Record Office, 1566-1855* (plus supplements: 1952, 1964 and 1968)

Emmison, F.G. (1947) *The Art of the Map-Maker in Essex*

Emmison, F.G. (ed.) (1955) *County Maps of Essex, 1576-1852* (Essex Record Office)

Emmison, F.G. (1974) *Archives and Local History*

Emmison, F.G. and Fowler, G.H. (1930) *Catalogue of Maps in the Bedfordshire County Muniments*

Emmison, F.G. and Smith, W.J. (1980) 'Material for theses in local record offices and libraries' *Hist. Assoc.* (Helps for Students of History Series), **87**

Evans, E.J. and Crosby, A.G. (1997) *Tithes: Maps, Apportionments and the 1836 Act* (Chichester)

Evans, G.L. (1968) 'Richard Norwood, Surveyor of Stephenage' *Hertfordshire Past and Present*, **8**, 29-32

Evans, G.L. (1978) *Tithes and the Tithe Commutation Act, 1836*

Evans, I.M. and Lawerence, H. (1979) *Christopher Saxton, Elizabethan Map-Maker* (Wakefield). See also Lawrence (1981)

Field, J. (1972) *English Field-Names* (Newton Abbot)

Fletcher, D.H. (1995) *The Emergence of Estate Maps, Christ Church, Oxford, 1600 to 1840* (Oxford)

Fletcher, J. (1849) 'Moral and educational statistics of England and Wales' *J. Statistical Soc. of London*, **12**, 151-76; 189-335

Foot, W. (1994) *Maps for Family History* (PRO)

Fordham, A. (1965) 'Town plans of the British Isles' *Map Collectors Circle*, **22**

Fordham, H.G. (1914) *Studies in Carto-Bibliography* (reprinted 1969)

Fordham, H.G. (1924) *The Road-Books and Itineraries of Great Britain, 1570-1850* (Cambridge)

Fordham, H.G. (1925) *Paterson's Roads—Daniel Paterson, his maps and itineraries, 1738-1825*

Fordham, H.G. (1927) 'The road-books of Wales with a catalogue, 1775-1850' *Archaeologia Cambrensis*, **82**

Foster, J. (1989) *British Archives*

Freeman, M. and Aldcroft, D. (1985) *The Atlas of British Railway History*

Fried, A. and Elman, R.M. (1969) *Charles Booth's London*

Frostick, R.A. (forthcoming) *Printed Maps of Norfolk, 1574-1800*

Garnett, D. (1984) 'John Airey's undated early railway maps' *The Map Collector*, **26**, 28-31. See also several articles on other early railway maps in *J. Railway and Canal Hist. Soc.*, **21** (1975) and **23** (1977)

Gilbert, E.W. (1958) 'Pioneer maps of health and disease in England' *Geog. J.*, **124**, 172-83

Glanville, P. (1972) *London in Maps*

Goad, Chas. E. Ltd. (1984) *Goad Fire Insurance Plans Catalogue 1984*

Goldmark, M. and Traylen, A.R. (1985) *Maps of Rutland* (Stamford)

Gough, R. (1780) *British Topography*

Hadfield, C. (1955-6) 'Sources for the history of British canals' *J. Transport History*, **2**, 80-89

Hadfield, C. (1972-3) *The Canals of Yorkshire and North East England* (2 vols) (Newton Abbot)

Hadfield, C. and Biddle, G. (1970) *The Canals of North West England* (2 vols)

Handford, C.C. (1971) 'Some maps of the County of Derby' *Derbys. Misc.* (Supplement)

Harley, J.B. (1962) *Christopher Greenwood—County Map-Maker, and his Worcestershire Map of 1822* (Worcester)

Harley, J.B. (1963-64) 'The Society of Arts and the surveys of English counties, 1759-1809' *J. Royal Soc. of Arts*, **112**, 43-46; 119-124; 269-275; 538-543

Harley, J.B. (1964) *The Historian's Guide to Ordnance Survey Maps*

Harley, J.B. (1965) 'The re-mapping of England, 1750-

1800' *Imago Mundi*, **19**, 56-67

Harley, J.B. (1968) 'The evaluation of early maps: towards a methodology' *Imago Mundi*, **22**, 62-74

Harley, J.B. (1968a) 'A map of the county of Lancashire, 1786, by William Yates' *Hist. Soc. Lancs. and Cheshire* (reduced facsimile and introduction)

Harley, J.B. (1971) 'Place-names on the early Ordnance Survey maps of England and Wales' *Cartog. J.*, **8/2**, 91-104

Harley, J.B. (1972) *Maps for the Local Historian*

Harley, J.B. (1975) *Ordnance Survey Maps—a Descriptive Manual* (Southampton)

Harley, J.B. (1979) 'The Ordnance Survey and land-use mapping: Parish Books of Reference and the County Series 1:2500 maps, 1855-1918' *Historical Geography Research Group: Research Paper Series*, **2**

Harley, J.B. (1982) 'The Ordnance Survey 1:528 Board of Health town plans in Warwickshire, 1848-1854' in Slater, T.R. and Jarvis, P.J., *Field and Forest* (Norwich)

Harley, J.B. (1983) 'Meaning and ambiguity in Tudor cartography' in Tyacke (1983), 22-45

Harley, J.B. (1988) 'Maps, knowledge and power' in Cosgrove, D. and Daniels, S. (eds), *The Iconography of Landscape* (Cambridge), 277-312

Harley, J.B. (1989) 'Deconstructing the map' *Cartographica*, **26, 1**-20

Harley, J.B. and Dunning, R.W. (1981) 'Somerset Maps—Day and Masters 1782; Greenwood 1822' *Somerset Rec. Soc.*, **76**

Harley, J.B. and Laxton, P. (1974) 'A Survey of the County Palatine of Chester, P.P. Burdett, 1777' *Hist. Soc. of Lancs. and Cheshire* (Occasional Series **1**)

Harris, A. (1961) *The Rural Landscape of the East Riding of Yorkshire, 1700-1850* (Oxford)

Harrison, B. (1976) 'Pubs' in Dyos, H.J. and Woolf, M. *The Victorian City*, **1**, 161-90 (originally published in 1973)

Harvey, P.D.A. (1965) *A Medieval Oxfordshire Village*

Harvey, P.D.A. (1965a) 'An Elizabethan map of manors in north Dorset' *The British Museum Quarterly*, **29**

Harvey, P.D.A. (1980) *The History of Topographical Maps: Symbols, Pictures and Surveys*

Harvey, P.D.A. (1981) 'The Portsmouth map of 1545 and the introduction of scale maps into England' in Webb, J. *et al*, *Hampshire Studies*, 33-49

Harvey, P.D.A. (1985) 'Estate surveyors and the spread of the scale-map in England, 1550-80' Paper presented at 11th International Conference on the History of Cartography, Ottawa

Harvey, P.D.A. (1993) *Maps in Tudor England*

Harvey, P.D.A. and Thorpe, H. (1959) *The Printed Maps of Warwickshire, 1576-1900* (Warwick)

Higham, J. (1997) *The Antique County Maps of Cumberland* (Carlisle)

Hindle, B.P. (1980) 'The towns and roads of the Gough Map (c.1360)' *The Manchester Geographer*, **1/1** (1980) 35-49

Hindle, B.P. (1982) *Medieval Roads* (Shire Archaeology, Princes Risborough) Revised 1998 as *Medieval Roads and Tracks*

Hindle, B.P. (1984) *Roads and Trackways of the Lake District* (Ashbourne) Revised 1998 as *Roads and Tracks of the Lake District* (Carnforth)

Hindle, B.P. (1985) 'The contextual study of atlases' *The Manchester Geographer*, **6**, 7-10

Hindle, B.P. (1993) *Roads, Tracks and their Interpretation*

Hodson, D. (1974) *The Printed Maps of Hertfordshire, 1577-1900* (originally in the *Map Collectors' Circle*, 1969-72)

Hodson, D. (1978) 'Maps of Portsmouth before 1801' *Portsmouth Rec. Ser.*

Hodson, D. (1984, 1989) *County Atlases of the British Isles published after 1703* (2 vols) (Tewin)

Hodson, D. (1984a) 'Dating county maps through mapsellers' advertisements' *The Map Collector* **26**, 16-18

Hodson, Y. (1987) 'The military influence on the official mapping of Britain in the eighteenth century' *IMCoS Journal* [International Map Collectors' Society] **27**, 21-31

Hodson, Y. (1989) *The Ordnance Surveyors' Drawings 1789-c.1840: the original manuscript maps, with an introduction, summary listing and indexes by Tony Campbell* (Reading)

Hodson, Y. (1991a) *'An Inch to the Mile': the Ordnance Survey One-inch Map, 1805-1974*

Hodson, Y. (1991b) *Board of Ordnance Surveys 1683-1820. Ordnance Survey: Past, Present and Future*

Hooke, J.M. and Perry, R.A. 'The planimetric accuracy of tithe maps' *Cartog. J.*, **13**, 177-83

Hoskins, W.G. (1955) *The Making of the English Landscape*

Hoskins, W.G. (1967) *Fieldwork in Local History*

Hoskins, W.G. (1972) *Local History in England*

Howgego, J. (1978) *Printed Maps of London, 1553-1850* (2nd edition)

Hull, F. (1973) *Catalogue of Estate Maps 1590-1840 in the Kent County Archives Office*

Hull, F. (1992) *Kentish Maps and Map-Makers, 1590-1840* (Maidstone)

Hunt, J. and Smith, R. (1985) 'Nineteenth-century maps: some cartographical problems and solutions' *Cartog. J.*, **22/1**, 50-6

Hyde, R. (1967) 'Ward maps of the City of London' *Map Collectors' Circle*, **38**

Hyde, R. (1970-73) 'Notes on a collection of London insurance surveys, 1794-1807' *J. Soc. of Archivists*, **4**, 327-9; 523

Hyde, R. (1975) *Printed Maps of Victorian London*

Hyde, R. (1975a) 'Reform Bill plans' *Bull. of the Soc. of Univ. Cartographers*, **9**, 1-9

Hyde, R. (1976) 'The "Act to Regulate Parochial Assessments", 1836, and its contribution to the mapping of London' *Guildhall Studies in London History*, **11/2**, 54-68

Hyde, R. (1978) 'Cartographers versus the Demon Drink' *The Map Collector*, **9**, 22-7

Hyde, R. (1979) 'Maps that made cabmen honest' *The Map Collector*, **9**, 14-17

Hyde, R. (1994) *A Prospect of Britain—the Town Panoramas of Samuel and Nathaniel Buck*

Iredale, D. (1974) *Local History Research and Writing*

Johnson, L.C. (1953-4) 'Historical Records of the British Transport Commission' *J. Transport History*, **1**, 82-96

Jones, I.E. (1985) 'Montgomeryshire on old maps' *Montgom. Collections*, **75**, 9-28

Kain, R.J.P. (1984) 'The Tithe files of mid-nineteenth century England and Wales' in Reed, M. *Discovering Past Landscapes*

Kain, R.J.P. (1986) *An Atlas and Index of the Tithe Files of Mid-Nineteenth Century England and Wales* (Cambridge)

Kain, R.J.P. and Baigent, E. (1992) *The Cadastral Map in the Service of the State—a history of property mapping* (Chicago)

Kain, R.J.P. and Oliver, R. (1995) *The Tithe Maps of England and Wales* (Cambridge)

Kain, R.J.P. and Prince, H.C. (1985) *The Tithe Surveys of England and Wales* (Cambridge)

King, G. L. (1988) *The Printed Maps of Staffordshire* (Stafford)

Kingsley, D. (1982) 'Printed maps of Sussex, 1575-1900' *Sussex Rec. Soc.*, **72**

Kitchen, F. (1997) John Norden (*c*.1547-1625): estate surveyor, topographer, county mapmaker and devotional writer' *Imago Mundi*, **49**, 43-60

Koeman, C. (1968) 'Levels of historical evidence in early maps (with examples)' *Imago Mundi*, **22**, 75-80

Lambert, A. (1956) 'Early maps and local studies' *Geography*, **41**, 167-77

Lawrence, H. (1981) 'New Saxton discoveries' *The Map Collector*, **17**, 30-31

Lawrence, H. and Hoyle, R. (1981a) 'New maps and surveys by Christopher Saxton' *Yorks. Arch. J.*, **53**, 51-56

Laxton, P. (1976) 'The geodetic and topographical evaluation of English county maps, 1740-1840' *Cartog. J.*, **12**, 37-54

Lee, J. (1957) *Maps and Plans of Manchester and Salford, 1650-1843* (Altrincham) (note also a set of 6 facsimiles published as *Maps of Manchester, 1650-1848* by Manchester Public Libraries, 1969)

Leighfield, J. (forthcoming) *Printed Maps of Oxfordshire*

Lewis, M.G. (1949) 'The printed maps of Merioneth, 1578-1900' *J. Merioneth Hist. & Rec. Soc.* **1**

Lewis, M.G. (1955) 'The printed maps of Cardiganshire, 1578-1900' *Ceredigion*, **2/4**, 244-76

Lewis, M.G. (1972) 'The printed maps of Breconshire, 1578-1900' *Brycheiniog*, **16**, 139-71

Lewis, M.G. (1977) T*he Printed Maps of Radnorshire, 1578-1900* (Aberystwyth)

List and Index Society (1971, 1972) *Inland Revenue Tithe Maps and Apportionments* (**68**, **83**)

List and Index Society (1986) *Tithe Files, Beds-Leics., 1836-1870* (**219**)

Lobel, M.D. (1968) 'The value of early maps as evidence for the topography of English towns' *Imago Mundi*, **22**, 50-61

Lobel, M.D. (1969, 1974, 1989) *Historic Towns* (3 vols)

Lynam, E. (1936) 'Maps of the Fenland' in *The Victoria History of the Counties of England: Huntingdonshire*, **3**

Lynam, E. (1944) *British Maps and Map-Makers*

Lynam, E. (1953) *The Mapmaker's Art: Essays on the History of Maps*

MacEachran, A.M. and Johnson, G.B. (1987) 'The evolution, application and implications of strip format travel maps' *Cartog J*, **24/2**, 147-58

Margary, H., Lympne Castle, Kent, publishes reproductions of various maps, usually with an introduction [author's name in square brackets below]. His list includes:

County maps
Berkshire: Rocque, 1761 [P. Laxton]; Essex: Chapman and André, 1777 [F.G. Emmison]; Kent: Andrews, Dury and Herbert, 1769; Stafford: Yates, 1775 [A.D.M. Phillips]; Yorkshire: Jefferys, 1775 [J.B. Harley]

Collections of county maps
Hampshire, 1575-1826 (includes Taylor, 1759; Milne, 1791) [P. Laxton]

Surrey, 1575-1825 (includes Rocque, 1768; Lindley and Crosley, 1792; Greenwood, 1823) [W. Ravenhill]

Sussex, 1575-1825 (includes Yeakell and Gardner, 1783; Gream, 1793; Greenwood, 1825) [R. A. Skelton]

Maps of London
Collection, 1553-1667 [R. Hyde]; Agas, 1562 [J. Fisher] An A-Z of Elizabethan London; Ogilby and Morgan, 1676 [R. Hyde]; Morgan, 1681-2 [R. Hyde];

Rocque, 1746 [R. Hyde] An A-Z of Georgian London; Rocque, 1746 [J. Howgego] Ten miles around London; Horwood, 1813 [P. Laxton]; Greenwood, 1827; Stanford, 1862 [R. Hyde]; Bacon, 1888 [R. Hyde] An A-Z of Victorian London

Others
Saxton's S. E. England, 1579; Van den Keere's County Atlas, 1605; Wren and Andrews' Canterbury, 1768

Ordnance Survey Old Series One-Inch (1975-87) **1**: Kent, E. Sussex, Essex and S. Suffolk (includes the Mudge map of Kent). **2**: Devon, Cornwall & W. Somerset. **3**: South Central England. **4**: Central England. **5**: Lincs., Rutland & East Anglia. **6**: Wales. **7**: North Central England. **8**: North England & I.O.M. (Reproductions of early states of the maps, with introductions and carto-bibliographies by J.B. Harley, Y. O'Donoghue, R.R. Oliver, J.B. & B.A.D. Manterfield.)

Mason, A.S. (1990) *Essex on the Map—the Eighteenth Century Land Surveyors of Essex* (Chelmsford)
Michael, D.P.M. (1985) *The Mapping of Monmouthshire* (Bristol)
Morden, R. (1965) *The County Maps from William Camden's Britannia, 1695* (Newton Abbot, 1972)
Morgan, M. (1979) *Historical Sources in Geography*
Moule, T. (1990) *The County Maps of Old England* [reprint of 1830s maps and text]
Munby, L.M. (1969) 'Tithe apportionments and maps' *History*, **54**, 68-71

Needell, K. (1995) *Printed Maps of Somersetshire, 1575-1860*
Newton, K.C. (1969-70) 'The Walkers of Essex' *Bull. of the Soc. of Univ. Cartographers*, **4**, 1-6
Nicholson, T.R. (1983) *Wheels on the Road: Road maps of Britain, 1870-1940* (Norwich) (note that this book reproduces no maps—only their covers)
Nicolson, N. and Hawkyard, A. (1988) *The Counties of Britain—a Tudor Atlas by John Speed*
Norden, J. (1966) *Orford Ness* (a selection of maps, mainly by John Norden)
Norden, J. (1966a) *A Topographical and Historical Description of Cornwall* (1584) (Newcastle) (originally published in 1728)
North, F.S. (1935) *The Maps of Wales* (Cardiff)
Norton, J.E. (1950) *Guide to the National and Provincial Directories of England and Wales*

O'Donoghue, Y. (1977) *William Roy, 1726-1790, Pioneer of the Ordnance Survey* (British Library)
Ogilby, J. (1675) *Britannia* (Reprinted Amsterdam, 1970; London 1939)
Oliver, R. (1982) 'What's what with the New Series' *Sheetlines*, **5**, 3-8
Oliver, R. (1983) 'The Ordnance Survey in Lancashire in the 1840s' *Sheetlines*, **8**, 2-8
Oliver, R. (1991a) *Ordnance Survey ... Indexes to the 1/2500 and 6-Inch Scale Maps* (c.1905-6)
Oliver, R. (1991b) 'More than a thumb nail: the large scale plans of the Ordnance Survey' *The Map Collector*, **54**, 36-40
Oliver, R. (1993) *Ordnance Survey Maps—a Concise Guide for Historians*
Ottley, G. (1983) *A Bibliography of Railway History* (revised second edition)
Ottley, G. (1988) *A Bibliography of Railway History: Supplement* (covers publications 1963-80)
Oxfordshire County Council (1983) *A Handlist of Plans, Sections and Books of Reference for the proposed Railways in Oxfordshire, 1825-1936* (Oxford)
Owen, T. and Pilbeam, E. (1992) *Ordnance Survey—Map Makers to Britain since 1791*

Parsons, E.J.S., *The Map of Great Britain c.A.D.1360, known as the Gough Map* (Oxford, Bodleian Library) (commentary and facsimile)
Pawson, E. (1977) *Transport and Economy—The Turnpike Roads of Eighteenth Century Britain*
Phillips, A.D.M. (1980) 'The seventeenth-century maps and surveys of William Fowler' *Cartog. J.*, **17/2**, 100-110
Phillips, A.D.M. (1981) 'William Fowler's Staffordshire maps' *Trans. South Staffs. Arch. Soc.*, **25**, 21-33
Phillips, A.D.M. (1984) *A Map of the County of Stafford by William Yates, 1775* (Staffordshire Record Society/Harry Margary) (a reproduction with a commentary)
Phillips, C.W. (1980) *Archaeology in the Ordnance Survey* (Council for British Archaeology)
Powell, R.F.P. (1978-9) 'The printed road maps of Breconshire, 1675-1870' *Brycheiniog*, **18**, 85-99
Pritchard, J.E. (1928) 'Old plans and views of Bristol' *Trans. Bristol and Gloucs. Arch. Soc.*, **48**. See also facsimiles in the same society's *A Gloucestershire and Bristol Atlas* (1961)
Public Record Office (1967) *Maps and Plans in the P.R.O. I. British Isles c.1410-1860*

Rackham, O. (1986) *The History of the Countryside*
Raistrick, A. (1969) *Yorkshire Maps and Map-Makers*
Ravenhill, W.L.D. (1965) *Benjamin Donn—A Map of the County of Devon, 1765* (facsimile and commentary)
Ravenhill, W.L.D. (1972) *John Norden's Manuscript Maps of Cornwall and its Nine Hundreds* (Exeter) (facsimile and introduction)
Ravenhill, W.L.D. (1973) 'The mapping of Great Haseley and Latchford' *Cartog. J.*, **10/2**, 105-11
Ravenhill, W.L.D. (1983) 'Christopher Saxton's

surveying: an enigma' in Tyacke (1983), 112-119

Ravenhill, W.L.D. (1985) 'Mapping a United Kingdom' *History Today*, **35**, 27-33

Ravenhill, W. (1992) *Christopher Saxton's 16th Century Maps—The Counties of England and Wales*

Ravenhill, W.L.D. and Padel, O.J. (1991) 'Joel Gascoyne: a Map of the County of Cornwall, 1699' *Devon and Cornwall Rec. Soc.* (NS) **34**, (facsimile and commentary)

Rawnsley, J.E. (1970) *Antique Maps of Yorkshire and their Makers* (Guiseley)

Record Repositories in Great Britain—A Geographical Directory (published every three or four years by the Royal Commission on Historical Manuscripts, with the HMSO)

Return of all Tithes Commuted and Apportioned under the Acts for Commutation of Tithes (1887) British Sessional Papers, House of Commons, **64**, 239-533

Richeson, A.W. (1966) *English Land Measuring to 1800; Instruments and Practices* (M.I.T.)

Riden, P. (1983) *Local History*

Riden, P. (1987) *Record Sources for Local History*

Robinson, A.H.W. (1962) *Marine Cartography in Britain* (Leicester)

Rodger, E.M. (1972) *The Large Scale County Maps of the British Isles, 1596-1850* (Oxford) 2nd edition

Rodger, E.M. (1989-95) 'Large scale English county maps and plans of cities not printed in atlases' (Parts 13-17; continuation of Tooley (1978-87)) *The Map Collector*, **47** (1989) Hants; **53** (1990) Hereford; **58** (1992) Herts; **63** (1993) Hunts; **71** (1995) IOW.

Rogers, A. and Rowley, T. (1974) *Landscapes and Documents*

Rowley, G. (1984) *British Fire Insurance Plans* (Hatfield). See also Rowley, G. (1984a) 'An introduction to fire insurance plans' *The Map Collector*, **29**, 14-19

Rowley, G. (1985) 'British Fire insurance plans: the goad productions, c.1885-c.1970' *Archives*, **17/74**, 67-78

Rowley, T. (1972) *The Shropshire Landscape*

Russell, E. and Russell, R.C. (1982) *Landscape Changes in South Humberside* (Hull)

Russell, E. and Russell, R.C. (1983) *Making New Landscapes in Lincolnshire* (Lincoln)

Russell, E. and Russell, R.C. (1985) *Old and New Landscapes in the Horncastle Area* (Lincoln)

Russell, R.C. (1974) 'Parliamentary enclosure and the documents for its study' in Rogers, A. and Rowley, T. (1974)

Russell, R.C. (1977) 'Parliamentary enclosure' in Rogers, A., *Group Projects in Local History* (Folkestone)

Schofield, J. (1983) 'Ralph Treswell's surveys of London houses c.1612' in Tyacke (1983), 86-92

Seymour, W.A. (ed.) (1980) *A History of the Ordnance Survey* (Folkestone)

Sharp, H.A. (1929) *An Historical Catalogue of Surrey Maps* (Croydon)

Shaw, G. (1982) 'British directories as sources in historical geography' *Hist. Geography Research Group: Research Paper Series*, **8**

Shaw, G. and Tipper, A. (1989) *British Directories— a Bibliography and Guide to Directories published in England and Wales (1850-1950) and Scotland (1773-1950)* (Leicester)

Shirley, R.W. (1980) *Early Printed Maps of the British Isles: A Bibliography, 1477-1650* (revised 1991)

Shirley, R.W. (1988) *Early Printed Maps of the British Isles, 1650-1750*

(Shropshire) 1. Shropshire Record Office (1902), *Plans and Documents relating to Roads, Bridges, Railways, Canals ... etc., deposited with the Clerk of the Peace*; 2. Shropshire Record Office (1969), *Canals and Railways: A List of Plans ... deposited at the Shirehall*; 3. Local Studies Department, Shropshire Libraries (1978), *Railway Plans ...*

Simmons, J. (1953-4) 'Railway history in English local records' *J. Transport History*, **1**, 155-69

Simmons, J. (1968) *The Railways of Britain*

Skelton, R.A. (1952) *Decorative Printed Maps*

Skelton, R.A. (1952a) 'Tudor town plans in John Speed's Theatre' *Arch. J.*, **108**, 109-20

Skelton, R.A. (1962) 'The origins of the Ordnance Survey of Great Britain' *Geog. J.*, **128/4**, 415-26

Skelton, R. A. (1970) County Atlases of the British Isles, 1579-1850. A Bibliography, 1579-1703

Skelton, R.A. and Harvey, P.D.A. (eds.) (1986) *Local Maps and Plans from Medieval England* (Oxford)

Smith, B.S. (1967) 'The Dougharty family of Worcester; estate surveyors and mapmakers, 1700-60 (catalogue of Maps and Plans)' *Worcs. Hist. Soc. Misc.* II (NS), **5**, 138-80

Smith, B.S. (1967a) 'The business archives of estate agents' *J. Soc. Archivists*, **3**, 298-300

Smith, D. (1982) *Antique Maps of the British Isles*

Smith, D. (1985) *Victorian Maps of the British Isles*

Smith, D. (1985a) 'The social maps of Henry Mayhew' *Map Collector*, **30**, 2-7

Smith, D. (1988) *Maps and Plans for the Local Historian and Collector*

Smith, D. (1990) 'The representation of industry on large scale county maps of England and Wales, 1700-c.1840', *Ind. Arch. Rev.* **12/1**, 153-77

Smith, D. (1992) 'Inset town plans on large scale maps of Great Britain' *Cartog. J.*, **29/2**, 118-136

Smith, D. (1994) Public health and the large-scale mapping of British towns' *IMCoS J.* [International Map Collectors' Society] **56**, 28-46

Steer, F.W. (1962, 1968) 'A catalogue of Sussex estate and tithe award maps' *Sussex Rec. Soc.*, **61** and **66**

Stephens, W.B. (1977) *Teaching Local History* (Manchester)

Stephens, W.B. (1994) *Sources for English Local History* (Chichester)

Symonson, P. (1968) *A New Description of Kent, 1596* (Southampton) (facsimile of 1650 edition by Stent)

Tate, W.E. (1948) 'Somerset Enclosure Acts and Awards' *Somerset Arch. and Nat. Hist. Soc.*

Tate, W.E. and Turner, M.E. (1978) *A Domesday of English Enclosure Acts and Awards* (Reading)

Taylor, C. (1974) *Fieldwork in Medieval Archaeology*

Taylor, I. (1961) Map of Gloucestershire, 1777 in 'A Gloucestershire and Bristol Atlas' *Bristol and Gloucs. Arch. Soc.* (reduced facsimile)

Thomas, C. (1966) 'Estate surveys as sources in historical geography' *Nat. Lib. of Wales J.*, **14**, 451-68

Thomas, D. (1963) *Agriculture in Wales during the Napoleonic Wars*

Thomas, H.M. (1992) *A Catalogue of Glamorgan Estate maps* (Glamorgan)

Tooley, R.V. (1970) *Maps and Map-Makers*

Tooley, R.V. (1978-87) 'Large-scale English county maps and plans of cities not printed in atlases', (Parts 1-12) *The Map Collector*, **5** (1978) Beds.; **6** (1979) Berks.; **14** (1981) Bucks.; **15** (1981) Cambs.; **17** (1981) Ches.; **21** (1982) Cornwall; **24** (1983) Cumb.; **27** (1984) Derbyshire.; **30** (1985) Devon; **32** (1985) Dorset; **34** (1986) Durham; **36** (1986) Essex; **38** (1987) Gloucestershire. Continued in Rodger (1989-95).

Tooley, R.V. (1979) *Tooley's Dictionary of Mapmakers* (Tring). See also *Supplement* (1985).

Torrens, H.S. (1974) 'Early maps of the Somersetshire Coal Canal' *Cartog. J.*, **11/1**, 45-7. See also response by J.M. Eyles and reply by Torrens in the same journal, **12/1** (1975) 47-9

Turner, M. (1980) *English Parliamentary Enclosure*

Turner, M. (1984) 'The Landscape of Parliamentary Enclosures' in M. Reed, *Discovering Past Landscapes*

Turner, P.M. (1981) *Transport History: Railways (A contribution towards a Lancashire Bibliography)*, **10** (Manchester)

Turnock, D. (1982) *Railways in the British Isles*

Tyacke, S. (ed.) (1983) *English Map-Making, 1500-1650*

Tyacke, S. and Huddy, J. (1980) *Christopher Saxton and Tudor map-making*

Van Eerde, K.S. (1976) *John Ogilby*

Wadsworth, F.A. (1930) 'Nottinghamshire maps of the 16th, 17th and 18th centuries' *Trans. Thoroton Soc.*, **34**, 92-132

Wallis, H. (1981) 'The history of land-use mapping' *Cartog. J.*, **18/1**, 45-8

Wallis, H. (1994) *Historians' Guide to Early British Maps* (Royal Historical Society)

Walne, P. (1969) *A Catalogue of Manuscript Maps in the Hertfordshire Record Office* (Hertford)

Walters, G. (1968) 'Themes in the large scale mapping of Wales in the eighteenth century' *Cartog. J.*, **5**, 135-46

Walters, G. (1970) 'The Morrises and the map of Anglesey' *Welsh Hist. Rev.*, **5**, 164-71

Wardle, D.B. (1955-6) 'Sources for the history of railways at the Public Record Office' *J. Transport History*, **2**, 214-34

Warren, K.F. (1965) 'Introduction to the map resources of the British Museum' *Professional Geographer*, **17**, 1-7

Welch, E. (1964) *Southampton Maps from Elizabethan Times* (Southampton) (an introduction to 24 facsimiles)

West, J. (1997) *Village Records* (Chichester) 3rd edition

West, J. (1983) *Town Records* (Chichester)

Whitaker, H. (1933) 'A descriptive list of the printed maps of Yorkshire and its Ridings, 1577-1900' *Yorks. Arch. Soc.*, **86**

Whitaker, H. (1938) 'A descriptive list of the printed maps of Lancashire, 1577-1900' *Chetham Soc.*, **101**

Whitaker, H. (1948) 'A descriptive list of the printed maps of Northamptonshire' *Northants. Rec. Soc.*, **14**

Whitaker, H. (1949) 'A descriptive list of the maps of Northumberland, 1576-1900' (Newcastle)

Whittington, G. and Gibson, A.J.S. (1986) 'The Military Survey of Scotland, 1747-1755; a critique' *Hist. Geography Research Group: Research Paper Series*, **18**

Willan, T. S. (1936) *River Navigation in England, 1600-1750* (Oxford)

Williams, A.F. (1962) 'Bristol port plans and improvement schemes of the 18th century' *Trans. Bristol and Gloucs. Arch. Soc.*, **81**, 138-88

Winterbotham, H. St J. L. (1934) 'The National Plans' *Ordnance Survey Professional Papers* (N.S.) **16**

Woolgar, C.M. (1985) 'Some draft estate maps of the early seventeenth century' *Cartog. J.*, **22/2**, 136-43

Wyatt, G. (1978) *Maps of Buckinghamshire* (Buckingham)

Yelling, J.A. (1977) *Common Field and Enclosure in England*

INDEX

Subjects

accuracy, ix
archaeology, 130

bird's eye views, 30, 54
Board of Health plans, 84-5, 131, 134, 136
building plans, 73-4, 88-90

cab-fare maps, 28
canals, 24, 26-7, 101-6
cataloguing maps, x
cholera plans, 82-4
civil boundaries, 130
coastal charts, 107
context, vii-viii
contours, 121
conventional signs, 8-9
county maps, 6-28
    bibliographies, 13
    canals on, 104-5
    early, 6-14
    large scale, 14-28
        list of, 15-16
    roads on, 94-6
    town plans on, 64-6
    see also under individual map-makers, including Bryant, Greenwood, Norden, Saxton and Speed
Courts of Sewers maps, 35
crime maps, 85
cycling maps, 28

demolition plans, 82
deposited plans, 79-80, 82, 98-9, 101-2, 108-10
directory maps, 70-2
distance tables, 9
drink maps, 86

early maps, 1-5
electoral boundaries, 72-3
enclosure maps, 29-30, 41-8, 99-100
enumeration district maps, 77-8
environs maps, 28, 60
estate plans, 29-42
excursion maps, 28

field names, 38, 52, 130
fields, 20-3, 33-4, 36-9, 42-3, 45-7, 50, 52, 56
Finance Act maps, 125
finding maps, ix-x, 42, 45-8, 53, 73, 77, 88, 90-1, 105-6, 111-2, 137
five-foot plans, *see* Ordnance Survey

generalisation, ix
Goad maps, *see* insurance plans

improvement maps, 79-81
industry, 23-4, 38-40, 102
insurance plans, 88-90

keys, 8, 25

land ownership, 35-8, 43-4, 65, 73-4, 98
Land Registry maps, 131
land use, 21-3, 29, 38, 49, 127
land use maps, 61

map-makers and the map trade, vii-viii, 11-12, 14, 17-18, 21-4, 26-8, 59-61, 94-5
maps as historical evidence, vii
medical maps, 82-5
medieval maps, *see* early maps
military surveys, 30, 114-5
mills, 24
mining, 38-9

omission of features, ix, 29, 39
Ordnance Survey, ix, 27-8, 73, 114-37
    6-inch & 25-inch, 106, 122-30
        list of, 126-7
    'Battle of the Scales', 115, 122
    field drawings, 22-3, 29, 117-20
    five-foot plans, 84, 106, 130-6
        list of, 131
    one-inch map, 113, 115-22
    other scales, 136-7
    ten-foot / 1:500 plans, 84, 131-6
        lists of, 131, 133-4
ownership, *see* land ownership

Parish Area Books, 127
parish boundaries, 25, 38, 120, 130
parish plans, 74-7, 125-7
Parliamentary plans, *see* deposited plans

parochial assessment maps, 74-7
perspectives, 54, 63, 67
place names, 11-12, 130
planning maps, 79-81
poverty, 85-6
prospects, *see* perspectives

Quarter Sessions plans, *see* deposited plans

railway junction diagrams, 112-3
railways, 81-3, 107-13
rating maps,
    see parochial assessment maps
religion, 86-7
rivers, 31-2, 35, 101
road-books, 92, 97
road strip maps, 92-4, 97
roads, xii, 1-5, 8-9, 11-12, 14, 17-18, 24, 26-7, 38, 39, 44, 92-100

sale plans, 39, 41, 74
scales, 138
school maps, 87
settlement, 2, 6-7, 25-6, 38
sewer maps, 80, 131
social maps, 82, 85-7
Society of Arts prizes, 17-19
sugar-loaf hills, 6, 31-2
surveys and surveying, viii, 5-6, 11, 14-27, 29-30, 33-5, 43, 49, 54-7, 59-61, 67-70, 73-4, 76, 84, 86, 96-7, 108, 115, 117-9, 121, 123-7, 130-4
survival of maps, viii-ix, 42

ten-foot plans, *see* Ordnance Survey
tithe maps, 29-30, 48-53, 76
town plans, 54-91
    early, 54-5
    London, 59-61
    Manchester, 67-70
    other towns, 61-7, 71-3
    Speed, 55-9
trees, 36
turnpikes, 23-4, 96, 98-9

urban estate plans, 59, 73-4

ward maps, 77

Map-makers